BUSINESS STUDIES

David Floyd
Senior Lecturer, University of Wolverhampton

EDUCATIONAL

Letts Educational
Aldine Place
London W12 8AW
Tel: 020 8740 2266
Fax: 020 8743 8451
e-mail: mail@lettsed.co.uk

Every effort has been made to trace copyright holders and to obtain their permission for the use of copyright material. The author and publishers will gladly receive information enabling them to rectify any reference or credit in subsequent editions.

First published 1994
Second edition 1997
Reprinted 1998, 1999, 2001

Text: © David Floyd 1994, 1997

Design and illustrations: © Letts Educational Ltd 1994, 1997

Typeset by Jordan Publishing Design

Illustrations Barbara Linton, Tek-Art, Catherine Bourne, Nigel Jordan

British Library Cataloguing in Publication Data
A CIP record for this book is available from the British Library

ISBN 1 85758 394 9

Note for readers: Some of the information in this book is liable to change, particularly that which is directly influenced by Government policy. Such information is correct at the time of going to press but the reader should keep in touch with current affairs to ensure an up-to-date knowledge of the subject.

Printed and bound in Great Britain by Bath Press Colourbooks, Glasgow

Letts Educational Ltd, a division of Granada Learning Ltd. Part of the Granada Media Group.

Acknowledgements
The author and publishers gratefully acknowledge the following for permission to use questions in this book:
Illustrative questions 1 (Chapters 5, 6, 7 and 9) and 2 (Chapter 8); practice questions 2 (Chapter 7) and 1 (Chapter 9): Reproduced by kind permission of the Associated Examining Board. Any answers or hints on answers are the sole responsibility of the author and have not been provided or approved by the Board. Illustrative questions 4 (Chapters 5, 6, 7, 8 and 10), 5 (Chapter 7) and 3 (Chapter 10); practice question 5 (Chapter 5); mock exam questions 1–5 (Section 3, paper 2): Reproduced by kind permission of London Examinations, a division of Edexcel Foundation. Edexcel Foundation, London Examinations accepts no responsibility whatsoever for the accuracy or method of working in the answers given. Illustrative questions 5 (Chapter 1), 2 (Chapters 2 and 10) and 3 (Chapter 8); practice questions 3 (Chapters 1 and 7), 4 (Chapter 6) and 1 and 2 (Chapter 10): Reproduced by kind permission of Northern Examinations and Assessment Board. The author accepts responsibility for the answers provided, which may not necessarily constitute the only possible solutions. Illustrative questions 1 and 5 (Chapter 2): Reproduced by kind permission of the Northern Ireland Council for Curriculum, Examinations and Assessment. Illustrative questions 3 (Chapters 4 and 9); practice questions 4 (Chapters 4 and 7), 5 (Chapter 6) and 3 (Chapter 9): Reproduced by kind permission of the Scottish Qualifications Authority. Questions used are solely for illustrative purposes and suggested answers are the responsiblity of the author and do not emanate from the Scottish Qualifications Authority. Illustrative questions 4 (Chapter 2), 2 (Chapter 3) and 5 (Chapter 8); practice question 3 (Chapter 6): Reproduced by permission of the University of Cambridge Local Examinations Syndicate. The University of Cambridge Local Examinations Syndicate bears no responsibility for the example answers to questions taken from its past question papers which are contained in this publication. Illustrative questions 4 (Chapter 1), 3 (Chapters 5, 6 and 7) and 6 (Chapter 10); practice questions 2 (Chapter 2) and 4 (Chapters 5 and 9): Reproduced by kind permission of the Welsh Joint Education Committee.

CONTENTS

SECTION 3: TEST RUN

PREFACE

In writing this Study Guide I have tried to provide readers with an insight into the Advanced, Advanced Supplementary and Scottish Higher-level examinations in Business Studies. Although these examinations have been with us for many years, they have undergone a number of changes, and continue to be updated and revised regularly. As an experienced Chief Examiner who has worked closely with three examining boards over a number of years, I have written the Guide to help Business Studies students cope with the demands made by these examinations.

I am most grateful to the examination boards for giving permission to reproduce questions set by them in previous examinations. The answers to the questions are entirely my own and none of the boards can accept any responsibility whatsoever for the method or accuracy of working.

I am also most grateful to various companies and other sources, who have kindly permitted the inclusion of illustrative material in the Study Guide. Business is 'real', and I have therefore used real-life examples to illustrate general 'textbook' theories. My thanks are therefore recorded to the following:

Barclays Bank plc
BICC plc
Birmingham Chamber of Commerce and Industry
British Petroleum Company plc
Cadbury Schweppes plc
Camelot Group plc
Co-operative Union Ltd
CWS Ltd
Department of Trade and Industry (DTI)
Department for Education and Employment
Esso UK plc
Eurostat
Ford Motor Co Ltd
Guardian Newspapers Ltd
J Sainsbury plc
Lloyds Bank plc
Marks and Spencer plc
McDonald's
NatWest Bank plc
Office for National Statistics (ONS)
Office of Population Censuses and Surveys (OPCS)
Organisation for Economic Co-operation and Development (OECD)
Royal Dutch/Shell Group
RTZ Corporation plc
Sears plc
Shropshire Newspapers Ltd
THORN EMI plc
UNISON

I wish also to express my thanks to the support received from the staff at Letts Educational, and to my colleague Phil Jackson for his invaluable advice. Most of all I thank Emily and Laura for their tolerance in letting their father get on with the task of writing the Guide, and Val for her continuing support.

David Floyd

STARTING POINTS

In this section:

How to use this book

    The structure of this book

    Using your syllabus checklist

Syllabus checklists and schemes of assessment

    Examination boards and addresses

Studying and revising Business Studies

    The difference between GCSE and A/AS Level

    Study strategy and techniques

    Subject-specific skills

    Coursework

    Revision techniques

The examination

    Question styles

    Examination techniques

    Final preparation

HOW TO USE THIS BOOK

THE STRUCTURE OF THIS BOOK

The key aim of this book is to guide you in the way you tackle A-level Business Studies. It should serve as a study guide, work book and revision aid throughout any A-level/AS-level Business Studies course, no matter what syllabus you are following. It is not intended to be a complete guide to the subject and should be used as a companion to your textbooks, which it is designed to complement rather than duplicate.

We have divided the book into three sections. **Section 1, Starting Points**, contains study tips and syllabus information – all the material you need to get started on your A-level study – plus advice on planning your revision and tips on how to tackle the exam itself. Use the **Syllabus Checklists** to find out exactly where you can find the study units which are relevant to your particular syllabus.

Section 2, the main body of the text, contains the core of A-level Business Studies. It has been devised to make study as easy – and enjoyable – as possible, and has been divided into chapters which cover the themes you will encounter on your syllabus. The chapters are split into units, each covering a topic of study.

The **Chapter Objectives** direct you towards the key points of the chapter you are about to read. The **Chapter Roundup** at the end of the chapter gives a summary of the text just covered, brings its topics into focus and links them to other themes of study. To reinforce what you have just read and learned, there are **Illustrative Questions** at the end of each chapter. All questions are actually taken from those recently set by the examination boards (including Scottish Higher). The tutorial notes and suggested answers provided give you practical guidance on how to answer A-level questions, and give additional information relevant to that particular topic. There are also **Practice Questions**, which are further examples of A-level exam questions for you to attempt, with the key points and potential pitfalls emphasised.

In **Section 3, Test Run**, we turn our attention to the examination you will face at the end of your course. First, you can assess your progress using the **Test Your Knowledge Quiz** and analysis chart. Then, as a final test, you should attempt the **Mock Exam**, under timed conditions. This will give you invaluable examination practice and, together with the specimen answers specially written by the author, will help you to judge how close you are to achieving your A-level pass.

USING YOUR SYLLABUS CHECKLIST

Whether you are using this book to work step-by-step through the syllabus or to structure your revision campaign, you will find it useful to use our checklist to record what you have covered – and how far you still have to go. Keep the checklist at hand when you are doing your revision – it will remind you of the chapters you have revised, and those still to be done.

The checklist for each examination – A, AS or Higher Grade – is in two parts. First there is a list of topics covered by this book which are part of the syllabus. Although the checklists are detailed, it is not possible to print entire syllabuses. **You are therefore strongly recommended to obtain an official copy of the syllabus for your examination and consult it when the need arises.** The examination board addresses are given after the syllabus checklists.

When you have revised a topic make a note of the date in the column provided and, if there are questions elsewhere in the book, try to answer them, putting the date or dates in the final column.

The second part of the checklist gives you information about the examination, providing useful details about the time allocated for each paper and the weighting of the questions on each paper. The different types of questions which may be set are explained in detail later in this section under the heading The Examination.

SYLLABUS CHECKLISTS AND SCHEMES OF ASSESSMENT

ASSOCIATED EXAMINING BOARD
A-level (0650)

Syllabus topic	Covered in Unit No	✓
SECTION 1: MARKETING		
Market analysis	7.1, 9.2	
Marketing strategy	7.1, 7.3	
Marketing planning	1.3, 7.2, 7.3	
SECTION 2: ACCOUNTING AND FINANCE		
Budgeting	6.3	
Cost centres, profit centres, overheads	6.3	
Company accounts	6.1, 10.1	
Ratio analysis	6.2	
Classification of costs	6.3, 8.1	
Investment decision-making	10.2	
SECTION 3: OPERATIONS MANAGEMENT		
Facilities	1.4, 3.2, 8.1, 8.2	
Productive efficiency	3.2, 7.3, 8.2, 10.3	
Controlling operations	8.1, 9.1	
Lean production	8.1	
SECTION 4: PEOPLE		
Management structure and organisation	2.2, 5.2	
Motivation	5.2	
Communication	5.2, 9.1	
Employer/employee relations	5.3, 5.5	
Human resource management	5.1, 5.3, 5.4	
SECTION 5: EXTERNAL INFLUENCES		
Economic opportunities and constraints	1.4, 4.1, 4.3	
Governmental constraints	4.1, 4.2	
Social constraints	4.3	
Other opportunities and constraints	4.4	
SECTION 6: OBJECTIVES AND STRATEGY		
Starting a small firm	2.1	
Impact upon firms of a change in size	2.1, 3.2	
Business objectives	2.1, 2.2	
Business strategy	7.2, 10.3	

Scheme of assessment

There are four Assessment Patterns available:

Versions A and B (Non-modular) — Three examination papers (Version A) *or* two papers plus coursework (Version B)

Paper 1   *3 hours*   50% of the total marks
Syllabus sections 1–5 assessed
Six compulsory stimulus-response questions.

Paper 2   *1¹/₂ hours*   30% of the total marks
Syllabus Section 6 used to integrate questions from the other 5 syllabus sections
Candidates collect information from a case study in the paper and answer about four compulsory questions

Paper 3   *1¹/₂ hours*   20% of the total marks
Section A (10%) requires candidates to write a report from a numerical data-based case study
Section B (10%) contains a choice of four essay questions from which candidates select one

OR

Paper 4   *Coursework*   20% of the total marks
An independently researched written assignment of about 3000 words.

Versions C and D (Modular)   Five module papers (Version C) *or*
four papers and coursework (Version D).

Papers 5, 6 and 7: each is 1 hour long and receives one-sixth of the total marks. Paper 5 covers syllabus sections 1 and 2, Paper 6 covers sections 3 and 4, and Paper 7 sections 5 and 6. The questions are identical to those in Paper 1.

Version C also includes Papers 2 and 3 (see above), and Version D includes Papers 2 and 4 above.

ASSOCIATED EXAMINING BOARD
AS-level (0957)

Syllabus topic	Covered in Unit No	✓
SECTION 1: MARKETING		
Market analysis	7.1, 9.2	
Marketing strategy	7.1, 7.3	
Marketing planning	1.3, 7.2, 7.3	
SECTION 2: ACCOUNTING AND FINANCE		
Budgeting	6.3	
Company accounts	6.1, 10.1	
Ratio analysis	6.2	
Classification of costs	6.3, 8.1	
Investment decision-making	10.2	
SECTION 3: OPERATIONS MANAGEMENT		
Productive efficiency	1.4, 3.2, 8.1, 8.2	
Controlling operations	8.1, 9.1	
Lean production	8.1	
SECTION 4: PEOPLE		
Management structure and organisation	2.2, 5.2	
Motivation	5.2	
Employer/employee relations	5.3, 5.5	
Human resource management	5.1, 5.3, 5.4	
SECTION 5: EXTERNAL INFLUENCES		
Economic opportunities and constraints	1.4, 4.1, 4.3	
Other opportunities and constraints	4.1, 4.2	
SECTION 6: BUSINESS OBJECTIVES AND STRATEGY	2.1, 3.2, 7.2, 10.3	

Scheme of assessment

Paper 1   *3 hours*   100% weighting
Section A (50%): about four compulsory questions
based on a case study
Section B (50%): two essay questions from six

LONDON EXAMINATIONS (Edexcel Foundation)
A-level (9075)

Syllabus topic	Covered in Unit No	✓
SECTION 1: BUSINESS ENTERPRISE		
Structure of business activity	1.2, 2.1	
Types of private sector business	2.1, 4.2	
Business objectives	4.3	
Process of decision making	9.2, 10.1, 10.3	
The planning process	7.2	
Data collection and presentation	9.2, 10.3	
SECTION 2: EXTERNAL ENVIRONMENT OF BUSINESS		
Macro-economic environment	4.1	
Micro-economic environment	1.3	
Legal, political, social, technological environments	1.2, Chapter 4	
International environment	1.4, 3.3, 4.1, 4.3	
SECTION 3: ACCOUNTING AND FINANCE		
Purposes and conventions	6.1	
Final accounts	6.1, 6.2	
Budgeting, costing	6.1, 6.3	
Sources and uses of funds	3.1, 10.1	
Break-even analysis	8.1	
Investment appraisal	10.2	
SECTION 4: PRODUCTION AND OPERATIONS		
Patterns of production	1.3, 8.2	
Location	4.1, 4.4, 8.2	
New product development	7.2	
Economies of scale	3.2	
Stock control	8.1	
Critical path analysis	10.3	
Quality assurance	8.1	
SECTION 5: MARKETING		
Market research	7.1, 7.2, 9.2	
Marketing plans	7.1, 7.2	
Product	7.3	
Pricing policies	7.3	
Promotion	7.3	
Distribution	7.3	
International marketing	1.4, 3.3	
SECTION 6: HUMAN RESOURCES IN BUSINESS		
Supply of human resources	5.3	
Human resource planning	5.3, 5.4, 5.5	
Organisational structure of the firm	2.2	
Motivation and leadership	5.2	
Communication	9.1	
Trade unions and employers' associations	5.5	
Changing nature and pattern of work	5.3	

Scheme of assessment

Paper 1	*2³/₄ hours*	40% weighting All questions (compulsory) are based on a pre-seen case study issued to candidates
Paper 2	*2¹/₂ hours*	40% weighting Section A: three quantitative data response questions, from which candidates select two Section B: three comprehension data response questions, from which candidates select two
Paper 3	*Coursework*	20% weighting Two assignments chosen from 5, each approximately 3000 words

LONDON EXAMINATIONS (Edexcel Foundation)
NDTEF A-level (9078)

Syllabus topic	Covered in Unit No	✓
MODULE 1: MARKETING		
Market research	7.1, 7.2	
Marketing	1.3, 4.2, 6.2, 7.3	
MODULE 2: BUSINESS RESOURCES		
Investment and production	6.1, 8.1, 8.2, 10.1, 10.2	
Human resources	2.2, 5.2, 5.3, 5.4, 5.5	
MODULE 3: BUSINESS PERFORMANCE		
Implementation of business decisions	10.3	
Financial control and accounting	6.2, 6.3, 8.2	
MODULE 4:		
Element (a): The Business Plan	(All chapters)	
Element (b): Optional Study	(All chapters)	
Module 5: Change and Development in Business	All above units plus: 10.4	

Scheme of assessment

Module 1 *1¹/₂ hours*   15% of total marks
Unseen written examination

Module 2 *1¹/₂ hours*   15% of total marks
Unseen written examination

Module 3 *1¹/₂ hours*   15% of total marks
Unseen written examination

Module 4 *2 hours*   20% of total marks
Coursework: candidates submit a business plan (a report of 5000 words maximum) and an optional study chosen from:
      Business and the law
      Business and media design
      Community leisure industries
      Business and the environment
      Language in business
      Structured work experience

Module 5 *2¹/₂ hours*   35% of total marks
Unseen written examination in the form of a case study focusing on an organisation in the process of change
The content of Modules 1–3 is also examined

NORTHERN EXAMINATIONS AND ASSESSMENT BOARD
A-level (4411)

Syllabus topic	Covered in Unit No	✓
MODULE 1: ECONOMIC AND SOCIAL ENVIRONMENT		
Nature of an economy	1.2, 1.3	
Framework for management decisions	7.2, 10.3	
Impact of government policy	1.4, 4.1	
Influence of the environment	4.1, 4.2, 4.3, 4.4	
MODULE 2: ACCOUNTING AND FINANCE		
Financial management	10.1, 10.2	
Financial framework	6.1, 6.2, 8.1	
Accounting systems in decision making	4.4, 10.2	
MODULE 3: HUMAN RESOURCES		
Role of employees and managers	2.2, 5.3, 5.4	
Motivation	5.2	
Nature of leadership	5.2	
Employer-employee negotiation	5.5	
Management of change	5.3, 10.4	
MODULE 4: OPERATIONS MANAGEMENT		
The operations environment	8.1	
The production and service functions	8.1, 8.2	
Planning, forecasting and control	8.1, 10.3	
MODULE 5: MARKETING		
Nature and role of marketing	7.1	
Processes and strategies of marketing	7.1, 7.3	
Collection and processing of marketing information	7.2	
Constraints on marketing	4.3	
MODULE 6: COURSEWORK	(All chapters)	

Scheme of assessment

Option 1: terminal examination and coursework

Paper 1	*3 hours*	40% weighting Section A (20%): three compulsory questions requiring short answers set on any part of the syllabus Section B (20%): twelve questions requiring short answers set on any part of the syllabus
Paper 2	*3 hours*	40% weighting Section A (20%): compulsory questions based on an unseen case study Section B (20%): a choice of six questions from any part of the syllabus; two essay-style answers
Coursework		20% weighting One assignment involving the production of a business plan

Option 2: modular assessment and coursework

Modules 1–5 (see chart above) each have a 75-minute examination worth 16% of the total marks. Each paper will consist of a series of questions based on given data in written, numerical or diagrammatic form. Coursework (details see above) is Module 6.

UNIVERSITY OF CAMBRIDGE LOCAL EXAMINATIONS SYNDICATE (part of OCEAC)
A-level (9370) Linear scheme

Syllabus topic	Covered in Unit No	✓
A: DECISION MAKING IN BUSINESS		
Phases of decision making	2.2, 5.2, 5.5, 8.1, 9.1, 10.3	
Information and analysis of information needs	7.2, 9.2	
Deciding between alternatives	8.1, 9.2, 10.2, 10.3	
Implementation and control	6.3, 10.4	
B: THE ORGANISATION AND ITS ENVIRONMENT		
Business units	2.1, 3.1, 3.3	
Objectives	2.1, 5.2, 7.2	
Structure of organisations	2.1, 2.2, 7.1, 9.2	
National and international environment	1.4	
C: THE DYNAMICS OF BUSINESS		
People in business	5.1, 5.2, 5.3, 5.4, 5.5, 9.1	
Marketing and production	1.3, 7.1, 7.2, 7.3, 8.1, 8.2	
Finance	6.2, 10.1	
Accounting for business activity	6.1, 6.2, 6.3	

Scheme of assessment

Component 1   *3 hours*   40% of total marks
Structured questions: four from a choice of six

Component 2   *3 hours*   40% of total marks
Case study and essay: six compulsory questions, including one essay.

Component 3   *Project*   20% of total marks
A report of between 4000 and 5000 words on a subject (chosen by the candidate) related to a business or organisation problem

UNIVERSITY OF CAMBRIDGE LOCAL EXAMINATIONS SYNDICATE (part of OCEAC)
A-level (9542) and AS-level (8542 and 8442) Modular schemes

Syllabus topic	Covered in Unit No	✓
MODULE: BUSINESS ORGANISATION		
1 The nature of business	1.2, 1.3, 2.1	
2 Objectives	2.1, 5.2, 7.2	
3 Internal organisation of business	2.2	
4 Information and business decision making	4.4, 7.2, 9.2	
5 Functional areas of business	3.2, 4.4, Chapters 5 to 8, 10.1, 10.3	
MODULE: BUSINESS CONTEXT		
1 Nature of the business environment	4.1, 4.2, 4.3, 4.4, 7.3	
2 Objective of the state	1.3, 1.4, 2.1	
3 Financial control of business	10.1	
4 Employer/employee relations	5.5	
MODULE: HUMAN RESOURCE MANAGEMENT		
Management and leadership	3.2	
Organisation structures	2.2	
Workforce planning	5.3, 5.4	
Communication	9.1	
Motivation, leadership	5.2	
Industrial relations	5.5	
The law	4.2	
MODULE: MARKETING		
The market	7.1	
The marketing mix	7.2, 7.3	
Marketing planning	1.4, 7.2	
MODULE: OPERATIONS MANAGEMENT		
The production process	4.2, 8.2	
The costing of production	8.1	
Improving productive efficiency	4.4, 5.4, 8.1, 10.3	
MODULE: ACCOUNTING AND FINANCE IN BUSINESS		
Accounting concepts	6.1, 6.2	
Financial statements	6.1	
Analysis and interpretation	6.2	
Classification of costs	6.3	
Budgets and decision making	6.3, 8.1	
Sources of finance	10.1	
Investment appraisal techniques	6.1, 10.2	

Scheme of assessment for A-level candidates

There are three compulsory Modules:

Business Organisation *3 hours* (Double Module)   33.3% of total marks
Compulsory questions based on a pre-issued case study

Business Context	*1¹/₂ hours*	16.7% of total marks The first question is worth 25% of the total available, and requires candidates to relate their answers to firms of which they have direct knowledge
Research Assignment		16.7% of total marks 4000–5000-word report

Option Modules: any two from Human Resources Management, Marketing, Operations Management, and Accounting and Finance in Business. Each is examined over 90 minutes and generates 16.7% of the total marks. The first three are structured in the same way as the Business Context paper; the Accounting and Finance paper contains compulsory questions related to the pre-issued case study.

Scheme of assessment for AS-level candidates

These candidates must take the Business Organisation Double Module (66.7% of total marks) and the Business Context Module (33.3% of total marks).

WELSH JOINT EDUCATION COMMITTEE
A-level and AS-level (Modular)

Syllabus topic	Covered in Unit No	✓
1: BUSINESS CORE		
Impact on business of external factors	1.3, 1.4, Chapter 4, 5.3, 7.1	
Marketing	Chapter 7	
People	Chapter 5	
Accounting and finance	Chapter 6	
Operations management	Chapter 8	
Integrating business activity	Chapters 9 and 10	
OPTION: MARKETING		
Nature of marketing	7.1	
Marketing planning	7.3	
Market research, consumer behaviour	7.2	
The marketing mix	7.3	
Marketing and sales departments	7.3	
International marketing	1.4, 3.3	
OPTION: HUMAN RESOURCE MANAGEMENT		
People and performance	5.3, 5.4	
Motivation	5.2	
Learning	5.4	
Individual differences	4.2	
Work	5.2, 5.3	
Leadership	4.2, 4.3, 5.2	
Management skills, communication	9.1, 10.4	
Changes in employment patterns	5.3	
OPTION: THE ECONOMIC ENVIRONMENT		
The economic problem	1.1, 1.2	
Elasticity	1.3	
Government intervention	1.4	
Factors of production, economies of scale	3.2	
Cost, revenues and profit	4.2, 6.2	
Macro-economic objectives	1.4, 4.1	
OPTION: BUSINESS STATISTICS		
Model building	10.3	
Sources	9.2	
Index numbers	9.2	
Forecasting	Chapter 10	
Presentation of data	9.2	
Information technology	9.1	

Scheme of assessment

AS-level candidates must study Module 1. A-level candidates must study Module 1 and three option modules.

Module 1   *3 hours*   50% weighting A-level; 100% weighting
(Business Core)   AS-level

Section A: compulsory case study including numerical data

Section B: five, two-part structured questions, from which candidates select and answer two

Option Modules (each is equally weighted and carries one-sixth of the total assessment at A-level):

2 Marketing
3 Human Resource Management
4 The Economic Environment
5 Statistics and Decision Making
6 Coursework

For coursework, candidates produce an assignment of between 3000 and 4000 words. Options 2–5 are examined by a written paper of 75 minutes, with two compulsory stimulus-response questions and a compulsory essay question.

SCOTTISH CERTIFICATE OF EDUCATION (HIGHER GRADE)
Management and Information Studies

Syllabus topic	Covered in Unit No	✓
MANAGERS AS DECISION MAKERS		
The nature of management	5.1, 5.4	
The nature of decisions	Chapter 10	
Effective decision making	Chapter 10	
EFFECTIVENESS		
Personal	Chapter 5	
Group	5.4	
INFORMATION MANAGEMENT		
Types of information	9.1, Chapter 10	
Information technologies	9.1	
Use and communication of information	Chapter 9	
MANAGEMENT DECISION AREAS		
Marketing	Chapter 7	
Human resources	Chapter 5	
Finance	Chapter 6	
Operations	Chapter 8	

Scheme of assessment

Paper 1   *2½ hours*   40% of the total marks
Ten structured or essay-type questions testing knowledge and understanding, from which candidates select four

Paper 2   *2½ hours*   40% of the total marks
Case study assessing problem-solving and decision-making skills

Paper 3   *Project*   20% of the total marks
Candidates write a report on a project which addresses a situation, problem or issue relating to work undertaken
Written content between 1500 to 2000 words

NORTHERN IRELAND COUNCIL FOR THE CURRICULUM, EXAMINATIONS AND ASSESSMENT
CCEA A-level

Syllabus topic	Covered in Unit No	✓
BUSINESS ENVIRONMENT AND ENTERPRISE		
Structure of business activity	1.2, 1.3, 1.4, 2.1	
Private sector	2.1	
External environment	4.1	
MARKETING		
Market segmentation	7.1	
Market research	7.1, 7.2, 9.2	
The marketing plan	1.3, 7.2, 7.3	
The marketing mix	7.3	
Marketing strategy	7.3	
International marketing	1.4, 3.3	
ACCOUNTING AND FINANCE		
Functions and conventions	6.1	
Final accounts, assets	6.1, 6.2	
Analysis and interpretation	6.2, 10.1	
Budgeting, costing	6.1, 6.3	
Sources and uses of funds	3.1, 10.1	
Break-even analysis	8.1	
Investment appraisal	10.2	
HUMAN RESOURCE MANAGEMENT		
Supply of human resources	5.3	
Organisational structure	2.2	
Motivation, leadership, groups	5.2	
Human resource planning	5.3, 5.4, 5.5	
Managing change	5.3, 10.4	
Employer/employee relations	5.5	
Communication in business	9.1	
OPERATIONS MANAGEMENT		
Decisions on how to produce	8.1, 8.2	
Decisions on where to produce	4.1, 4.4, 8.2	
New product development	7.3, 8.2	
The scale of production	8.1, 8.2	
The control of stock	8.1	
Critical path analysis	10.3	
Quality management	8.1	
Information management	9.1, 9.2, 10.3	

Scheme of assessment

Paper 1   *3 hours*   40% of the total marks
Section A (20%): candidates answer two compulsory questions
Section B (20%): candidates answer two comprehension-type questions from four

Paper 2   *3 hours*   40% of the total marks
Section A (20%): case study (pre-seen) with compulsory questions
Section B (20%): candidates answer two from three data-response questions

Paper 3   *Project*   20% of the total marks
3000-word report on research into an issue the candidate selects

EXAMINATION BOARDS AND ADDRESSES

AEB   The Associated Examining Board
                     Stag Hill House, Guildford, Surrey GU2 5XJ

                     Tel: 01483 506506

Cambridge   University of Cambridge Local Examinations Syndicate
(OCEAC)   Syndicate Buildings, 1 Hills Road, Cambridge CB1 2EU

                     Tel: 01223 553311

London   Edexcel Foundation
Examinations   Stewart House, 32 Russell Square, London WC1B 5DN

                     Tel: 0171 393 4444

NEAB   Northern Examinations and Assessment Board
                     Devas Street, Manchester M15 6EX

                     Tel: 0161 953 1180

NICCEA   Northern Ireland Council for the Curriculum, Examinations and
                     Assessment
                     29 Clarendon Road, Belfast BT1 3BG

                     Tel: 01232 261200

Scottish   Scottish Qualifications Authority
                     Ironmills Road, Dalkeith, Midlothian EH22 1LE

                     Tel: 0131 663 6601

WJEC   Welsh Joint Education Committee
                     245 Western Avenue, Cardiff CF5 2YX

                     Tel: 01222 265000

STUDYING AND REVISING BUSINESS STUDIES

THE DIFFERENCE BETWEEN GCSE AND A/AS LEVEL

Before explaining the differences between GCSE and A/AS-level, it is important to recognise the similarities:

- all major Business Studies syllabuses contain key economic, financial and other business concepts;
- much of the content is similar, though more depth is required for A-level;
- the examining processes tend to be similar.

There have been moves at both GCSE and A/AS-levels to produce 'modular' syllabuses. The range of content and modules tends to be similar – Marketing, Accounting/Finance, Production etc. – although A-level syllabuses normally have a wider content coverage than GCSE ones.

There have also been moves in recent years to rationalise the status of the dozens of different 'academic' and 'vocational' courses. As a result, GCSE courses are regarded as equivalent to an 'Intermediate GNVQ' performance, while A-level and similar courses overlap with 'Advanced GNVQ' (or 'Applied A-levels'). This confirms that the principal difference between A/AS and GCSE Business Studies is in the levels of skill and knowledge that the student is expected to demonstrate. GCSE candidates must show that they can recall information, state and describe what they know and understand, and explain how general 'theory' points apply to specific (real or realistic) situations. A/AS-level candidates must demonstrate to a greater depth the higher-level 'thinking' skills of understanding and analysis when answering examination questions. Many of the A-level and GCSE questions are related to actual or simulated business situations, but an A-level examination question or coursework assignment expects much greater analysis and more detailed explanations from you.

The various syllabuses explain the demands made at your level. The knowledge and abilities tested can be classified under the following headings. You will see that there is greater emphasis on explaining and analysing what you know than on just recalling facts and figures. Popular headings used are:

- **Knowledge**: your ability to recall specific terms, techniques, principles and facts,
- **Comprehension**: understanding which you demonstrate by selecting and interpreting information (in both written and graphical forms),
- **Application**: using your knowledge (of terms, techniques, etc.) to explain unfamiliar business matters and situations,
- **Analysis and synthesis**: your ability to distinguish between fact and opinion, to make generalisations, to reorganise information and to test hypotheses,
- **Evaluation**: demonstrating reasoned judgement and reaching suitable conclusions.

> When levels of response marking is used, from 1988, it will be essential for candidates not only to apply their theoretical knowledge... but to proceed to analyse and evaluate the material in order to enter the highest mark bands.
>
> (Extract from London Examinations A-level report)

You will also use high-level communication skills, to organise and present information and to ensure this information is accurate and complete.

The following extract gives a typical indication of what you are expected to achieve by the end of your A, AS or Higher Level study. It is from the Northern Examination and Assessment Board (NEAB) A-level syllabus. NEAB states in the introduction that:

Business Studies at Advanced Level should enable candidates to develop a critical understanding of organisations, the markets they serve and the process of adding value...

NEAB points out in its section on relevant skills that:

... candidates should acquire and demonstrate skills of communication, critical understanding, investigation, numeracy and problem solving.

A summary of the assessment objectives identified by NEAB shows that you will have to:

1 demonstrate knowledge and understanding of the syllabus content, and apply this to problems and issues;

2 collect, collate, organise and present information, ideas and arguments;

3 analyse problems, issues and situations; and

4 evaluate, to distinguish between fact and opinion.

STUDY STRATEGY AND TECHNIQUES

General hints

You must plan well ahead to do yourself justice in the examination. To pass it, you not only have to make notes throughout the course, but you also have to carry out regular revision. The amount and nature of this revision is influenced by the time available and the demands made by the examination. You can concentrate solely on learning subject-matter when revising for short-answer or restricted-response question papers: but your approach to revising for data response and essay papers should also involve constructing and writing actual answers.

We advise you to think about revision at the start, rather than towards the end, of the course. Many A-level and similar courses include a form of 'revision' as part of learning. This occurs when teachers use an **integrative** approach to teach Business Studies: you revise and build on previously learnt content by having to relate it to new content being studied. If you have to complete coursework, you will also revise by researching and writing up the assignments.

We also advise you to plan some active revision sessions during the course. This should:

- take some pressure (and anxiety) off you at examination time, by spreading your workload;

- improve the quality of your coursework;

- identify any learning problems and subject-matter difficulties in time for your teacher to help solve them;

- lead to a more thorough learning of new Business Studies content because you have a better foundation of knowledge on which to build.

There are various methods of revising, and what suits one candidate does not suit another. As a basic principle there is not much benefit to be gained from memorising Business Studies content, but you have to learn key concepts and the occasional definition, even though it is often more important to know how to apply them.

You can vary your revision once the examination requirements are known. Some sessions could concentrate on learning content: on other occasions you can practise answering relevant types of question. To carry out the latter approach I suggest you collect some past papers from your teacher or your school or college library: if necessary, they can be purchased from the examining board (see page 16 for a list of addresses).

SUBJECT-SPECIFIC SKILLS

A-level candidates are assessed on both their subject knowledge and their ability in the **key skills**. There are three particularly important skill areas in Business Studies.

Communication

Examinations in all subjects at this level expect you to demonstrate a good standard of communication. Chief Examiners sometimes comment that candidates' communication skills are weak:

> The standard of English was generally very poor indeed, and shows some signs of deterioration. Since communication skills are central to business studies this is a trend which all should seek to reverse.

> (Extract from AEB A-level report)

Specific communication skills in Business Studies include report writing. Advice on constructing reports is given in the next section on Coursework (see page 20).

Numeracy

Business Studies examinations and coursework include numerical and diagrammatic information. This information is given in table or diagram (chart or graph) format and you must interpret or restructure it. The skills needed here include the ability to:

● perform simple and complex calculations (normally done with the aid of a calculator); and

● present and label tables and diagrams appropriately.

The general standard of numeracy is also often commented on in Chief Examiner Reports.

> The standard of numeracy appears to be inadequate... Since business depends as much on quantitative as qualitative information... candidates will lose the opportunity to achieve high grades unless they are clearly able to demonstrate such a skill.

> (Extract from AEB A-level report)

Examiners are interested in the thinking which lies behind your answer: this is emphasised in the comments below on data handling. There are two easy ways to improve your chances of getting good marks for numerical questions.

❶ Where there are computations, all workings should be shown – even when calculators are used – because there are marks awarded for both accuracy and method of approach. Errors in computation lose the 'accuracy' marks, but the examiner can still award you the 'method' marks from your workings and layout of the answer.

❷ Estimating the correct numerical answer, for example the proportions of a pie chart or the percentage breakdowns of a total, is a useful technique to use in the examination. This applies especially when you use a calculator. If the answer does not look right, it encourages you to check workings: it could be that you have pressed a wrong button or mispositioned the decimal point.

Data handling

Increasingly, Business Studies examinations ask you to handle data. Such questions require you to relate *general* theory and textbook points to the *particular* situation - the 'data' - in the question.

The most common failing of candidates is a 'clear inability... to manipulate data' (extract from AEB A-level report). The AEB report points out that data handling 'is a central business studies skill'. It also comments that 'there is more to it than simple manipulation [of the data]'.

An A-level report from London Examinations also noted that 'many candidates were unable to combine theoretical knowledge with evidence taken from the Case Study... candidates merely repeated statements from the Case Study rather than extracting key points to present as evidence to support their case.'

Section 3 contains a mock examination and the second paper illustrates how question data can be extracted and used. The basic principles are:

● do not simply copy out chunks of the data;

- extract what is required to illustrate the points you are making;
- comment on how the data relate to these points.

COURSEWORK

The requirements for coursework vary from board to board (see pages 3-15). The Northern Examination and Assessment Board (NEAB), for example, requires its candidates to submit one assignment which forms 20 per cent of overall assessment.

The boards usually provide advice not only in terms of what is required, but also of what to avoid when selecting and completing coursework. For example, the NEAB advises its candidates how to prepare the business plan required for the coursework assignment. The University of Cambridge A-level syllabus also gives an outline of what is required for its coursework assignment (a report). Cambridge examiners assess their candidates by awarding marks for:

- the skill with which the problem has been put into context and considered;
- evidence of personal research;
- evidence of understanding of relevant Business Studies concepts and ideas;
- application of Business Studies concepts and ideas to the problem;
- the logic, depth and breadth of the analysis undertaken;
- evaluation of alternatives and conclusion related to problem set;
- quality of language; and
- other aspects of presentation, including appropriate use of tables, graphs and charts, etc.

The following comments are often made by examiners and teachers:

1 You gain little credit from just repeating information produced by others. This can form the basis of the coursework's 'information component', but it is insufficient by itself. You are expected to select, interpret and apply this information, for example in solving the problem on which your coursework is based. You must also distinguish between 'fact' and 'opinion' when repeating information.

2 Credit is given for appropriate organisation and presentation of facts, figures and ideas. The coursework may have to be presented as a business report: if so, you must use an acceptable structure which contains suitable headings. Your syllabus might help: an example is the Cambridge A-level syllabus which suggests that the report should include:

> a title which accurately reflects the work undertaken,
> a setting for the problem,
> a clear definition of the problem, the candidate's objectives in relation to the problem,
> relevant information collected in a suitable manner...

Examiners have commented that most of the better projects submitted at this level are structured along the lines of a business report.

3 Many candidates ignore the variety of presentation methods which are available to them. A coursework assessor expects to see a suitable range of explanatory and summary diagrams, charts and graphs which demonstrate that you know how to construct them and when to use them. The use of different forms of presentation breaks up the text and improves the appearance of your work.

4 The better assignments show evidence of extensive reading, not just of textbooks but also of specialist publications and 'quality' newspapers. They also have arguments which are clearly presented and which move towards a conclusion.

5 Selecting a suitable coursework topic or area is crucial to the quality of the end result. Coursework is likely to be 'suitable' if:

- it will maintain your interest and attention;
- it can be completed in the time available;
- it does not demand too many resources;
- the information on which it is based is easily available to you; and
- (most importantly) it meets the examining board's requirements.

A business problem should be featured, but many firms are not prepared to disclose information (particularly on financial matters) to you which might be needed for your research into the 'problem'. Your choice of topic will therefore be determined largely by the availability of information on it.

Examiner reports suggest that weak coursework is based on badly selected topics which are:

- unmanageably large;
- likely to be inconclusive;
- based on information that is largely unavailable;
- likely to stray away from Business Studies.

Topics which often cause difficulty include those based on:

1 **'Green' issues** These issues are only valid when they are analysed from a Business Studies perspective and are also related to the external environment of a particular organisation. One examiner's report mentioned that '...examiners are not impressed by the repetition of public relations statements and naive accounts of how a famous name is helping to save the planet'.

2 **Sociological issues** These can also be acceptable, but over-concentrating on aspects such as equal opportunities risks diverting the assignment away from a sufficiently broad Business Studies perspective.

REVISION TECHNIQUES

When you revise is up to you, but it pays to **plan a revision programme** well before the examination, to identify when you are free for two or three hours at a time. Experiment with the time of day that you revise: some people work better early in the day, others later on, and the number and intensity of distractions also varies throughout the day. Find times that suit you and try to stick with them. This will enable you to establish a basic routine which will operate through to the examination.

Each revision session can be structured to include a number of short breaks after, say, twenty or thirty minutes spent working. Everyone has a limited concentration span, and the thought of hour after hour of solid revision can demotivate even the keenest student. You should also **vary your methods of revising** to help maintain concentration (and it will improve your examination techniques and skills):

- read aloud;
- make summary notes;
- plan a skeleton answer to a past question;
- answer a question under examination conditions.

If you have to answer restricted response and short-answer questions, you need to spend some revision time writing down concise answers to questions from past papers and this Guide. You might also restructure some of your notes to practise summarising points briefly.

Once you are happy with your knowledge of a particular topic, you should test how well you approach essay questions by **drafting out skeleton answers**. This tests your ability to recall information and structure it appropriately. When revising to answer data response papers, you should practise applying general information to a specific situation to become familiar with this technique.

If you propose to use this Guide as the basis of a revision programme, we suggest that you concentrate on one or two topic areas only at each revision session:

- read the topic detail;
- attempt one or more of the questions provided by drafting out a planned answer;
- check your answer against the one provided;
- identify any differences or omissions (remember that you may have included correct information which is not included in the Guide's suggested answer);
- go back quickly over the topic unit again to reinforce your knowledge and to correct any misunderstandings.

Following this it should be easy for you to recall the main concepts and - importantly - describe them using your own (written) words without relying on the Guide. Having done this you should again compare your work to the Guide's content. If you treat this as a continuing process, you can quickly master the topics.

THE EXAMINATION

QUESTION STYLES

We can classify the forms of Business Studies questions as:

1 restricted response and short-answer;

2 data response and essay.

Restricted response questions

Most of the examining boards include in their examination a section of questions testing recall and comprehension. The advantage to examiners of using these questions is that they allow all syllabus areas to be tested in the time available.

One form of restricted response question is the 'multiple choice' type. Here you are given a question or statement which is followed by (typically) four options or alternatives, only one of which is correct. Although these are used in some A, AS or Higher Level examinations, they are rarely found at present in Business Studies.

A more popular form asks you to read a short question and then write an answer limited to a few words or a sentence. You are more likely to be asked 'what', rather than 'why', because a detailed explanation is not needed.

An example of this type of question is:

> State TWO factors which influence the method a business person uses to obtain finance.

The answer should consist of two brief statements, such as 'The cost of finance' and 'The nature or form of the business (such as a share issue by a PLC)'.

Key words used in restricted response questions include

- STATE
- NAME
- OUTLINE
- LIST

Characteristics Because these restricted response questions are limited in scope and therefore take little time to answer, you can expect to face a lot of them. They tend to be compulsory: there is usually no choice of questions to answer.

You can obtain full marks for these questions by stating general points of content which you have learnt. The skills the examiner tests in restricted response questions are those of recalling and describing factual knowledge. These questions will only have a few marks awarded to them, and so only short answers are required.

Another feature of these questions concerns the guidance received on the length of answer. Some examining boards ask you to write answers in the answer book provided and advise you that complete sentences are not required as answers. The alternative approach is to write answers on the examination paper itself, the paper doubling as the answer book. An advantage of this approach is that you can see clearly the maximum length of answer expected by the examiner.

Short-answer questions

These questions fall between the restricted response type and the full essay. They vary in detail and number of marks allocated, but typical examples of such questions are:

> In your answer book, sketch a diagram based on the statistics provided to show a comparison between the regions.

> Explain why an increase in general interest rates might cause a fall in consumer spending.

The examiner uses words such as

- EXPLAIN
- DESCRIBE
- COMPARE
- CONTRAST

to indicate to you that the answers expected are longer and more detailed than those for restricted response questions.

Short-answer questions are popular in Business Studies examinations. A short-answer element often forms the first part of a more extensive question: by structuring questions in several parts, starting with the easier short-answer element, the examiner is setting questions with an 'incline of difficulty', meaning they get more difficult as you proceed through the parts. The examiner can still set a large number of these questions and therefore cover all major syllabus topics.

Characteristics The similarities between short-answer and restricted response questions are that the answers required tend to be limited in:

- scope;
- depth;
- volume of information.

There are also important differences. Short-answer questions place three extra demands on you. You could be asked to:

- explain or analyse a general Business Studies idea or concept;
- apply this general principle to a given situation;
- construct answers which more fully test your ability to communicate.

Data response questions

We use many real-life illustrations and case histories when learning about Business Studies. Examiners use data response questions to bring the real world into the examination room.

All the boards now use data response as a key part of their assessment. A popular approach for examiners is the 'incline of difficulty', mentioned above, where easy questions based on the data are followed by more difficult ones. The precise use varies from board to board: some papers consist of a single case study with a series of compulsory questions, whereas other papers mix essay-style and data response questions. You will find information on the boards' assessment structures on pages 3-15.

Data response questions often contain phrases such as:

> What arguments could the board of directors in this company put forward to support the merger with...?

Using material from the case study:
(a) explain the differences between...

Discuss what is revealed by this balance sheet about the sources of finance for this business.

Characteristics These questions require you to organise your answers: this is less of a problem here than with essays, because data response questions are themselves structured using parts (a), (b), (c), etc. Both data response and essay questions focus on the higher-level thinking skills of application, analysis, evaluation and judgement. In answering data response questions, you will use these higher-level skills to analyse data presented in numerical and/ or diagrammatic form, unlike the more general approaches in essays. This characteristic means that data response questions require you to demonstrate a wide range of skills. Many Business Studies teachers and examiners felt for a long time that limiting A-level and similar examinations to an essay format was inappropriate, and did not allow candidates to be tested on relevant business-related skills such as summary and presentation of information. This also partly accounts for the growth in the use of project and assignment work.

Essay questions

Higher-order skills are also tested by traditional essays. These often concentrate on a major aspect of Business Studies theory. Examples of these questions are:

Discuss the likely effect on business of the increasing awareness of environmental issues.

Explain the concept of cost-benefit analysis. To what extent is the concept relevant to the UK economy of the 1990s?

Characteristics Essay questions require descriptive and analytical answers. At A-level or equivalent, you are expected to organise the answer logically and to include real-life illustrations if possible and where relevant.

Essays are less 'applied' than data response questions: partly because of this, their relative importance has declined in recent years, but the examining boards still use them in Business Studies assessment.

Unlike the typical data response/case study papers, many essay papers allow you a choice of questions.

EXAMINATION TECHNIQUES

If your examining board allows a choice of questions, it is worth spending some time making your decision. Factors influencing this decision should be your **familiarity with and confidence in the different topics**, and the **amount of time** that each question is likely to take to answer. Some candidates find that computational questions, or ones requiring diagram construction, take longer to complete.

Restricted response and short-answer questions do not normally require you to organise your answer, and other communication skills (such as sentence construction) may not be tested. The major challenge is to complete the section in the time allowed. Some candidates ignore the instructions or mark allocation and write unnecessarily long answers. You must also move on quickly from any question proving difficult or involving over-lengthy calculations. If you have, say, half an hour for the section, you could allow twenty minutes as a first run-through, leaving ten minutes for completing answers to any difficult, partly-completed questions. This ensures that you have attempted all questions, including the later (and possibly easier) ones.

Good answers demonstrated an ability to express facts briefly and concisely. Poorer candidates tended to ignore instructions and wrote long sentences or relied on one-word answers that were too vague.

(Extract from AEB A-level report)

Here are some tips to help you answer the longer (essay and data response) questions successfully.

❶ **Study the key words.** Essays often include a key word giving an indication of how to approach the answer. The use of words such as 'outline', 'state' and 'describe' suggests that the examiner expects you to give information without having to argue a case or make a judgement. Where the essay asks you to 'explain', 'justify', 'evaluate' or 'argue', you are expected to provide a more reasoned and developed answer.

> A major problem was the failure to read questions so that key words were missed and thus questions were misinterpreted. In addition, candidates need to understand words such as 'distinguish', 'explain', 'discuss', 'outline' etc. and to relate the length of their answers to the marks allocated.
>
> (Extract from AEB A-level report)

❷ **Do not spend a disproportionate amount of time on any one answer.** If you have spent too much time on one question, you will need to recover the situation. This can be done by selecting one of the later questions and summarising your answer as a series of points. Though not ideal, this is acceptable where the examiner is testing your ability to list and explain relevant points. If you can select a question which asks you to 'compare' or 'contrast' rather than 'discuss', you can provide a good summary of points without having to elaborate arguments (which takes time).

> Poor candidates failed to allocate time appropriately – often providing lengthy answers to questions carrying few marks and superficial, short answers to questions with a large mark allocation.
>
> (Extract from AEB A-level report)

You must also pay close attention to the mark allocation where the question is divided into parts. For example, a question worth 25 marks might read:

(a) Outline the work of TWO of the following management theorists... (10 marks)

(b) Explain why....(15 marks)

If you have forty minutes available for the answer, the first part should be completed in approximately sixteen minutes (40 per cent of the time available): the work of each theorist should be outlined in about eight minutes only.

❸ **Avoid repeating points.** There is a given number of marks for each point made, and you gain nothing by repeating information which has already been explained clearly and fully. The examiner always prefers to mark clear and concise essays, rather than over-long, repetitive and rambling ones. In essay answers, the opening paragraph could be used to define terms (see point 6 below) to avoid repetition. Any closing paragraph should also avoid over-repeating arguments and information for which marks will already have been given.

❹ **Do not start a major question without first constructing a plan.** This provides a source against which you can check that all points are included, and also helps avoid repetition.

❺ **Avoid merely writing down all you know and can recall about a topic.** If a question includes general terms such as 'marketing' or 'investment', there is a danger that you will provide an answer which is not required. You should check carefully to see if the question focuses on one particular aspect of a topic. If it does, the examiner expects you to select and apply relevant details from this topic.

❻ **Define any terms you regard as ambiguous.** General essay questions are sometimes open to more than one interpretation. In such a situation I would advise you to use the first paragraph to define any terms you regard as ambiguous and/or to explain to the examiner any assumptions you are making. There can be several 'right answers where different assumptions are made, all... quite legitimate, as long as such assumptions were made specific' (extract from an examiner's report).

Study the data carefully. Careful study of the question is important, especially when it contains a substantial data component. Whether you are given real-life or hypothetical data, the examiner expects you to be able to apply your general Business Studies knowledge to the situation outlined in the data. We can distinguish between a question phrased as: 'Why do such firms...', and one asking 'Why does this firm...'. The first question allows you to generalise to a greater extent than the second, where you should phrase your comments from the point of view of the given firm.

> ... candidates are not expected to read and re-read the Case Study until word perfect, but are expected to identify the major issues, consider causes and assess possible solutions...

> ... candidates often failed to do themselves justice by... not reading the question carefully – for example if a report is asked for, that is what is expected.

(Extracts from London Examinations A-level report)

FINAL PREPARATION

The week before the examination

Are you sure that you know the exact requirements of the examining board?

- How many questions are there on the paper(s)?
- Is there a choice?
- What type(s) of question do I have to answer?
- How many sections are there in each paper?
- What is the time limit for each section and paper?
- Is a calculator permitted?
- Does the question paper double as an answer book?
- What overall weighting do the papers have?

It is worth carrying out a 'minutes per mark' calculation for the more demanding papers. As an illustration, if an A-level Business Studies Paper 1 lasts two and a half hours and contains 100 marks, a question worth twenty marks should take about thirty minutes to plan and answer. If you are still working on it after, say, forty minutes you must consider starting another question, because:

- you should allocate some time for checking answers and computations;
- you can still obtain most of the marks even though the question is left unfinished; and
- time pressure in Business Studies examinations is quite severe and the opportunity cost of spending too long on one question is the loss of time available to answer others.

With only a week to go, you should know most of the syllabus content. Some of the time spent revising this week should be spent practising your examination technique.

We suggest that, if possible, you check the examination room in advance. If it is a room you know, you will be aware of environmental factors such as heat, draughts, sunlight and ventilation. If you do not know the room, checking it before the examination means anticipating problems of noise and heat. This is also a valuable psychological ploy, because you will arrive on the day with a 'feel' for what to expect.

The night before the examination

Sitting an examination paper is a tiring business: and you will have at least two papers to sit. Perhaps the most important thing to do the night before is to get a reasonable amount of rest, to allow you to think clearly throughout the examination.

Most people like to spend the evening doing last-minute revision. This is fine, as long as you acknowledge that 'last-minute' is the key phrase. Assuming that you have planned and done your revision, the work the night before plays an important psychological role in boosting your confidence. I suggest that you concentrate on areas you are least happy with. Whilst this might seem demoralising rather than confidence-boosting, there are good educational reasons for suggesting it.

All students must expect to struggle with some syllabus topics: this influences your choice of questions to answer. By concentrating your last-minute revision on weaker areas, you should be able to commit many difficult points to short-term memory (with tomorrow's examination in mind). This should be a better use of your time than rechecking content which you already know thoroughly.

You should test how much content you can remember from these difficult areas by trying to recall and write down key points. I suggest that a **checklist of key words and phrases** is constructed to 'trigger' your memory. This can be referred to on the morning of the examination and also just before entering the room, to reinforce short-term learning. (The idea of using abbreviated notes and lists is not of course restricted to the topics you find difficult: your topic content summaries will have been used as revision sources.)

The day of the examination

Even at this late stage of the process you can still carry out some limited revision. Benefits from checking notes and summaries 'on the day' are:

● they boost your confidence;

● reinforcement of short-term learning takes place.

Before setting out for the examination you will obviously check you have everything required. Typical items include pens (blue or black: not red), a ruler, a watch and a calculator. You should know the time it takes to get to the examination centre. Planning to arrive well in advance gives you time to settle down, as well as allowing for any unforeseen delays.

The confidence you now have in your subject knowledge will be a great boost at the start of the examination.

BUSINESS STUDIES TOPICS

In this section:

Each chapter features:

- *Units in this chapter:* a list of the main topic heads to follow

- *Chapter objectives:* a brief comment on how the topics relate to what has gone before, and to the syllabus. Key ideas and skills which are covered in the chapter are introduced.

- *The main text:* divided into numbered topic units for ease of reference.

- *Chapter roundup:* a brief summary of the chapter.

- *Illustrative questions:* typical exam questions, with tutorial notes and our suggested answer.

- *Practice questions:* further questions, with tutorial comments on the pitfalls to avoid and points to include in framing your own answers.

THE ECONOMIC ENVIRONMENT

Units in this chapter

Chapter objectives

All Business Studies syllabuses include a section which acts as an introduction to the business world. A typical example is the Welsh Joint Examination Committee (WJEC) A-level Business Core, based on the Subject Core common to A-level Business Studies syllabuses. This module starts with 'The Individual, the Organisation and the Environment of Business' which sets the scene of business in society.

The purpose of this chapter is therefore to give an overview of business activity within the UK economy. It also explains the international economic situation which influences, and is influenced by, the United Kingdom. The chapter provides background information which is drawn on throughout the Guide, and links closely with the next two chapters. Chapter 2 explains the nature of business organisations, and Chapter 3 concentrates on how organisations grow in our economy.

The key topics and concepts covered in this chapter are:
● opportunity cost;
● supply, demand and price determination;
● elasticity;
● specialisation, exchange and trade;
● protectionism;
● regional economic groupings;
● balance of payments;
● exchange rates.

1.1   SCARCITY, CHOICE AND OPPORTUNITY COST

The science of Economics concentrates on the allocation of **scarce resources** between **competing alternative uses**. As production takes place, the goods created – known as economic goods – use these scarce resources. These resources have costs associated with them: an accountant measures the costs in purely financial terms, whereas an economist considers the **opportunity cost** of production. Resources which are allocated to one use cannot simultaneously be used elsewhere. For example, the opportunity cost of spending an evening at the cinema includes not going bowling and not attending a concert.

The use of land provides a good illustration of opportunity cost in action. If an area of land contains a number of office blocks, it cannot be used at the same time for alternative purposes such as housing, a shopping complex, or agriculture. The use of this plot of land can change at a later date: if the offices are demolished to make way for a new road, the opportunity cost of the land used for this road is the loss of office space. Opportunity cost is therefore concerned with the loss of the value of the next best use at any particular time.

Given that there are scarce resources, choices have to be made between their alternative uses. Different economic systems approach this problem in different ways, but all systems must consider how to answer the basic question of what to produce. The concept of opportunity cost is particularly important here, when a government considers, for example, how to share its taxation revenue between defence, education, health, and other competing uses.

1.2 TYPES OF ECONOMY

In any economic system there is some form of mechanism to allocate both the scarce economic goods and the scarce resources used to make these goods. All economies must solve the problems of

- *What* do we produce?
- *How* do we produce it?
- *For whom* do we produce?

The types of economy described below differ according to the mechanism they use for allocating scarce resources. The theoretical extremes of pure 'market' or 'command' economies are not found in real life, although these terms are used when referring to economic systems dominated by one or other of these extremes.

THE MARKET ECONOMY

The price mechanism is used to allocate scarce resources in a market economy. Production decisions are made by firms and/or private individuals, not by a central planning authority. The profit motive is important and influences demand, supply and price. Private ownership of resources, commonly known as 'free enterprise', is associated with these economies.

The price mechanism works efficiently when it carries out its two functions.

1. **Signalling** Stable or changing prices give signals to buyers and sellers, conveying information which is acted upon by them.

2. **Incentives** Price increases or reductions should act as incentives. For example, greater demand for a product should encourage existing firms to employ more resources in increasing their output, leading to economies of scale.

Advantages of a market economy

1. **Efficiency** A market economy can achieve great efficiency in production and in the allocation of resources.

2. **Decentralisation** Decision-making takes place through the price mechanism, thereby avoiding a cumbersome and slow central bureaucracy.

3. **Consumer sovereignty** Producers have to satisfy their clients in order to make a profit, and the consumer therefore has the power to determine what is produced.

Disadvantages of a market economy

1 **Inefficiency** Few 'perfect' markets exist in the real world, and distortions such as collusion amongst competitors, limited knowledge on the part of consumers, barriers to entry, and taxes and subsidies mean that economic efficiency may not exist in practice.

2 **Under-use of resources** There should (theoretically) be full employment of labour (and all other resources) in a perfectly competitive market, but unemployment still persists.

3 **Inappropriate use of resources** The price mechanism and profit motive can result in social judgements being ignored, with scarce resources not being allocated to socially beneficial projects because of these market factors. This results in non-profitable goods or services such as universal health care not being supplied without state intervention.

4 **Inequality** Where the price mechanism is used as the basis for allocation, those who are priced out of the market cannot obtain many of the goods or services.

5 **Market realities** The distortion of certain markets by monopolies, cartels and other forms restricting the workings of the market results in the producer and not the consumer being sovereign. Other factors such as persuasive advertising can also increase the power of the producer.

6 **Cost-benefit** Without state influence, external costs such as pollution might be ignored by a producer when price and profit are calculated.

THE MIXED ECONOMY

In practice there are often publicly owned enterprises (such as the UK's nationalised industries) which form an important part of market economies. Their existence leads to the economy being called 'mixed'. A distinction is made between the two sectors, public and private, using ownership as the basis: we also differentiate on how goods and services are allocated by using the terms 'market sector' and 'non-market sector'. Political or social decisions might lead to a product being provided by only one sector, although both sectors can often produce the same item. For example, health services are available in both sectors of the UK economy.

Throughout the 1980s and 1990s, the UK economy saw a growth in the private sector at the expense of the public sector. **Privatisation** (see page 70) and other economic policies of the Conservative government led to the market economy becoming increasingly important: the role of the State is seen as providing a 'safety net', creating an environment within which market conditions can flourish, whilst at the same time undertaking some regulation of the market.

Reasons for the existence of mixed economies

1 Because public goods are produced through the central planning system and private goods through the operation of the price mechanism, a wider range of goods is provided.

2 State regulation helps overcome many of the socially undesirable results of a market economy. Examples include the legal control of UK monopolies, and health and safety legislation protecting employees and consumers.

3 In a pure market economy, income distribution would not be affected by non-economic factors. The State has to make decisions on how taxation and other influences on income affect its distribution.

THE COMMAND ECONOMY

A centrally planned, or 'command', economy is the opposite theoretical extreme to the pure market economy. As an approach to the allocation of resources it tends to be widely discredited in the West, but we should note that there is no reason why, in theory, a command economy cannot be just as efficient as a market-based one.

Command economies which have existed in practice, such as those in the former Soviet Union and Eastern Europe, have concentrated on the **central control** of what is produced, how it is distributed and at what price. This is usually implemented by utilising some form of central plan.

Advantages of a command economy

1 Cost considerations   The central planning agency takes into account social and other costs which are not easily measurable in financial terms.

2 Public goods   Provision of goods and services can be made on the basis of need rather than profit.

3 Income distribution   The State can make decisions concerned with the fairness of income distribution, through its decision-making role relating to taxation levels.

Disadvantages of a command economy

1 Bureaucracy   The number and frequency of decisions which have to be made centrally lead to extremely complex administrative systems, time delays and inevitable mistakes in resource allocation.

2 Lack of incentive   Producers are not rewarded to the same extent as in a market economy, and there is also a lack of incentive for employees. Innovation of new products, services and systems is not encouraged and products tend to be 'standardised'.

3 Price signals   Because prices do not depend to the same extent on the interaction of demand and supply, there are no signals available to producers from price movements. Producers have to meet production targets and the economy experiences surpluses and shortages because of planning imperfections.

1.3   PRODUCTION AND THE MARKET

FORMS OF PRODUCTION

Production can be classified under the three headings shown in Fig. 1.1.

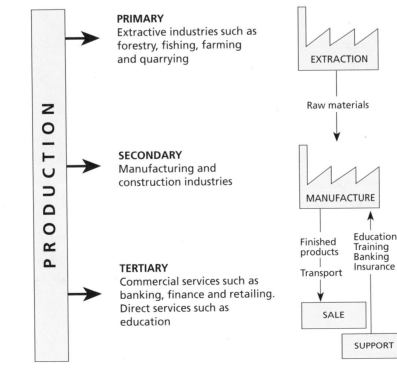

Fig. 1.1 Primary, secondary and tertiary production

The UK economy

Table 1.1 illustrates the change in the relative importance of the primary, secondary and tertiary sectors in the UK economy.

Table 1.1 *Employees in employment by Standard Industrial Classification and sex, 1981 and 1995*

	PRIMARY	SECONDARY		TERTIARY			
	Agriculture, forestry, fishing, energy and water supply (%)	Manufacturing (%)	Construction (%)	Distribution, hotels and catering (%)	Transport and communication (%)	Banking, finance, insurance, business services (%)	Public administration and other services (%)
Males 1995	2.9	26.3	6.5	20.3	8.4	16.5	19.1
(1981)	(7.1)	(35.2)	(8.1)	(15.2)	(9.1)	(7.2)	(18.1)
Females 1995	0.9	11.1	1.2	24.5	3.2	17.0	42.1
(1981)	(2.0)	(19.2)	(1.2)	(24.3)	(3.0)	(9.0)	(41.3)

Source: Office for National Statistics

Manufacturing industry has declined in relative importance in the UK since 1980. This **deindustrialisation** reflects a long-term move towards tertiary production. The first Industrial Revolution led to many workers moving from the country to the towns and changing to employment in secondary production. The trend away from agriculture and extraction has continued since the Second World War, together with a major shift in recent years from employment in manufacturing to employment in the service sector. This is typical of developed Western economies, whereas a number of countries in the Far East are experiencing the move from primary to manufacturing employment. Fig. 1.2 suggests that this trend is likely to continue.

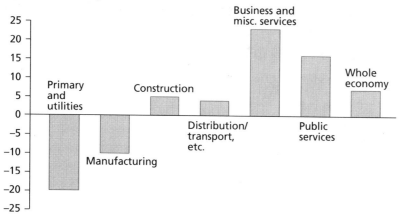

Fig. 1.2 Sectoral employment projections, percentage change, 1991–2000

Source: Department for Education and Employment

Reasons for deindustrialisation in the UK include:

● The increasing substitution of capital for labour in the production process in both the primary and secondary sectors.

● The fall in the UK's competitiveness in secondary production, resulting in more manufactured goods being imported.

● The increased number of newly industrialised countries such as Taiwan and Malaysia.

MARKETS

Buyers purchase from the range of goods and services available from producers. In order to supply goods, these producers must themselves buy factors of production – land, labour and capital – which are for sale in the market-place.

In the manufacturing sector, goods produced are classified as either consumer goods (bought for final consumption, e.g. televisions) or capital goods such as industrial machinery, which are bought to make other goods. This classification can also be applied to markets.

Consumer market	Industrial market
Buying and selling of consumer goods	Buying and selling of producer goods

A market is therefore a meeting of buyers and sellers, where goods or services are exchanged for other goods or services. This exchange is indirect, the products being exchanged for money: this money is used at a later date to buy other products. Economists emphasise this role of the market as **a system of exchange based on demand, supply and price**. All forms of market are seen as having price determination as a common factor.

DEMAND

The fundamental law of demand is:

As price increases, quantity demanded falls
As price decreases, quantity demanded rises

We make the assumption that this demand is effective, i.e. it is backed by money and a willingness to buy.

When a demand curve is plotted to show consumer behaviour in a single market, it appears as in Fig. 1.3.

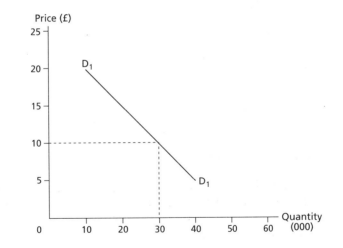

Fig. 1.3 Demand curve

The graph shows that at a price of £10, 30,000 items are demanded. The curve is constructed from the individual demand curves of all consumers in the market. The gradient of the curve's fall from left to right varies according to the elasticity of demand for the item (see page 41).

The downward-sloping demand curve confirms that consumers demand more of the item as its price falls. In the above illustration an expansion of quantity demanded occurs if the price falls from £10 (when 30,000 are demanded) to £5 (when 40,000 are demanded). A contraction of quantity demanded occurs when the price increases.

These movements along the existing demand curve are due solely to price changes for the product, and are referred to as changes in quantity demanded. The demand curve itself does not change position on the graph.

Shifts in the demand curve

Changes in demand also occur, resulting in the demand curve moving position. These are known as shifts in demand: the curve either moves to the right (an increase in demand) or to the left (a decrease in demand), as shown in Figs. 1.4 and 1.5.

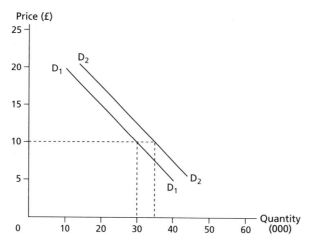

Fig. 1.4 Increase in demand

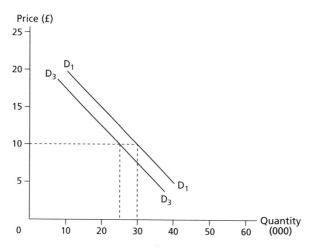

Fig. 1.5 Decrease in demand

In Fig. 1.4 the demand curve has moved to the right. The increase in demand, shown by curve D_2, at a price of £10 is from 30,000 to 35,000. Fig. 1.5 illustrates a fall in demand: at a price of £10 demand has fallen from 30,000 to 25,000 (on curve D_3).

Shifts in the demand curve are due to changes in:

1 **Taste or fashion**   This is often associated with clothing or particular trends in youth markets, such as the fashion in the early 1990s for mountain and sports bikes. It is also found when health-related information is made available on certain foodstuffs or other products, such as tobacco. The effectiveness of a product's advertising in shaping consumer tastes can have an influence here. The effect on demand can be short-term, such as a scare which took place over the safety of apple juice in the early 1990s, or long-term, for example the steady increase in demand for low-fat 'healthy' varieties of some foods.

2 **Price of substitutes**   Many products have close substitutes. This is the case for foodstuffs (meat, spreads, etc.) or most branded products such as soap, toothpaste and washing-up liquids. In such cases an increase in the price of one good is likely to increase the demand for its substitute, the demand curve for the substitute shifting to the right even though its price has not altered.

❸ Price of jointly demanded products   Where one product is in joint or derived demand with another (vehicles and petrol, or CD players and compact discs), a change in the price of one product will affect the demand for its joint product. As CD players and computer games hardware prices fall, the demand for CDs and computer games increases.

❹ Income   Effective demand must be backed by money, and so any increase in real disposable income normally shifts the demand curve to the right, as consumers can now afford more of the product. 'Real disposable income' refers to net personal income after allowing for deductions and price changes. It is affected by government direct and indirect taxation policies or changes in employment and general wage levels. Increases in income might result in less of a good being demanded if it is an inferior good; consumers switch their attention to substitutes felt to be superior, for example by buying cars (private transport) to replace the use of public transport. We should also remember that individuals and households are not the only important groups demanding goods and services. Firms create demand for labour, capital and land in the 'factor' (of production) markets. The relative level of firms' income through profitability and investment is therefore also important.

❺ Population   Changes in the total population, its age or other structure and geographical situation influences demand. The UK has an ageing population, which has caused increasing demand for health care and other products used by this sector of the population. A fall in the school-age population during the 1980s led to a reduced demand for a range of school education services. Fig. 1.6 shows the expected growth in the over-65 sector of Europe's population.

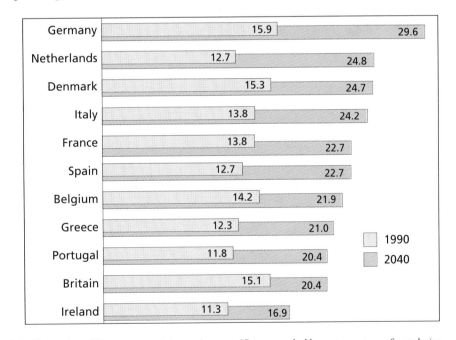

Fig. 1.6 The ageing of Europe: growth in pensioners – 65 years and older as percentage of population

Source: OECD

The UK population movements towards urban areas and away from the countryside have changed the demand for public and private transport in different parts of the country. Changes in society and social attitudes also affect demand: an increase in the number of single-parent families increases demand for smaller properties, and any changes in the number of couples both working can affect the demand for convenience and 'fast' foods. Table 2 highlights the growth of one-person households and the fall in the number of 'traditional' households. In 1961, over three in ten households consisted of a married couple with two or more dependent children: by 1990 this had fallen by a third. Factors leading to smaller household sizes include increasing divorce rates and an increasing elderly population.

Table 1.2 *Household size, 1961 and 1994–5*

Size of household	1961 (%)	1994–5 (%)
1 person	14	27
2 people	30	34
3 people	23	16
4 or more people	33	23
Average size	3.1	2.4

Source: OPCS

⑥ Innovation   As new goods and services are introduced, they influence the demand for products currently on the market. Good examples come from the entertainment sector, where compact disc developments have affected demand for media such as vinyl records and magnetic tape in the music sector, and microchip-based computer games.

SUPPLY

Fig. 1.7 shows that the direction of the supply curve is opposite to that of the demand curve, because

> **As price increases, quantity supplied rises**
> **As price decreases, quantity supplied falls**

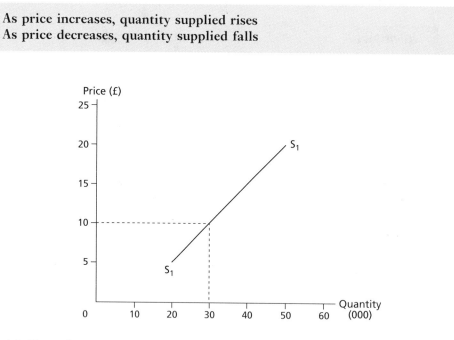

Fig. 1.7   The supply curve

Therefore the higher the price, the greater will be the quantity supplied. Higher prices enhance profits so the existing firms in the market increase output and new firms enter the market. The market supply curve in Fig. 1.7 shows the amount that will be supplied at any given price: at £10 for example, firms are prepared to supply 30,000 items of the product.

Shifts in the supply curve

Movements along an existing supply curve – expansions or contractions of quantity supplied – occur when the price of the good or service alters. The supply curve itself might also move, due to a number of factors. When this occurs we refer to it as a shift in supply, and it is due to non-price factors.

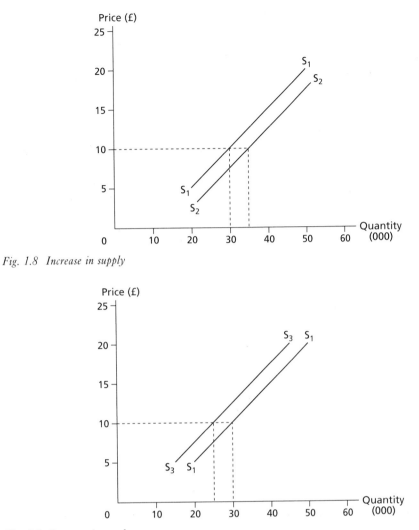

Fig. 1.8 Increase in supply

Fig. 1.9 Decrease in supply

A change from supply curve S₁ to S₂ shown in Fig. 1.8 illustrates that at a price of £10, firms are now prepared to supply 35,000 items. Where supply changes from S₁ to S₃ (Fig. 1.9), firms will now supply 25,000 rather than 30,000 items.

Shifts in the supply curve are due to changes in:

❶ **Factor inputs** A change in the price of individual factors of production used, their quality, or the ratio in which they are used all cause a change in production costs. This in turn affects a firm's profit margins and supply levels. A good illustration occurs with technological developments, where cost-saving new machinery and automated processes replace labour and lead to improved productivity, reduced unit costs and increased output. Improvements in the quality of labour, for example through better training, can have a similar effect.

❷ **Competition** The existence of major competitors should lead to increased efficiency in the use of resources; this in turn results in higher output at given cost levels and increases the supply of the product.

❸ **Other products** Where jointly supplied products exist – for example, petrol, paraffin and other oils all have joint production processes – an increase in the price of one product will lead to an increased supply not only of it, but also of any product which is jointly produced with it.

❹ **Natural factors** The recent exploitation of North Sea oil illustrates how the discovery of new sources of a primary product increases the supply of that product. Changes in climate, such as the possible global weather changes now taking place, influence levels of agricultural production through affecting harvests, or the ability of a country to continue growing its present range of crops.

⑤ Government policies   Levels of taxation affect firms as well as individuals. Direct (corporation) and indirect (VAT) tax changes affect total costs and thus supply levels. Changes in the law, such as 'clean air' legislation, also affect production methods and costs. Governments might decide to control levels of production or impose subsidies or quotas to influence prices.

MARKET PRICE

The market, or **equilibrium**, price is established when demand equals supply. The term 'equilibrium' indicates a state of rest, where price stays the same unless there is a change in either supply or demand.

If the demand and supply curves shown in Figs. 1.3 and 1.7 are combined, the equilibrium price will be £10 (see Fig. 1.10). Consumers demand 30,000 at this price and producers are prepared to supply the same amount.

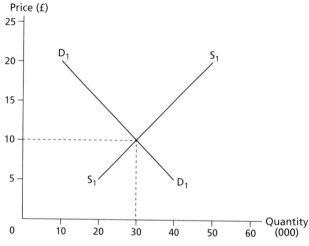

Fig. 1.10 Equilibrium

Prices are allowed to change freely. Fig. 1.11 shows that if the price rose to £15:

- consumers would only demand a quantity of 20,000
- but producers would supply 40,000
- thus creating a surplus
- causing the price to fall
- leading to increased demand
- and reduced supply
- and establishing the equilibrium position

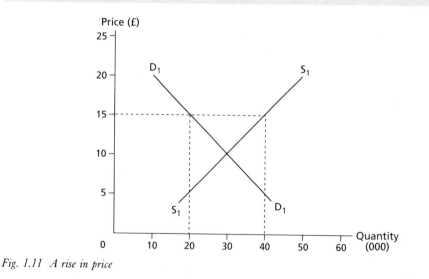

Fig. 1.11 A rise in price

If the price was set below the equilibrium, shortages would result due to demand exceeding supply. The effect of the shortage would be to encourage firms to put up their prices, and so reduce demand and increase supply until equilibrium was again established.

In reality, prices do not always rise and fall freely. Where they are fixed, for example through European Union decisions regarding agricultural product prices, surpluses such as the 'wine lakes' may remain; where there are shortages, 'black market' or other rationing operations can develop.

The equilibrium changes when there is a change in demand or a change in supply. The resulting new demand or supply curve produces a new equilibrium price.

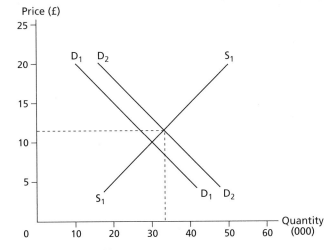

Fig. 1.12 Changes in demand and equilibrium

In Fig. 1.12 the increase in demand from D_1 to D_2 – due to one of the reasons given on pages 36-8 – raises the equilibrium price from £10 to £11.25. Fig. 1.13 illustrates a fall in supply – for one of the reasons given on pages 39–40 – which also raises the equilibrium price from £10 to £11.25 (the equilibrium quantity is 28,000 compared with 32,000 shown in Fig. 1.12).

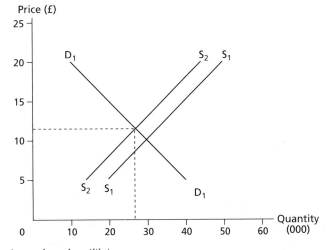

Fig. 1.13 Changes in supply and equilibrium

ELASTICITY OF DEMAND

The measure of the change taking place in the quantity supplied or demanded as a result of some external factor is known as elasticity. Elasticity of demand is affected by one of three influences:

❶ changes in its price = PED;

❷ changes in income = YED;

❸ changes in the price of other goods = CED.

Price elasticity of demand

The price elasticity of demand (PED) for a product measures the responsiveness of the quantity demanded to a change in its price. We are examining **movements along the product's demand curve**, and not changes in demand. Using Fig. 1.14 as an illustration we apply the following formula to calculate PED.

$$\text{PED} = \frac{\textbf{Percentage change in quantity demanded}}{\textbf{Percentage change in price}}$$

The price has risen from £20 to £30 and the quantity demanded has fallen from 400 to 300; applying the formula gives us:

$$\text{PED} = \frac{25}{50} = 0.5$$

(The negative sign is normally ignored in PED calculations.)

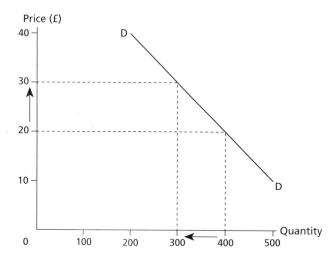

Fig. 1.14 Price elasticity of demand

PED > 1

When PED is greater than one, the supplier knows that a change in price will bring about a more than proportionate change in quantity demanded. The product is **price-sensitive** and demand is said to be **price-elastic** due to this sensitivity.

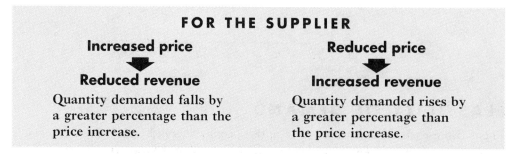

PED < 1

If PED is less than one, the change in price is proportionally greater than the resultant change in quantity demanded. Demand is said to be **price-inelastic**.

FOR THE SUPPLIER

Increased price	**Reduced price**
Increased revenue	**Reduced revenue**
Quantity demanded falls by a lower percentage than the price increase.	Quantity demanded rises by a lower percentage than the price increase.

PED = 1

This is known as **unitary elasticity**. Any given percentage price change results in the same percentage change in the quantity demanded.

Price elasticity is influenced by:

- **Availability of substitutes**   Where a product has a close substitute, such as margarine and butter, demand tends to be elastic since it is easy for the user to switch between the substitutes. Where substitutes do not exist there is less competition and demand is therefore more inelastic.

- **Percentage of spending on the product**   Inexpensive products have inelastic demands because increases in price have little effect on consumers' spending plans. Where higher prices are involved, potential consumers will search harder for substitutes or alternatives. Consumer durable goods and the more expensive foodstuffs often have price-elastic demands because consumers delay expenditure or go without the item.

- **Addiction**   Where consumers are prevented from making price-rational decisions, for instance through alcohol or other drug addiction, price movements have little effect and price tends to be inelastic.

Price elasticity is a valuable measuring tool. It influences the decisions of producers because total revenue is affected by the level of the product's elasticity. Government decisions on taxation levels are also affected by price elasticity. Products subject to taxation which have inelastic demands (petrol and tobacco are examples) will yield extra revenue if the indirect tax levels on them are increased: the relative fall in sales is lower than the rise in income generated from the price (tax) increase.

Income elasticity of demand

This form of elasticity – YED (sometimes called IED) – is a measure of how demand responds to changes in consumer incomes. It is measured by:

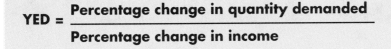

$$\text{YED} = \frac{\text{Percentage change in quantity demanded}}{\text{Percentage change in income}}$$

If consumer incomes rise by 3 per cent and demand for a product then rises by 9 per cent:

$$\text{YED} = \frac{9}{3} = 3.0$$

We normally expect a positive result, because demand for most products rises and falls with income. Inferior goods such as some staple foodstuffs, however, may have a negative YED because the amount demanded falls as real income rises and the consumers can afford more appealing alternatives.

Demand is **income-elastic when YED is greater than 1**, and **income-inelastic when YED is less than 1**. The higher the percentage of income spent on the product, the more income-elastic that product's demand tends to be.

YED can also be associated with shifts in the demand curve: page 37 identifies changes in real disposable income as one of the influences causing a shift in the curve.

Cross-elasticity of demand

This form of elasticity – known as CED – measures how a product's demand responds to changes in the price of a related (substitute or complementary) good. It is associated with shifts in the demand curve and is calculated by:

$$\text{CED} = \frac{\textbf{Percentage change in product A's demand}}{\textbf{Percentage change in product B's price}}$$

Product A could be either a complementary or a substitute good for product B. If it is a complementary good, the cross-elasticity will be negative: a fall in the price of Nintendo or Sega hardware will increase demand for the associated software. If product A is a substitute for product B, there will be a positive value for the cross-elasticity: an increase in the price of Nintendo machines will lead to greater demand for Sega hardware. The closer the complement or substitute, the higher the cross-elasticity value will be. We would therefore expect a higher cross-elasticity value for different brands of jam than for the more distant substitutes of strawberry jam and cheese spread.

Price elasticity of supply

Price changes affect both quantity demanded and quantity supplied. The price elasticity of supply (PES) measures the responsiveness of the quantity supplied to a change in price. It is calculated by using the formula:

$$\text{PES} = \frac{\textbf{Percentage change in quantity supplied}}{\textbf{Percentage change in price}}$$

In the very short term, suppliers cannot respond in full to price changes. Over a longer period, however, the elasticity is influenced by:

- **The industry** If firms find it easy to set up in or leave the industry, the more elastic the supply will be.
- **The factors of production** Firms having factors of production readily available can respond more easily to price signals. However, if labour is not available or requires training, or capital equipment is not readily available, the response to price changes is more inelastic.

1.4 INTERNATIONAL TRADE

SPECIALISATION AND EXCHANGE

Modern-day mixed economies are based on specialisation. Specialists working within the UK include plumbers, carpenters, computer programmers, doctors and dentists. People become interdependent as a result: they have to rely on others either to produce what they cannot produce themselves, or to buy their expertise or surplus.

Money and barter

Specialisation within an advanced economy such as that of the United Kingdom has led to the need for an accepted medium of exchange (money). The old system of exchange using barter presented certain problems:

1. **Lack of coincidence of wants** A carpenter having a table to barter and who needs food must find a farmer with surplus food who also needs a new table.

② **Indivisibility**   The carpenter may want only a small amount of food, but because of the relative value of his table the farmer might be asked to part with far more than he would wish to.

③ **Valuation**   The value of tables in chickens or beans must be agreed by both parties.

Money as a universally recognised medium of exchange does not solve all these problems, especially when trade between nations takes place (each nation must establish the value of its own currency against that of other nations, for example). It does, however, perform several valuable functions. It is a:

- **medium of exchange**
- **measure of value**
- **store of value**

SPECIALISATION OF ECONOMIES

Countries specialise as a result of factors such as the nature of the land and its climate, the availability of raw materials, and the level of training and expertise of the labour force. Specialisation leads to mass production, the purpose being to produce a substantial amount which is surplus to the producer economy's needs. This surplus is produced at a competitive cost through the existence of economies of scale (see pages 83-4).

The problem for an economy of using scarce resources to produce a surplus it does not need is that it no longer has the resources to make the other items needed. Exchange of surpluses therefore takes place between countries. Interdependence between countries exists through trade in the same way that individuals within a country become interdependent. Table 1.3 summarises the trade between the UK and the rest of the world.

Table 1.3 *UK imports (cif) and exports (fob) by country groupings, 1996 (Quarter 1)*

	EXPORTS £ million	IMPORTS £ million
European Union	22,956	23,992
Other Western Europe	1,718	2,985
North America	5,374	5,977
Other OECD Countries (Japan, Australia, New Zealand)	1,842	2,811
Oil-exporting Countries	1,737	891
Rest of the World	6,489	7,791

Source: Office for National Statistics

FREE TRADE

Free trade occurs when the movement of goods and services between countries is not restricted in any way. The advantage of free trade is explained by the theories of absolute advantage and comparative advantage.

Absolute and comparative advantage

Let us assume that the UK and Denmark both devote half their available resources to produce televisions and half to produce textiles (the same total resources are used). If production is as shown below, the UK has an absolute advantage in making televisions and Denmark has an absolute advantage in producing textiles. Output is:

	UK (thousand units)	Denmark (thousand units)	Total
Televisions	10	6	16
Textiles	3	5	8

If each country decides to specialise in the product for which it has an absolute advantage, the result of using all resources to produce it is now shown:

	UK (thousand units)	Denmark (thousand units)	Total
Televisions	20	0	20
Textiles	0	10	10

Trade will benefit both countries. Assuming an exchange rate of one television for two units of textiles, the trade of eight thousand televisions results in:

	UK (thousand units)	Denmark (thousand units)	Total
Televisions	12	8	20
Textiles	4	6	10

We can compare this with the original position. Both countries have now gained through trade. The conclusion is that where two countries trade and each has an absolute advantage in different products, total output increases when each country specialises in producing that product for which it has the absolute advantage.

One country might have an absolute advantage in the production of **both** products. Specialisation and trade still benefits both countries, as long as each has a comparative advantage. If we now assume that the UK has an absolute advantage over Denmark in the production of food and cars, and that both countries are devoting half their resources to the production of each commodity:

	UK (thousand units)	Denmark (thousand units)	Total
Food	12	6	18
Cars	16	4	20

The UK has an **absolute advantage in both** products, but a **comparative advantage** in cars: its advantage is greater, producing four times as many cars as Denmark compared with twice as many units of food. Denmark has a comparative cost advantage in food, since its disadvantage is less than with car production. If the UK now specialises further in the product for which it has the comparative advantage (cars) and Denmark does the same with food, total output increases. If the UK devotes three-quarters of its resources to car production and Denmark all its resources to food:

	UK (thousand units)	Denmark (thousand units)	Total
Food	6	12	18
Cars	24	0	24

An exchange rate of one car per unit of food, trading six thousand units results in this position:

	UK (thousand units)	Denmark (thousand units)	Total
Food	12	6	18
Cars	18	6	24

Both countries have gained (two thousand cars) through specialising where comparative advantage exists.

The benefits from free trade can be summarised as follows:

- **Countries specialise and gain from absolute and comparative advantage.**
- **Their specialisation leads to mass production and economies of scale taking place.**
- **Consumers gain from the efficient use of resources through mass production and economies of scale.**

The existence of trade encourages competition, leads to a greater range of products being available and improves cooperation and goodwill between countries, all of which benefit consumers.

PROTECTIONISM

Countries may prevent free trade from taking place. Protectionism occurs when a country places restrictions on free trade. This has one or more purposes:

- to improve the country's balance of payments, by increasing exports and/or reducing imports;
- to protect the country's exchange rate;
- to raise revenue (from tariffs);
- to restrict the 'dumping' of goods from overseas competitors who export at low prices to establish a position in the market;
- to safeguard domestic employment and industries, such as those 'infant' industries not yet strong enough to compete with established overseas firms.

The main methods of protectionism include

1 Tariffs   These are taxes placed on imports to make them comparatively more expensive than home-produced products.

2 Quotas   A physical limit is placed on the amount of a good or service which can be imported. A quota might be agreed between two countries: for example, the VERA (Voluntary Export Restriction Agreement) between the UK and Japan to limit the import of Japanese cars to 11 per cent of the previous year's total UK car sales.

3 Subsidies   Governments might decide to give financial support to certain industries, improving their competitive position in the home and/or export market.

4 Embargoes   These occur where a country refuses to trade in certain items with another country, often for political or military reasons. Recent examples include the trade embargoes against Iraq (military items) and Libya.

5 Government procurement policies   A government could have a policy of 'buying from within', using domestic firms to supply its goods or services, wherever possible.

6 Exchange controls   A government might limit the amount of foreign currency that can be bought by firms or individuals, to prevent the exchange rate of its currency being put under pressure through the purchase of imports. The UK government abolished exchange controls in 1980, but they exist in many developing countries.

Problems of protectionism

Where there is protectionism, the benefits of free trade described above will be negated: there is less choice, consumers face higher prices, and inefficiency increases due to reduced competition. There is also a danger that when one country adopts protectionist measures, other countries will follow suit, resulting in the reduction of world trade to the detriment of all. On average, trade accounts for about a quarter of UK economic output: expansion in world trade is an important source of growth and the United Kingdom is therefore keen to see world trade expand and not contract.

GATT

The General Agreement on Tariffs and Trade has operated since 1948. It is based on a set of principles, which include consultation between members and the reduction of tariffs through negotiation. There have been a series of negotiating 'rounds' devoted to reducing tariffs. The ninth GATT Round, the Uruguay Round, included discussions on agricultural tariffs and subsidies (such as the EU's Common Agricultural Policy) and world trade in services, two areas which had previously been largely ignored by GATT. In December 1993 the 117 countries involved in the Uruguay Round made trade agreements worth an estimated £150 million, and supported the **World Trade Organisation** to facilitate trade among countries.

REGIONAL ECONOMIC GROUPINGS

Free trade areas and customs unions have been allowed to develop. The European Union is an example of a customs union: these establish common policies on trade between members and with the outside world, and encourage this 'inward' trade between members.

Supplier organisations also exist. These often consist of producer countries who seek to exploit their dominance in the relevant world market, for example by establishing a cartel. An example is the Organisation of Petroleum Exporting Countries (**OPEC**), established in 1960 in an attempt to gain some measure of control over the world oil supply and price.

A recent illustration of a regional economic grouping is the agreement in August 1993 between the USA, Canada and Mexico to create the world's largest free trade zone, embracing 370 million people and with a combined gross national product of over £4 billion. **NAFTA**, the North American Free Trade Agreement, came into effect in 1994 and has a long-term expansion potential to include fast-developing South American economies such as Brazil. Note that NAFTA is a free trade agreement, not a customs union: there are no common political institutions.

THE EUROPEAN UNION (EU)

Although the USA and Japan are the world's two largest industrialised economies, the European Union as a whole is larger than either. It contains four of the 'G7' group of major industrialised countries: the UK, Germany, France and Italy. Seven of the twelve largest industrial economies are EU Members. The EU was established in 1957 by the Treaty of Rome and now contains nearly 400 million consumers in fifteen member states.

EU MEMBERSHIP

Original members:	Members from 1973:	Members from 1986:	Members from 1995:
Belgium	Denmark	Portugal	Austria
France	Ireland	Spain	Finland
Germany	United Kingdom		Sweden
Italy	**Member**	**1991:**	
Luxembourg	**from 1981:**	The former German	
Netherlands	Greece	Democratic Republic	
		was incorporated	

The Single Market from 1992

Promotion of trade between members was a major reason behind the formation of the then European Community. The 'Common Market' is now the Single European Market, following the 1986 Single Market Act which sought to:

Remove	<ul><li>administrative barriers to trade</li><li>controls on the flow of capital</li><li>abuse of market power</li></ul>
Establish	<ul><li>free movement of labour</li><li>free movement of goods</li><li>common technical standards</li><li>parity of professional qualifications</li></ul>

The Influence of the Single Market on UK businesses

1 Common standards Community-wide standards of quality and safety have been established. UK manufacturers must ensure their products meet these EU requirements. For example:

- the Directive on food labelling harmonises food labelling;
- the Toy Safety Directive harmonises toy safety standards;
- the Safety Framework Directive provides a framework for other directives on health and safety.

2 Open markets These now exist in areas such as information technology, telecommunications and financial services (see below). UK firms face increased competition through these open markets with their common standards.

3 Free movement of labour The free movement of individuals is one of the EU's basic principles, set out in its Social Charter (Table 1.4). The increased recognition of professional qualifications between member states affects employment opportunities for UK citizens and the recruitment policies of UK firms. Professions presently covered by directives include doctors, dentists and architects.

Table 1.4 UK nationals working in EU states and EU nationals working in the United Kingdom, 1995

	UK nationals working in EU states (thousands)	EU nationals working in the UK (thousands)
Austria	4	4
Belgium	10	3
Denmark	7	9
Finland	1	5
France	28	35
Germany	63	27
Greece	3	7
Irish Republic	21	217
Italy	1	43
Luxembourg	2	–
Netherlands	23	13
Portugal	–	18
Spain	8	16
Sweden	6	8

Source: Eurostat

4 Free movement of goods The use of the SAD (Single Administrative Document) and simplified border formalities reduce delay in moving goods throughout the Union. Transport services have been liberalised: an illustration is the abolition of all road haulage permits and quotas.

The Single Market in practice

Eight of our EU partners are among our top ten trading partners. Table 1.3 (page 45) shows the importance of the Single Market to the United Kingdom economy.

The single market in financial services, based on the free movement of capital throughout the Union, came into effect from the end of 1992 (though Greece and Portugal were given extensions to this date). The aim of the financial services single market is that authorisation to conduct financial business (on investment, for example) in one member state acts as authorisation to conduct it in any member state, thus creating an EU financial 'passport'. This helps to increase competition by opening markets. It also allows firms to decide on the most efficient method of operation, by choosing whether to open branches in different member states or to supply services to these countries without having a physical presence in them.

In banking a number of Directives (legislative outlines which allow member states to decide the details of the legislation) have been established. They include the Second Banking Directive which has been in force from 1993.

- It includes lending, leasing, issuing credit cards and travellers' cheques, and money transmission services.

- Any credit institution authorised in its own country for these activities can supply them throughout the EU.

- It therefore provides a passport for credit institutions throughout the Union.

Other Directives include the Own Funds Directive, which harmonises the definition of bank capital, and the Bank Accounts Directive, which harmonises the content of banks' financial statements.

Insurance companies have been influenced by Directives covering life assurance, non-life insurance, motor insurance and reinsurance. Passports have been available from 1994 for firms selling life and non-life business. Other financial services such as pension funds are developing legislative frameworks to meet the requirements of the Single Market.

Other European Union activities

In addition to the Single Market, the European Union's other activities are a major influence on all UK businesses.

The European Investment Bank (EIB) and the European Monetary Institute

The EIB granted loans worth over 16 billion ECUs (about £12 billion) to member States in 1992. The UK received 2.4 billion ECUs (£1.8 billion), the approximate sharing being:

- 30 per cent going to finance construction and infrastructure projects such as the Channel Tunnel;

- 30 per cent for water supply and environmental protection, in particular sewage systems and waste water treatment;

- 30 per cent to develop North Sea oil and gas fields, and gas-fired power stations;

- 10 per cent for other projects.

The Bank raises funds on the capital markets and aims to finance EU projects related to its objectives:

1 Promoting European integration through:

- regional development – focusing on regions in structural decline or in rural areas;

- effective communications – to assist the efficient movement of goods and people associated with the Single Market, and to improve transport and telecommunications links;

- environmental protection and improving the quality of life;

- improving the international competitiveness of EU industry.

❷ Fostering cooperation with non–Member countries: this is likely to increase in importance as the Union establishes closer links with other European countries, following the political changes in Eastern Europe.

UK businesses qualify for EIB finance if they meet certain criteria, projects being judged not only on potential profitability, but also on the extent to which they meet one or more of the Bank's objectives above.

The **European Monetary Institute** has the task of coordinating monetary policy of the central banks of the member states, and to help prepare for the introduction of the single European currency.

The Common Agricultural Policy (CAP)

The CAP provides agricultural subsidies to EU farmers and seeks to:

- improve competitiveness with the rest of the world;
- increase earnings from agriculture;
- eliminate or reduce fluctuations in price and supply.

Farm subsidies in 1992 totalled $85 billion, an increase from $60 billion in 1989. It is a form of protectionism and critics point to vast surpluses – 'wine lakes' and 'butter mountains', for example – which are created by CAP subsidies and have to be financed by EU consumers. It is argued that the CAP has led to UK consumers facing higher food prices and disproportionately large budget contributions (which result in less money being available for other EU initiatives). The CAP formed a focus for the Uruguay Round of talks in GATT.

The Common External Tariff (CET)

Most imports from outside the Union have to bear this tariff, thereby encouraging member states to import from other members due to the relative price benefit.

The European Economic Area (EEA) Agreement

Signed in 1992, this extends the principles of the Single Market to the European Free Trade Area (EFTA) countries: Iceland, Liechtenstein, Switzerland and Norway. The Agreement advances existing trade links. Under the Agreement:

- EFTA countries adopt most of the Single Market legislation and will take on future measures;
- new EEA institutions will be set up to administer the Agreement;
- there will be closer EU/EFTA cooperation, for example in education and research and development.

THE BALANCE OF PAYMENTS

Whenever trade or movement of assets takes place between countries, payment is made. The balance of payments records the United Kingdom's payments to, and receipts from, the rest of the world.

The balance of payments on current account

The current account summarises the trade in goods ('visibles') and services ('invisibles'). The balance of visible trade, known as the 'balance of trade', measures the sterling value of goods exported against that of goods imported.

The balance of invisible trade measures the export of services against their import. About half the funds involved are under the headings of 'IPD' (interest, profits and dividends) and transfers – for example, the UK contributions to the EU.

Invisible exports include:

- spending by foreign tourists in the UK;
- net property income from abroad (net inflows from profits and dividends to UK residents owning capital assets overseas);

51

- earnings from the City of London: 'forex', the foreign exchange market, has been the City's main revenue earner.

The current balance is the most important part of the balance of payments because it reflects the UK's competitiveness and its ability to live within its means. Although a permanent surplus on current account cannot be expected, a period of surplus is important so that foreign currency reserves can be built up. The trend in the 1990s has been towards an increasingly large deficit on current account (see Fig. 1.15). Reasons for the UK experiencing greater pressure in maintaining a positive current account balance include:

1 A decline in importance of UK revenue from North Sea oil, even though it forms a significant proportion of overall visible exports (7 per cent in 1990 and 1991) – North Sea oil revenues have largely been used to fund improved short-term standards of living through importing consumer goods, rather than as the basis for long-term investment in the economy.

2 Deindustrialisation – the decline in manufacturing strength due to factors such as the loss of the UK's comparative advantage in manufacturing.

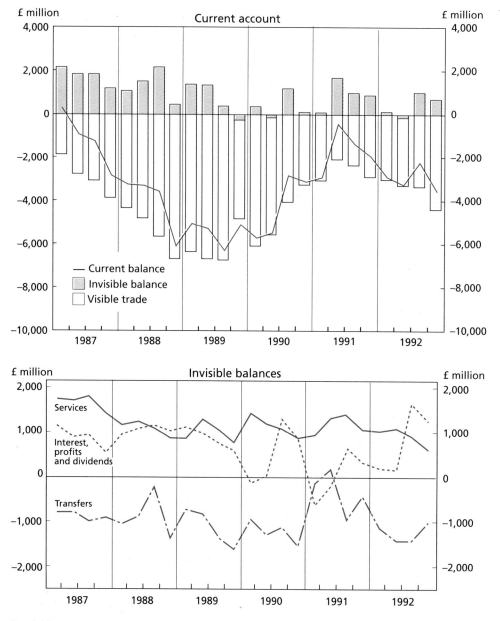

Fig. 1.15 UK balance of payments, 1987–92

Source: ONS

Although the importance of invisible trade and services continues to grow, service exports cannot easily replace those from manufacturing (which accounts for over 60 per cent of exports). This is because manufacturing exports tend to have a greater 'multiplier' effect. For example, the sale of UK-manufactured tanks to the Arabian Gulf countries generates visible export revenue. It also creates income for UK businesses through providing training for the engineers and tank crews, generating service contracts, providing insurance, transport and finance. There might also be overseas investment in the UK arms manufacturer as a result of exporting.

Table 1.5 UK current account performance

	1994 £ million	1987 £ million	1982 £ million
Current account			
Visible trade			
Exports	134,611	79,153	55,331
Imports	145,349	90,735	53,421
Visible balance	−10,738	−11,582	1,911
Invisibles			
Credits	123,046	79,826	65,162
Debits	114,136	72,726	62,423
Invisibles balance	8,910	7,099	2,741
Current balance	−1,828	−4,482	4,649

Source: ONS

Transactions in external assets and liabilities

This forms the second section of the balance of payments, following presentational changes which were made to it in 1987. Net capital flows are recorded, representing the difference between

❶ outward capital flows – where UK residents buy assets in another country; and

❷ inward capital flows – residents of other countries purchase UK assets.

Table 1.6 Transactions in UK external assets and liabilities, 1994

Transactions in major assets 1994	(£ million)
UK investment overseas	
Direct	−16,412
Portfolio	18,552
Lending abroad by UK banks	−49,967
Transactions in major liabilities 1994	**(£ million)**
Overseas investment in the UK	
Direct	6,677
Portfolio	31,836
Borrowing abroad by UK banks	41,121
Net sterling transactions of UK banks	6,553
Net transactions in assets and liabilities, 1994	−3,561

Source: ONS

Following the abolition of exchange controls in 1979, the UK has become a large net exporter of capital, and is now the world's second largest owner of external capital assets (after Japan).

Long-term capital flows occur when residents of one country invest in assets in another country, for example by a UK company establishing a foreign subsidiary overseas. Short-term capital flows are less stable and predictable, often involving speculation and the movement of 'hot money'. Speculation might result from factors such as an international event (e.g. conflict in the Middle East), the belief that a country's currency is over- or under-valued or as a response to the interest rates being offered in different financial centres. Such movements can have a destabilising effect on a country's balance of payments.

Policies to tackle a balance of payments deficit

Deflation   A government attempts to deflate its economy by reducing the level of demand. Measures include restricting bank lending and other forms of credit through high interest rates and controlling the levels of government borrowing (both being monetary measures), and raising taxes (a fiscal measure). Although imports of consumer goods are likely to fall due to lower demand levels, deflation also hits the home economy by reducing economic growth and investment and employment levels.

Devaluation   The devaluation of a country's currency – where the exchange rate against other currencies is lowered – results in more expensive imports and cheaper exports. A notable devaluation took place in 1967, when the UK altered the sterling–dollar exchange rate from $2.80 to the pound to $2.40.

When the UK was a member of the European Union's Exchange Rate Mechanism (see page 55), the value of the pound against the other countries' currencies 'floated' within agreed limits. **'Depreciation'** describes the situation where the exchange rate of a country's currency falls against other currencies, within an agreed range of values. This is a more gradual process than a devaluation.

Neither devaluation nor depreciation is guaranteed to succeed, for these reasons:

- Imported items such as food or oil might be necessities for a country, which must then meet a higher import bill.

- There is a connection between devaluation and inflation. About one-third of UK national income is spent on imported items: a 10 per cent devaluation is likely to increase the retail price index by about 3 per cent immediately. Also, the rise in the cost of imported raw materials and the increase in the RPI lead to increased pay demands, thus continuing the pressure on inflation.

- Because exports will be that much cheaper, more need to be sold to generate the same revenue (although increased export levels should increase domestic investment and employment).

EXCHANGE RATES

The exchange rate of a currency is expressed as its value in other currencies. The UK, when in the European Union's Exchange Rate Mechanism – the ERM – had an exchange rate of 2.95 Deutschemarks to the pound (within an agreed margin). The exchange rate is particularly important for importers and exporters, who could find that their profit margins are affected by the change in the relative prices of the different currencies used in international trade.

Floating exchange rates

Under this system the rate (price) is determined by the demand for and supply of the currency on the foreign exchange market. Government action is important: by buying or selling some of its reserves of foreign currency, the government can influence the exchange rate for its currency and even out fluctuations in the exchange rate. In addition it might alter domestic interest rates to control the short-term capital movements, which also affect the exchange rate.

A floating rate should help solve balance of payments problems. If the United Kingdom is becoming less competitive:

- it suffers a deficit in the balance of payments;
- the resulting increase in imports will increase the supply of sterling;
- and the fall in exports reduces the demand for sterling;
- so the value of sterling falls;
- which raises import prices and reduces export prices;
- leading back to equilibrium.

However, since only a small proportion of all currency transactions are to do with trade, a balance of payments deficit can still be accompanied by an increasing exchange rate. Exporters and importers may find that the fluctuations in rates under this system can wipe out the profits on their trading. Floating exchange rates also encourage speculation, with speculators gambling on future changes in these rates: their actions can influence the exchange rate of the currency which is the focus for speculation.

Fixed exchange rates

The fixed rate system operated from 1944 until 1972, and in the ERM from 1979. Under this system governments agree the rates at which their currencies are to be exchanged, within set limits. In the ERM, for example, sterling's 'parity' with the Deutschemark was fixed at DM2.95 to the pound. When trading conditions force a currency to the edge of its band, the government either buys some of the excess supply of its currency (raising demand for it) or sells some to reduce demand and raise supply. The advantage to firms trading in overseas markets is that a fixed exchange rate brings with it greater certainty that profit margins will be maintained.

The UK and the Exchange Rate Mechanism

In 1979 the member countries of the EU (but not the UK) adopted a central rate for their currencies in terms of the ECU (European Currency Unit). The rate for each currency was kept within narrow limits by market forces, buying or selling when necessary. Most currencies had a limit of + or - 2.25 per cent (the UK had a 6 per cent limit when it joined in 1990), and some non-EU currencies, such as those of Austria and Switzerland, were linked to the ERM through their links with the Deutschemark. Realignment of currencies was made possible, members adjusting the central rate by agreement: this would occur where differing internal inflation levels made one country less competitive.

It was hoped that the ERM would provide greater stability in exchange rates and thus encourage international trade. For the UK it was believed that interest rates – kept high to encourage people to hold sterling in times of poor current account performance – could be reduced. Arguments against the UK joining the ERM focused on the lack of freedom of action the government would have in economic policy: for example, it could not alter interest rates where the results of this would go against a policy of fixed exchange rates.

In its early years, the ERM was praised for its contribution to lower inflation rates and a reduced volatility of exchange rates (following a number of realignments in the currency rates). Since 1990, however, currency speculation and other problems led to countries leaving the ERM. Sterling was forced out of the ERM on 16 September 1992 by speculative pressure. The foreign exchange market was suspicious of the UK government's commitment to stick to the DM2.95/£ parity because of recession in the United Kingdom, and the German Bundesbank appeared to believe the pound should be devalued. On leaving the ERM the pound was allowed to float and find its own level.

By August 1993 the remaining ERM currencies were operating on a much wider 15 per cent trading range, which arguably meant that in reality they were floating. The United Kingdom still pursues the EMU 'convergence criteria' of reducing the PSBR, to help reduce international competitiveness of interest rates and devaluation. EU countries generally are pursuing lower PSBR requirements with the Single Currency criteria (established by Maastricht) in mind.

Chapter roundup

Chapter 1 has explained how the key economic concepts affect a business person's decisions on what to produce, for whom to produce and how to produce. Scarcity and choice influence the price, availability and mix of the factors of production used. In the United Kingdom's mixed economy:

- primary, secondary and tertiary production take place, with the tertiary sector becoming increasingly important;
- the free market element uses the price mechanism to determine prices through the interaction of supply and demand;
- firms are affected by changes in quantity demanded and changes in demand; the elasticity of demand for a firm's products is a major influence on its profits.

The UK economy does not operate in isolation from the rest of the world. The final section of the chapter explains how specialisation by individual countries results in trade between different countries, the increased output from specialisation benefiting all countries. The major present trading influence on the UK comes from its membership of the European Union.

Illustrative questions

1 Explain briefly how a firm might be affected by 'opportunity cost'. (2)

2 What is meant by *income elasticity of demand*? (2)

Tutorial note

These questions are short-answer but are phrased as essay-style: the clue to the length of answer required is the mark allocation. Your answer should be limited to two or three statements, which will be sufficient to gain full marks.

Suggested answers

1 It is the cost of an opportunity forgone. For example, a firm might have capital available to invest either in additional premises or in new machinery: the opportunity cost of buying the premises is the postponement in buying the new machines.

2 Income elasticity of demand refers to the responsiveness of demand to changes in income. It is calculated by dividing the percentage change in quantity demanded by the percentage change in income.

3 What advantages might European firms gain from the harmonisation of laws influencing their activities? (6)

Tutorial note

A rather more extended answer is required here. The question does not guide you on the number of 'advantages' required: I suggest two well-argued ones, or three which are described in reasonable depth, are enough for full marks.

Suggested answer

The first advantage likely to be enjoyed by European businesses is that of saving certain costs. Cost savings are likely to accrue from producing to a uniform standard, having a simplified set of laws applicable to all member countries (and their businesses), and reduced legal activity due to the new consistency and ease of interpretation. Businesses should also gain from greater clarity, because laws in one country will apply in all the others. Finally, these businesses will face fairer competition than before, on a 'level playing field', with all firms having to obey the same laws.

4 Study the following information and then answer the questions that follow.
   The diagram shows the demand and supply of tickets for a major sporting event. The sports' governing body has decided to introduce maximum prices for their tickets.

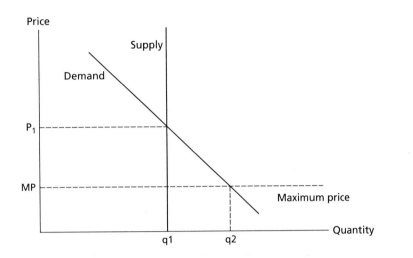

(a) Why is the supply curve drawn in the manner shown?   (3)

(b) Why do maximum prices lead to the development of a black market?   (3)

(c) How might the available tickets be allocated?   (6)

(d) With the use of **two** suitable examples, explain why governments sometimes choose to interfere in markets.   (6)

WJEC

Tutorial note

This question requires you to relate your knowledge of supply and demand theory to the specific case of a sporting event. In answering it, therefore, make sure you identify how such an event will be affected by the general theory.

Suggested answer

(a) The supply curve is vertical, which indicates perfectly inelastic supply at level q1. Since we are examining a sporting event, the supply of tickets is probably fixed by the seating capacity of the stadium where the event is to be held.

(b) The graph shows that, at maximum price, demand (quantity demanded = q2) is greater than supply (maximum supply level of q1). This results in a shortage of tickets (q2–q1). Since demand is greater than supply, some people will be prepared to pay above face value for the tickets, resulting in a 'black market'.

(c) One way of allocation is to use the 'first come, first served' approach which is commonly found with sporting and other major events where there is a limited number of tickets (supply). An alternative is to limit each buyer to, say, two tickets (a form of rationing): this is often applied to popular events when the organisers are confident that demand will greatly exceed supply, for example with major rock concerts.

(d) Governments choose to interfere in markets to regulate them. For example, the privatisation of the old state monopolies has led to the creation of privatised monopolies which might otherwise exploit consumers (government-established regulators such as Oftel control prices). Secondly, governments might choose to interfere in order to protect home-based industries through the use of tariffs, quotas or subsidies; examples are found in the Single Market, where EU governments use subsidies (eg the financial support for the Common Agricultural Policy), and have established tariffs for goods imported from outside the Union.

5 The table below shows UK activity rates for women in selected years. The figures indicate the percentage of women in the workforce aged 16 to 60 years (inclusive).

	1971	1976	1981	1986	1990
%	43.9	46.8	47.6	49.6	52.9

Source: *Social Trends*

(a) Give reasons for the trend in activity rates for women as shown in the table. (5)

(b) Since women make up some 47 per cent of the UK's workforce, why do you think there are so few women in senior managerial positions? (5)

(c) Women tend to be under-represented in trade unions. Why might this be the case? (5)

(d) Why is it that average female earnings are approximately 70% of average male earnings? (5)

NEAB

Tutorial note

This question focuses on a specific trend. In my outline answer I have included some examples of how society is changing to accommodate greater percentages of women workers.

Suggested answer

(a) The trend indicates increasing activity rates for women. Reasons include the change in society's attitudes towards married women working, an increased demand by women for careers, and increased numbers of single-parent mothers seeking work.

(b) There has been some evidence of bias stopping women being promoted at work; women are also more likely to take career breaks (e.g. to raise a family), which interrupts career progression.

(c) Many women are employed on a part-time basis, where unions are not heavily represented; they have also not made up this percentage of the workforce in the traditional union 'shop-floor' recruiting areas such as heavy engineering.

(d) Again, many women work part time, receiving lower average rates of pay; even though the UK has Equal Opportunities (sex discrimination) laws, some employers still fail to pay women the same rate as men doing equivalent work.

Practice questions

1 Identify **three** effects on a UK firm resulting from the increased mobility of labour within the European Union. (3)

2 If a government introduces tariffs on a range of imported goods, why might demand for these goods remain at the same level? (3)

Pitfalls

There is a danger that question 1 might be answered in too general a fashion by concentrating on the after-effects of 1992, rather than on particular labour-related issues. Compare how question 1 is phrased – asking for a specific number of points – with question 2 (and also the first two in the 'Illustrative questions' section). A common pitfall in answering these questions – pointed out in many Examiners' Reports – is that candidates spend far too long on the answer: a short paragraph at most is normally sufficient for all points to be made.

Key points

In question 1, three possible effects are:

(a) Increased competition in the labour market, leading to quicker labour turnover.

(b) This likely increased labour turnover leads to higher costs of recruitment and selection.

(c) A wider choice of candidates from across the EU.

In question 2, goods are necessities or essential raw materials; they are not available in the home country; they may be fashionable/unique.

3 (a) What factors might influence how the demand for a product reacts to a change in its price or in the price of another item? (5)

(b) How might the imposition of VAT on books affect their demand? (5)

NEAB

Pitfalls

Part (a) contains two questions in one, asking you to examine both a change in the product's price and a change in 'another item'; this other item may or may not be connected in some way to the product in question, which further complicates your answer.

Key points

(a) What proportion of disposable income is spent on the product; is there an available substitute; is it a necessity or a luxury (what is its price elasticity of demand); is the other item in some way connected (e.g. complementary demand)?

(b) Price will rise so the general effect is reduced demand (supply may remain constant since a price rise due to VAT does not greatly affect suppliers' profits). What type of books are being sold; e.g. textbooks (there may be substitute sources of information), leisure reading (demand on library services may rise as a result)?

CHAPTER 2

BUSINESS ORGANISATIONS

Units in this chapter

2.1 *The framework of organisations*
2.2 *The internal structure of organisations*

Chapter objectives

The purpose of this chapter is to explain the general nature of the different organisations in our economy, their common characteristics, and how they vary in purpose and structure. There are close links with other chapters. In particular:

- Chapter 3 explains how organisations grow in size;
- Chapter 5 includes a unit on the theory of organisational structure and operation;
- Chapters 5 to 8 examine the major functions of a typical organisation;
- Chapter 10 outlines how decisions affecting organisations can be made.

The key topics and concepts covered in this chapter are:

- profit;
- limited liability;
- incorporation;
- the public sector;
- organisation charts;
- line, staff and matrix structures;
- span of control and chain of command;
- centralisation;
- delegation.

2.1 THE FRAMEWORK OF ORGANISATIONS

PRIVATE SECTOR

Organisations in the UK fall into two main groups: private sector organisations and public sector organisations. Firms in the private sector are owned by private individuals who use this ownership to achieve various objectives:

- job satisfaction;
- security of employment;
- personal factors (prestige, self-esteem, power);
- income through profits made.

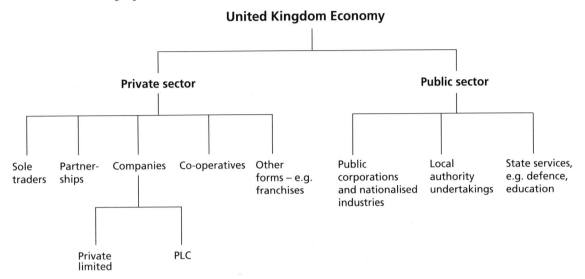

Fig. 2.1 Types of business in the UK economy

Profit, liability and incorporation

Individuals in the private sector seek to make profit by acting as entrepreneurs in the market-place. This 'profit motive' forms the foundation of the private sector.

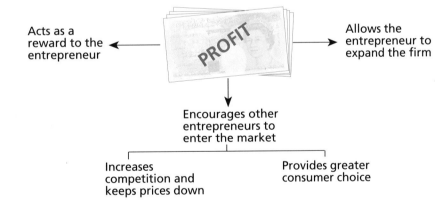

Fig. 2.2 Profit

Profit is the reward for the entrepreneur taking business risks. Some entrepreneurs fail: there has been a high rate of business failure in the last decade, especially during the recessionary periods. The rate of business failures is illustrated in Fig. 2.3.

Limited liability is a feature of the private sector. Most large commercial trading companies are **limited by share** and must include the word 'limited' or 'plc' in their name (in Wales the abbreviations 'cyf' or 'ccc' are allowed as alternatives). This acts as a warning to those who deal with such companies that any trading debts may not be fully recoverable, due to this limitation of liability. Other companies, for example most examination bodies and professional associations, are **limited by guarantee**. Members of such a company guarantee its business debts (up to a given maximum) on its being wound up. Liability is limited to the amount guaranteed.

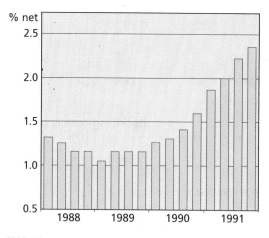

Fig. 2.3 Company failures, 1988–91

Source: *The Guardian*

The owners of a limited company are therefore only liable to lose their agreed investment in the company. Where the company cannot meet its debts from its own financial resources, it is unable to call upon the owners to meet its debts from their personal finances. Sole traders and partnerships have **unlimited liability**: where business debts cannot be met from the firm's own resources, the owner(s) can be forced to sell personal assets to cover business debts.

The benefit of limited liability to the economy is that it encourages people to take the risk of owning and/or investing in companies, in the knowledge that they can only lose a given amount of money. This leads to greater levels of investment than would otherwise take place and encourages the sale of stock and shares.

An illustration of the problem of unlimited liability is the recent difficulty experienced by many 'Names' of Lloyd's of London. The insurance market in which Lloyd's operates requires investment, and Lloyds investors had unlimited liability. This was of no concern when the company continued to make regular and high profits for these Names, but a series of recent natural and man-made disasters led to substantial losses by Lloyd's (about £8 billion from 1988 to 1992). These losses had to be met by the Names from their personal assets. Lloyd's now looks increasingly to institutional investors and offers them the safeguard of limited liability.

Another difference between companies and sole traders or partnerships is that **companies are incorporated bodies**. Incorporation means that a company has a separate legal existence from its members. It can:

- own property;
- enter contracts in its own name;
- sue or be sued in the courts.

Sole traders and partnerships are unincorporated businesses. These firms do not have a legal existence which is separate from that of the owners.

Sole traders

The sole trader (or sole proprietor) is a popular form of business ownership (see Fig. 2.4) where

- personal services are provided;
- little capital is needed to start up business;
- large-scale production is not a major feature or benefit.

This form of ownership is therefore widely found in service areas such as hairdressing, plumbing and window-cleaning.

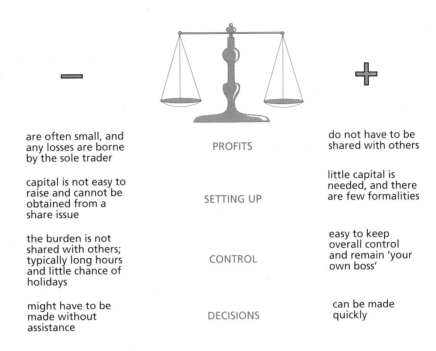

are often small, and any losses are borne by the sole trader	PROFITS	do not have to be shared with others
capital is not easy to raise and cannot be obtained from a share issue	SETTING UP	little capital is needed, and there are few formalities
the burden is not shared with others; typically long hours and little chance of holidays	CONTROL	easy to keep overall control and remain 'your own boss'
might have to be made without assistance	DECISIONS	can be made quickly

Fig. 2.4 Features of the sole trader

Partnerships

Partnerships are also unincorporated businesses with unlimited liability. Now that private limited companies are relatively easy and inexpensive to set up, the partnership as a form of business ownership has declined in popularity. Partnerships are traditionally associated with professions such as accountants and lawyers where capital outlay is small. The minimum number of partners is two and the normal maximum is twenty, though there are exceptions.

Partners usually draw up a written agreement, or partnership deed, which details the various rights and duties of each partner. The agreement covers:

- profit-sharing ratios;
- the amounts of capital to be contributed by each partner;
- rules concerning withdrawals in anticipation of profits;
- an outline of the partners' business responsibilities;
- regulations concerning the introduction of new partners and the dissolution (ending) of the partnership.

In the absence of a written agreement, and in the case of a dispute, the rules of the 1890 Partnership Act apply. This Act states that, in the absence of any agreement to the contrary, profits and losses are to be shared equally, each partner has the right to an equal say in how the partnership operates, and any loans made by partners to the partnership receive interest at 5 per cent.

Compared with sole traders:

- **partnerships can obtain capital more easily;**
- **individual partners can specialise in business functions;**
- **financial affairs can still be kept private;**
- **a partnership is just as simple to establish,**

BUT

- **decisions can take longer;**
- **unlimited liability is still a drawback;**
- **difficulties are created if one of the partners dies or wishes to leave.**

COMPANIES

Incorporation provides a company with a **separate legal existence** from its shareholders, who benefit from limited liability. There are over 1 million companies registered in the UK. These vary in size from small family-owned businesses with two owners also managing the firm, to large public companies having many thousands of shareholders.

Private and public companies

A limited company is deemed to be a private limited company unless its memorandum of association states that it is a public limited company. Private companies cannot advertise their shares for sale to the public or through the Stock Exchange.

Public limited companies are registered as such through their memorandum of association: they must have a minimum share capital of £50,000 and can sell their shares to the public and may be quoted on the Stock Exchange. PLCs therefore tend to be much larger than private companies, and ownership and control are more clearly separated. Few shareholders – owners – have a direct say in the daily running of the firm, because specialist directors are appointed to exercise management control.

Compared with sole traders and partnerships, a company:

- offers limited liability to potential investors which encourages investment;

- has a separate legal existence from its owners and can own assets and sue or be sued in its own name;

- is not affected by death or retirement of its owners because of its separate existence;

- finds it easier to obtain extra (share or loan) capital;

- can more easily benefit from economies of scale.

BUT

- there are many more formalities in creating this form of ownership;

- there is less privacy associated with its business affairs;

- its (normally) greater size leads to:
  slower decisions
  greater difficulty in adapting to market changes
  diseconomies of scale
  employees feeling isolated from the main decision-makers;

- the owners of private companies face difficulties in selling shares, especially where restrictions on this sale have been made by the company: and in PLCs the transfer of ownership (via the Stock Exchange) can take place without the support of the managers;

- many shareholders operate 'short-term' policies in the hope of making profits through buying or selling their shares: this encourages takeover bids and leads to a greater feeling of instability.

Registering a company

All companies must be registered at the Companies Registration Office (CRO): in Cardiff for companies incorporated in Wales and England, in Edinburgh for Scottish incorporation and in Belfast for Northern Irish companies.

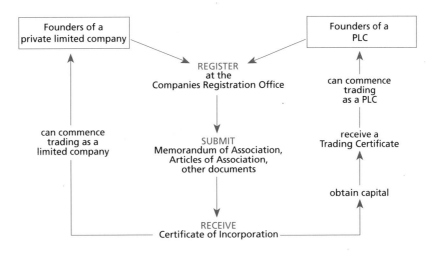

Fig. 2.5 Registering a company

The Memorandum of Association governs the relationship of the company with the outside world. Its clauses include:

1. **Name** The proposed company name, to differentiate it from other companies.

2. **Situation** The address of its registered office.

3. **Objects** The purpose for which it was formed (usually described in a very general fashion).

4. **Liability** A statement that its members have limited liability.

5. **Capital** The amount registered and type(s) of shares.

6. **Association** Directors' names and addresses.

The Articles of Association govern the internal workings of the company. They include details on directors (number, rights and duties), the conduct and calling of meetings and the division of profits.

On receiving a Certificate of Incorporation, the private company can commence trading. The PLC must first raise its capital from the public. It issues a prospectus, giving details of its plans and inviting the public to subscribe. Once sufficient capital has been obtained, the PLC receives a Trading Certificate from the Registrar and can start trading.

Companies must submit to the CRO an 'annual return', which summarises any changes in their affairs. All companies must also produce a set of annual financial statements, a copy of which is sent to each shareholder. These include the:

- directors' report;
- profit and loss account;
- balance sheet;
- notes on accounting policies used;
- auditors' report.

A copy of the financial statements is filed with the CRO, though firms defined as 'small' or 'medium' in size do not have to submit full accounts.

OTHER FORMS OF PRIVATE SECTOR ORGANISATION

Franchises

The British Franchise Association was established in 1977. Franchising is a major growth area of the economy: in the UK there were over 25,000 franchise businesses employing 220,000 people in 1996.

Types of franchise arrangments include:

- manufacturer–retailer: petrol stations and car dealers;
- wholesaler–retailer: Spar and other voluntary groups;
- trademark–retailer: 'fast-food' outlets.

Actual examples of franchise operations include The Body Shop, which opened its first franchise shop in 1977: of the 233 shops in the United Kingdom (1993), 176 (75 per cent) were franchised. McDonald's is another example of an organisation offering franchises: by the end of 1993, 67 of the 523 quick-service restaurants were run by franchisees and the stated plans are to have 40 per cent of the outlets franchised by the year 2000.

The franchisor:

- allows the tradename to be used;
- gives support through
  - local/national marketing
  - training
  - financial and other advice;
- supplies the decor and assists with layout;
- provides the product.

The franchisee:

- agrees to follow rules and to meet set standards;
- invests the capital required;
- purchases only from the franchisor or other recognised suppliers;
- pays royalties to the franchisor.

The franchisee agreement grants the right and authorisation to operate a specific McDonald's restaurant, usually for a period of 20 years. These rights include the use of McDonald's trademarks, restaurant decor designs, signage and equipment layout, the formula and specifications for menu items, use of McDonald's method of operation, inventory control, book-keeping, accounting and marketing and the right to occupy the restaurant premises.

In return, the franchisee agrees to operate the business in accordance with McDonald's standards of quality, service, cleanliness and value. The franchisee is expected to become involved in their community's civic and charitable activities. Training is a top priority to ensure the uniformity of the operation and the consistent quality of the staff.

Each franchisee has constant support through their own McDonald's consultant who is always available for help and advice, visiting the restaurant on a regular basis. Training facilities are free and available to the franchisee and their management team.

Fig. 2.6 Franchise agreement

Source: McDonald's

The franchisor can expand without the need for major capital investment. For example, the financial investment required to become a McDonald's franchisee starts at about £50,000. The franchisee gains a recognised product which is backed by expert support in all spheres of the business, although there are often long hours of work and tight constraints on what can be sold.

Co-operatives

The main purpose of a co-operative is to provide a service for its member-owners and customers. Although the large UK co-operatives are limited companies, capital ownership is not the dominating factor in the Co-operative movement. Control of co-operative societies is shared democratically, with each member having one vote. Any trade surplus is distributed to the members in proportion to their 'trade' with the society.

Consumer, **retail** and **producer** forms of co-operative exist. Consumer co-operatives, where customers collectively own the business, are found particularly in Europe and Japan. Other forms include housing co-operatives and credit unions (which allow people to enjoy the benefits of collective saving and borrowing).

There are nearly sixty local co-operative retail societies – 'the Co-ops' – operating almost 5,000 shops in the United Kingdom. Co-operative Retail Services Ltd (**CRS**) is one of the largest co-operatives in the United Kingdom, representing 20 per cent of the Co-operative movement and having an annual turnover of over £1 billion. It differs from most of the other retail societies in that it is nationwide and has a regional organisation.

Many of the products sold by these societies are procured by the Co-operative Wholesale Society Ltd (**CWS**). The role of the CWS is to buy (or make) in bulk and to supply the retail co-ops with its own (about 3,000 'own-brand') goods. The CWS is one of the largest businesses in the UK, and is Britain's largest farmer. Like a retail society, the CWS is democratically controlled by its members (who consist mainly of retail societies, electing the CWS Board). The CWS is itself the largest UK Co-operative retailer.

CWS ORGANISATION STRUCTURE

North Eastern Region	RETAIL	PRODUCTION	FINANCE & PROPERTY	CORPORATE AFFAIRS	SECRETARIAT
Associated Co-operative Creameries (ACC)	Food & Non-food Retailing	Milk	Chief Accountants	Public Affairs	Legal & Administration
Food & Non-food Retailing	Food Buying, Marketing & Distribution	Food Manufacturing	Computer	Market Research	Pensions & Insurance
Travel	Non-food Buying, Marketing & Distribution	Agricultural	Property	Design	Personnel Services
Funeral Services	Funeral Services	Engineering			Security
Garages	Travel	Co-op Brand			Membership Services
Milk Processing	Optical	Quality & Consumer Care			
Milk Distribution					
Fresh Food Distribution					

Fig. 2.7 CWS organisation structure

Source: CWS Ltd

Other co-operative activities include:

- **Banking** The Co-operative Bank started in 1872 and became the banker for the Co-operative movement: it now operates nationally from over 100 branches and 4,000 points located in Co-operative stores

- **Insurance** The Co-operative Insurance Society was formed in 1867: it is owned by the CWS and is now one of the largest UK business and domestic insurers.

These and other branches of the Co-operative movement are summarised in Figure 2.8.

UK CO-OPERATIVE MOVEMENT

Facts & Figures

Co-operative Retail Societies

Turnover	£7.8 billion
Trading surplus	£161 million
Staff	68,000
Number of societies	50
Members' benefits/dividend	£26 million
Number of shops	4,633 (79 Superstores)
Number of members	8,281,000

The Co-operative Wholesale Society

Turnover	£3.0 billion
Staff	35,000
Farms	50,000 acres
Distribution centres	9
Co-op Brand lines	4,500
Number of CWS food shops	658

The Co-operative Bank Group

Assets	£3.9 billion
Staff	3,800
Branches	158
Handybanks	290
Cash-a-cheque points	2,000
Customer accounts	1.5 million
Link cash machines	8,500

The Co-operative Insurance Society

Total income (premium income + investment income)	£2.0 billion
Assets (held on behalf of policyholders)	£12.8 billion (market value)
Number of families insured	3.5 million
Staff	12,000
Regional Claims and District Offices	201
Profits (1995) for benefits of life assurance and pension policy holders	£581 million
Profit sharing discounts on household and motor policies for the current year	£27 million

Co-operative Travel
(all societies inc. 240 CWS) — 480 branches

Shoefayre — 294 branches

Co-operative Opticians — 80 practices (58 CWS)

National Co-operative Chemists — 236 branches

Worker Co-operatives (UK) — 1,500 (ICOM Directory)

Fig. 2.8 The Co-operative movement, September 1996

Source: Co-operative Union Ltd

Producer co-operatives exist in the UK, usually in agriculture: the Milk Marketing Board is a good example. Worker co-operatives are not as popular here as in many other European countries but they have grown in popularity: there are over 2,000, many of them having existed previously in a different ownership form. Popular areas for establishing producer co-operatives are printing and publishing, textiles and fashion. ICOM, the federation of worker co-operatives, was formed in 1971 and supports its members by providing training and business support.

Management buy-outs

Another important development in our economy over the last decade has been the increase in the number of management buy-outs (**MBOs**). A management buy-out occurs when the managers of a business – often an existing subsidiary of a conglomerate – buy the business and take control of it. Finance for the MBO comes from:

- the managers' own resources – remortgaging, personal borrowing, selling personal investments, etc.;
- borrowing from financial institutions – normally in the form of debt rather than equity, which leads to high gearing levels (see page 155). The loans are secured on the firm's assets.

MBOs developed in the early 1980s as an alternative to full or partial closure of firms due to recession: since the mid-1980s they became less associated with failure and more with company restucturing through disposal of subsidiaries or divisions. Receivership reasons were responsible for less than 1 per cent of the MBO market in 1989, whereas 'going private' (management acquiring a public-quoted company) and privatisation deals – disposal of subsidiaries before privatisation – were more common reasons for undertaking MBOs. The mean value of MBOs in 1989 was £11 million, although the median value of £3 million indicates the small nature of most MBOs.

Table 2.1 *Management buy-outs, 1979–89*

Year	Number	Average buy-out value (£m)
1979	18	0.8
1984	238	1.7
1989	357	11.0

Source: M. Wright, S. Thompson, K. Robbie, NatWest Bank plc

MBOs have a good survival record. Their success is due to:

- acquiring the business at a price lower than the net asset values taken over;
- improved management motivation through substantial shareholding;
- a reduction in the height of the organisational pyramid, leading to more effective communication;
- share ownership extension to other employees, improving employee motivation;
- close monitoring by lending institutions and closer financial involvement.

THE PUBLIC SECTOR

This sector provides goods and services to the community through public corporations, local government and other statutory agencies. The profit motive does not feature so prominently, the emphasis here being on providing for the community by the community with funding through taxes and government borrowing.

Public corporations

A public corporation:

- is a firm whose assets are owned by the State on behalf of the community;
- has objectives influenced by commercial considerations but which are more likely to include greater emphasis on social aspects than those of private sector firms;
- normally has financial targets such as a target return on its capital;

- has a separate legal existence through the Act of Parliament which created it;
- is supervised by a government minister, who helps to provide overall policy direction.

The public corporation is controlled in a number of ways:

- the minister appoints a board to run the corporation;
- it is overseen by a consumer council protecting the interests of the consumers;
- the Monopolies and Mergers Commission audits its performance;
- MPs, through the Select Committee on Nationalised Industries, check financial performance and can question its overall efficiency.

Nationalisation and privatisation

Nationalisation has taken place through:

METHOD	EXAMPLE
Compulsory purchase of private sector assets	British Aerospace in the 1970s
Creating new firms	The creation of BNOC (British National Oil Corporation)
Reorganising existing public sector firms	British Gas Corporation (1965) from reorganisation of the gas industry

Arguments for nationalisation

1 **'Natural monopolies' (e.g. water)** Supply should be owned and controlled by the State for the benefit of all.

2 **Economic or defence considerations** Some industries (e.g. fuel) are vital to the economy and the survival of the country, and should be kept under public control.

3 **Regional arguments** Unprofitable or less profitable services (e.g. rural rail and postal services) would not operate under a private sector profit motive.

4 **Cost considerations** The extent of capital investment required in some industries might rule out private sector involvement due to risk and no guarantee of return.

5 **Social arguments** Some firms might be nationalised to avoid collapse and the creation of unemployment 'blackspots' (e.g. government support in the 1970s of Rover's predecessor, British Leyland based in the Midlands).

By the end of the 1970s nationalised industries were regarded as over-subsidised and generally inefficient. The response of the Conservative government was to privatise many of the industries, such as British Gas and BT, and to stiffen financial and efficiency targets for those industries remaining under public control.

Arguments for privatisation

1 **Raising revenue** A short-term one-off source of income for the government.

2 **Promoting competition** The Conservative government argued that nationalisation created inefficient monopolies and that privatisation would break up the monopolies and increase efficiency (see Table 2.2)

Table 2.2 *Labour productivity in utilities*

Privatised utilities	Year in which privatised	Average annual increase in labour productivity since privatisation
British Telecom	1984–5	7.0
British Gas	1986–7	3.7
Water	1989–90	1.7
National Power	1990–91	20.7
PowerGen	1990–91	15.5
Regional Electricity Companies	1990–91	6.0
Public sector utilities	Reference year	Average annual increase in labour productivity since reference year
British Rail	1984–5	0.7
Royal Mail	1984–5	3.3
Nuclear Electric	1990–91	24.7

Source: Company accounts to 1993–4; for Gas, Britsh Gas company accounts to December 1995 and Financial and Operation Statistics 1993; for water, *Waterfacts*, various years.

3 **Reducing the PSBR** The government's public sector borrowing requirement and the level of public spending has been reduced as a result of the way that privatisation income has been accounted for.

4 **Political considerations** The Conservative government of the 1980s and 1990s was committed to a 'popular capitalism' share-owning society, which has been encouraged by public purchase of shares in previously nationalised industries. In 1992 some 22 per cent of the adult population of the United Kingdom were shareholders, compared with 7 per cent in 1981.

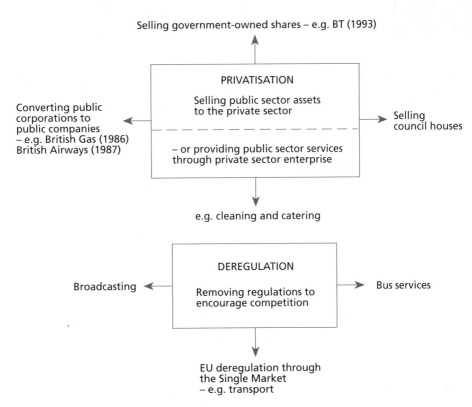

Fig. 2.9 Forms of privatisation

71

Arguments against privatisation

1 A number of privatisations to date have been in 'natural monopoly' industries, with a potential loss of economies of scale.

2 Those industries, such as gas, which have been sold off whole to the private sector have led to public monopolies being replaced by private ones, with little evidence to date of increased efficiency or competition. High profit levels in the early years of many privatised companies have led to much criticism, for example in 1993 when BT announced a 27 per cent increase in its first quarter earnings, to £757 million from £596 million.

3 Private monopolies are usually less well-regulated and less accountable to consumers than public sector ones.

4 'Selling off the family silver': revenue from the sale of previously state-owned assets has been used for current expenditure, and many financial experts believe that the assets were sold too cheaply (to ensure that their sale was a risk-free success). Government revenue was therefore lower than it might have been, and there is the additional cost to the government of the lost future revenue from industries which were previously state-owned.

5 The move towards a 'popular capitalism' society through increased share ownership has not been fully realised. Many people only bought shares in privatised industries because they knew these shares were competitively priced and they could make quick profits on the Stock Exchange. They therefore sold these shares and have not been willing to buy other shares with greater risks attached. Although there is wider share ownership than a decade ago, holdings by individuals only comprise a fifth of the total share market, compared with over a half of the market in 1963.

2.2 THE INTERNAL STRUCTURE OF ORGANISATIONS

Firms have the same influences on their internal organisation regardless of the differences in size, form of ownership or sector of the economy in which they are based.

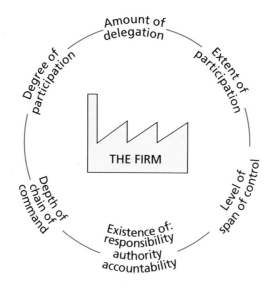

Fig. 2.10 Influences on a firm's internal organisation

ORGANISATION CHARTS

The purpose of an organisation chart is to outline the **formal structure** of a firm. It is associated with the larger firms because most smaller sole traders control all business functions themselves.

The organisation chart:

- provides a simplified and easily followed summary of the formal structure;
- can be used in induction training;
- draws attention to areas which are badly organised and which require review;
- acts as a record of any changes made.

The chart shows the degree of **specialisation** within an organisation, together with the resulting division of labour and formal channels of communication. Its limitations are that it can quickly become out of date as changes take place, and that it does not show the informal structures and channels of communication.

The traditional functional chart is based on the main business functions. Some organisations now use a matrix chart with its 'grid' approach highlighting how the various product managers coordinate the different functions.

LINE, STAFF AND MATRIX ORGANISATION

The main departments of an organisation reflect the key functions on which it relies. A typical manufacturing firm will have (at least) production, purchasing, accounts and sales departments. The system of organisation based on these functions is known as **line organisation**. The advantages of line organisations are that responsibilities are well-defined and understood, and the simple nature of the structure does not inhibit communication.

As they grow in size, organisations come to rely more heavily on specialist functions and personnel. A good illustration is the developed nature of the personnel function in medium-sized and large firms. A **line and staff** organisation recognises the importance of such specialists, although these problems can arise:

- a lack of 'line' understanding of 'staff' techniques, procedures and language;
- some line managers feeling inhibited or threatened by the existence and work of the 'staff' specialists;
- communication slowing down due to the increased complexity of the organisational structure.

The **matrix** structure originated in the USA and is increasingly found in UK firms. It combines the use of line departments – shown vertically on the chart – with project or task teams which are drawn from the various line functions as appropriate. These can be temporary in nature or they may have a permanent brief to follow. The advantage is that traditional (departmental) barriers are broken down, although there may be a clash of loyalties experienced by some of the team members.

Span of control

This is defined as the number of employees directly controlled by one person. The width (level) of an individual's span of control is influenced by three principal factors:

1. The degree of complexity of the work involved: simple tasks which are easily supervised are associated with wide spans; with more complex or advanced work, fewer employees are under the control of one person.

2. The level of staff skill and ability: well-trained and able employees can be supervised efficiently in larger groups compared with new or untrained staff.

3. The supervisor's training and ability levels.

Too narrow a span leads to employees being over-supervised and denied the opportunity to demonstrate initiative: too wide a span is associated with lack of control and the likelihood of costly mistakes being made by subordinates.

Chain of command

This identifies how power and control is passed downwards through the organisation. The chain becomes more complicated as the size of the organisation increases: whereas a sole proprietor might control and liaise with all employees, large companies have chains of command which go through a number of levels of authority.

Organisation structures can be analysed into 'tall' or 'flat' forms. Tall structures are associated with larger firms and illustrate long chains of command. As a result:

- high-level decisions take a long time to reach employees at the bottom of the chain, and to be actioned;
- there is often a 'them and us' feeling of remoteness between those at both ends of the chain;
- this feeling is reinforced by formal communication systems and methods being used;
- spans of control are often narrow;
- employees are highly task-specialised.

'Flat' structures are more popular nowadays and are associated with smaller organisations and shorter chains of command.

Centralisation

This term can be used to identify how a firm's services (such as reprographics) are organised, whether on a centralised or a departmental basis. When considering organisational structures, the degree of centralisation is a reference to the authority to make decisions. A highly centralised structure denies those lower down the chain of command the power or authority to make decisions for themselves. As an illustration, many of the well-known 'fast-food' outlets operating on a franchise basis have little or no scope regarding display, pricing policy and the style or amount of advertising. Other examples of centralised organisations include 'multiple' retailers, whose counter layout, prices, promotions and window displays are determined without the direct involvement of individual store staff.

Decentralised structures have become increasingly popular in recent years. They are associated with greater authority at 'unit' (e.g. shop) level and are said to:

- allow a quicker and more effective local response to local needs and conditions;
- improve employee motivation through greater involvement in the decision-making process;
- lead to more effective management by objectives (through decentralised and personally devised objectives being set), and better management by exception through more accurate budgeting and an improved control system through the use of variances (see pages 159–60).

Delegation

Delegation exists because no one person can effectively control all the functions of a large business. A manager delegates certain powers to subordinates: a side-benefit of delegation is that it results in the junior employee taking on additional responsibilities and therefore being trained for later advancement.

The success of delegation is influenced by the responsibility, authority and accountability of those involved with the tasks.

❶ **Responsibility**   If employees are to carry out tasks delegated to them, they must accept the responsibility for carrying out the tasks, and for any failure. As a result the responsibilities must be:
  - identified clearly (and recorded, for example in the job description);
  - reasonable in nature and scope, considering the subordinate's training, qualifications and experience.

❷ **Authority**   The employee who is to carry out the delegated work must be given the authority to do the work. This authority might have to be communicated to others, such as a manager holding information to which the employee would not normally have access.

③ **Accountability** Delegation which is correctly given will result in the subordinate being accountable to the superior – and, in turn, the superior to the next person up the chain of command – for the success of the work.

There are a number of widely acknowledged limits to delegation:

- The work itself might be unsuitable – too complex, too specialised, or highly confidential.
- The delegator might have difficulty in delegating, being unwilling to relinquish tasks to subordinates.
- The subordinate, through lack of training, confidence or motivation, might be unwilling to accept the tasks delegated.

Chapter roundup

Chapter 2 has explained the main types of organisation in the United Kingdom economy. It has included the main forms of ownership in both the private and public sectors and has described their individual features. The internal structures of these different organisations often have similar characteristics, which this chapter identifies and explains.

Illustrative questions

1 Identify two disadvantages which consumers might experience when buying from a monopoly. (2)

NICCEA

2 (a) What do you understand by the term delegation? (4)

(b) What would be the benefits to managers and subordinates from successful delegation? (6)

NEAB

Tutorial note

Question 1 requires a short answer only. You need to define 'delegation' and to provide illustrations in answering question 2.

Suggested answers

1 (a) There is little or no consumer choice.

(b) There are higher prices due to a lack of competition.

2 (a) Delegation involves a transfer of authority and accompanying responsibility from manager to subordinate to undertake given tasks: for example, an advertising manager might delegate a research task on some aspect of the firm's advertising to a deputy. The subordinate will be accountable to the manager for the success of the task.

(b) Managers: they gain from a reduced work load, and thus greater opportunity to focus on key areas of their work (strategic rather than routine); they also face less stress/pressure; as a result, they should be able to make more effective decisions.

Subordinates: they gain greater experience through doing new tasks; they benefit from this extra experience/training and therefore have enhanced promotion chances; they become more highly motivated (e.g. McGregor's 'Theory Y' person) to succeed and to support the firm.

3 What difficulties does a sole trader face? (10)

Tutorial note

The question is quite straightforward, although the number of 'difficulties' required is not stated. I suggest you identify at least four of them, giving clear arguments and drawing on any relevant examples to support your arguments. Where a term such as 'sole trader' is mentioned in a question, it is usually beneficial to include a (brief) definition of its meaning.

Suggested answer

Sole traders (i.e. single-owner businesses) suffer from many difficulties, which can be grouped under these headings:

(a) **Financial** Sole traders, due to relative lack of size and limited security to offer, often find it more difficult to raise additional finance from major lenders such as banks. This results in limited expansion possibilities, and the small size of many sole traders also stops them benefiting from economies of scale. Cash flow problems are often experienced by sole traders due to their typical lack of power or market control.

(b) **Personal** The time and effort required is substantial; there are usually few opportunities for holidays and time off, and continuity problems are faced due to the unincorporated nature of the sole trader. The main personal disadvantage is normally regarded as unlimited liability (personal liability for business debts).

(c) **Structural** The single-owner feature of sole traders means that they are 'Jacks of all trades', not having specialist expertise in all aspects of the business (although they can, of course, employ specialists). The sole trader, whilst being able to adapt quickly to market conditions, faces difficulties from competitors who might have more market control and greater resources (e.g. for advertising). The sole trader tends to be dependent on other, larger firms (e.g. suppliers).

4 Examine the main factors that should be considered by a company contemplating a change in its legal status from that of a private limited company to that of a public limited company. (10)

Cambridge

Tutorial note

The question does not state how many 'factors' are required. To answer it successfully you must apply the key principles of both ownership and growth (see Chapter 3 if necessary).

Suggested answer

The legal status remains that of an incorporated association; the private company still has the power to enter contracts and to take (and defend) legal action in its own name. The main differences that a change in status to a PLC will bring are in disclosure of information and financial trading.

It is likely that the change in status will bring about a change in size (an increase). As the company grows, the directors will find that they must disclose more of the company's financial information to the Companies Registration Office. Growth is likely because the PLC will be able to offer its shares for sale to the general public: it must have a minimum £50,000 share capital anyway. By doing this, the directors will find the division between ownership and control increases: takeover bids become more likely through the PLC's shares being available on the Stock Exchange, and the additional information now available about the PLC will also interest potential buyers.

The directors will therefore have to balance the potential advantages of becoming a PLC – greater share capital which is easier to obtain, and benefits of greater size – with the disadvantages – further disclosure of information, a loss of control, possible buy-outs, the 'short-termism' of the stock market, and the drawbacks (e.g. slow communication) that increased size often brings.

5 Many government-provided services are currently being privatised or have already been privatised.

    (i) Identify **two** advantages and **two** disadvantages of privatisation to:
        (a) the consumer, and
        (b) the privatised company.   (8)

    (ii) Under what circumstances might privatisation not be favourable to the interests of the consumer?   (8)

    (iii) The public are actively encouraged to invest in privatised companies. What advice would you offer to a friend who is interested in investing £1,000 in a privatised company?   (12)

NICCEA

Tutorial note

The question is structured clearly for you. It does not mention a particular privatised company, but you could refer to examples in your answer. Part (iii) of the answer below should be studied with Chapter 6 in mind, where we examine the role of accounting ratios in financial analysis. Although the question states investment in a privatised company, your answer should include points on investment decisions in general.

Suggested answer

(i) The consumer benefits from increased choice and increased competition (lower prices), but loses the previous consistency of service and no longer has a government 'watchdog' controlling the industry. The company can now issue shares to raise capital and is no longer under direct government policy control; however, it must survive in the market-place, there is not now any direct government support and it must satisfy its shareholders.

(ii) Privatisation can result in duplication of products or services for the consumer (privatisation of bus services has led to criticism here). In reality the 'monopoly' might still exist, with resultant higher prices or price increases due to policy implementation (e.g. the long-term benefits of improved water supply systems by the privatised companies are at the short-term cost to the consumer).

(iii) The friend should: check any past results available, compare the expected return on investment with that from a well-established PLC and a 'safe' alternative (e.g. a building society), and seek professional advice.

Practice questions

1 Explain the term 'chain of command'.   (2)

Pitfalls

Many candidates confuse this term with 'span of control'.

Key points

This refers to the number of steps of authority in the hierarchy of an organisation. Each employee (subordinate) carries out the instructions of his/her manager (superior).

2 (a) Describe **two** types of ethical policy that might be adopted by a large do-it-yourself retailer such as 'Do-It-All' or 'B&Q' stating the reasons why they might adopt such policies. (8)

(b) Evaluate the costs and benefits of one of these policies to the stakeholders of such a company. (12)

WJEC

Pitfalls

This question is quite specific: make sure your answer is in the context of a large retail DIY chain. General points must be put into context in both parts of the question.

Key points

(a) Policy 1: consider the effects on the environment; e.g. encourage customers to reuse plastic bags, sell environment friendly and repeat-use products where possible, do not trade with firms which exploit their local environment. Policy 2: support equal opportunities; e.g. apply rigorously relevant UK and EU legislation, support local and national equal opportunities initiatives.

(b) Benefits of Policy 2 to stakeholders (e.g. employees, shareholders): enhanced reputation and goodwill leads to positive publicity and more sales; helps frame advertising campaigns which also increase sales; higher profits should result; employees have greater sense of worth. Costs: monitoring and applying laws has a financial cost which affects profits; prices charged by 'acceptable' suppliers may be higher; some customers may go elsewhere for lower prices (price competitiveness may suffer); pressure on keeping jobs for employees, and reduced profit margins/lower share prices for shareholders.

3 (a) What is a business 'franchise'?

(b) Give **three** reasons why a person might take out a franchise.

(c) Why might firms sell franchises instead of opening the shops themselves?

Pitfalls

The definition of the term 'franchise' can vary according to the precise situation: here you are only required to provide a general statement and reasons, and you need not apply them to a particular situation. Parts (a) and (b) only need short answers, but your answer to (c) should be more extensive.

Key points

(a) Granting permission (licence) for a franchisee to make and/or distribute products in return for the franchisor's trade name, finance and expertise.

(b) Professional support; nationally known name/national advertising; avoids need for large-scale initial investment.

(c) Reduces capital investment required; guaranteed income; success of existing franchisees boosts value of unsold franchises; large-scale economies possible in the context of small-firm operations.

CHAPTER 3

THE GROWTH OF ORGANISATIONS

Units in this chapter

Chapter objectives

The purpose of this chapter is to explain how organisations grow in size, and the benefits and drawbacks associated with this growth. It develops the international trade unit in Chapter 1 by analysing the influence of multinational corporations. Chapter 3 also evaluates how small firms (which link with Chapter 2 on business organisations) continue to survive and flourish in our economy.

The key topics and concepts covered in this chapter are:

● measuring size;
● internal growth;
● integration and deintegration;
● economies and diseconomies of scale;
● multinational structure;
● survival of the small firm.

3.1 SIZE AND GROWTH

MEASURING SIZE

The size of an organisation can be measured using different indicators. Some are more suitable than others, depending on the nature of the organisation. Firms in the same industry should be compared using the same indicator.

❶ **Turnover**   The level of annual sales is the most widely used indicator of a firm's size: they indicate its ability to obtain finance and benefit from economies of scale. Limitations of using turnover as the measure of size include:

● turnover varies greatly from year to year;
● since profit margins vary between industries, firms with similar turnovers can have quite different profits;
● turnover is not necessarily an indicator of market share.

② **Capital employed**   The firm's capital employed (its net assets: see page 151) shows the amount of net investment and is compared with profit to illustrate profitability. 'Capital employed' is a difficult figure to measure: for example, two firms might have different asset valuation policies, which could then lead to an inaccurate comparison being made on this basis.

③ **Profits**   A firm's profit figure (such as profit before tax) is sometimes used to indicate its size. The drawbacks of using this measure are that different firms in the same industry may deliberately have different profit margins, and that a firm's profits vary from year to year.

Table 3.1   *The ten largest UK industrial companies in 1991, ranked by profits*

	Turnover £ billion	Profits £ billion
British Telecom	13.2	3.1
British Petroleum	33.0	2.8
British Gas	9.5	1.8
Hanson	7.2	1.3
Glaxo Holdings	3.4	1.3
Imperial Chemical Industries	12.9	1.0
BTR	6.7	1.0
BAT Industries	15.0	1.0
Grand Metropolitan	9.4	0.9
RTZ Corporation	3.9	0.9

Source: Lloyds Bank Plc

④ **Employees**   This is normally a straightforward indicator to use, but firms in different industries have different capital/labour ratios: for example, a service sector firm is normally much more labour-intensive than one based in the secondary (manufacturing) sector.

Profits before tax £ million		Turnover £ million			Capital employed £ million		Full-time equivalent employees	
Cadbury Schweppes	332	BICC	3,647	MANUFACTURERS: Cadbury Schweppes BICC	Cadbury Schweppes	1,214	BICC	40,118
BICC	77	Cadbury Schweppes	3,372		BICC	724	Cadbury Schweppes	36,570
M & S	994	Sainsbury's	13,499	RETAILERS: Marks & Spencer Sainsbury	M & S	4,142	Sainsbury's	95,519
Sainsbury's	712	M & S	7,209		Sainsbury's	3,534	M & S	65,498

Fig. 3.1 Problems of measuring size

Sources: Annual report information – Marks and Spencer and Sainsbury's (1996), Cadbury Schweppes and BICC (1992)

METHODS OF GROWTH

Most firms try to grow in size for specific reasons. Larger size brings with it:

● improved survival prospects through larger market share, diversification and greater finance;

- economies of scale (see page 83);
- an increased feeling of status and power for the directors.

Internal growth

This occurs when a firm expands using its own resources by

retaining its profits

⬇

preserving its liquid assets

⬇

using them to invest in additional fixed assets

⬇

improving its productive capacity

⬇

increasing market share and growth

Internal expansion avoids mergers and takeovers, which are not guaranteed to succeed, but it is a much slower method of growth and can be difficult in certain market conditions (e.g. where there is a saturated market for the product).

Integration

External growth, or integration, occurs when one firm takes over or merges with another. In the UK economy, takeovers and mergers are a popular way of firms increasing in size very quickly.

- A **takeover** occurs when one firm offers to buy – and then obtains – a controlling interest in another: it does not normally involve agreement between the firms.
- A **merger** takes place when two (or more) companies agree to combine their assets: the companies are completely reorganised as a result of the merger.

Horizontal integration

This occurs when firms making similar products or providing similar services join together. Examples include Sears plc acquiring Richard Shops in October 1992 'to give us a position in the growing 35+ sector' (extract from Sears plc Chief Executive Strategic Review) (see Table 3.2).

Table 3.2 Group profile, Sears plc 1995/6

Division/ Market	Footwear	Clothing	Home shopping	Selfridges
Companies	British Shoe – Dolcis Shoe City Shoe Express	Adams Wallis Miss Selfridge Richards Warehouse	Freemans	Selfridges
Profits 95/6 (93/4)	7.5 (32.9)	31.7 (26.6)	38.0 (31.0)	34.6 (21.0)
Sales 95/6 (£m)	604.8	533.3	531.0	278.0

Source: Sears plc

Because horizontal integration involves firms in the same industry or at the same stage of production, the results should be larger-scale production and economies of scale. The new company will have a greater market dominance since it has the previous market shares of the former companies. (In saturated markets this might be the only way to substantially increase market share.)

Companies in the same industry may decide to establish links but not join formally. Examples include the use by Rover of Honda expertise in car technology and design, and British Aerospace agreements operating in 1993:

- an agreement with Eurocopter SA on the possibility of co-operating on Ministry of Defence military helicopter programmes;
- a partnership with McDonnell-Douglas to develop and produce a Harrier II V/STOL combat aircraft and a Goshawk naval trainer;
- an agreement with Rombac to manufacture BAC One-Eleven airliners in Romania.

Such joint ventures:

- avoid the expense and permanent commitment of a formal merger;
- help reduce competition;
- improve competitiveness through the sharing of technology and other resources.

Vertical integration

This occurs when two firms which are at different stages of production amalgamate. **Vertical forwards** integration takes place when a firm amalgamates with one of its outlets, for example when an oil company acquires a chain of petrol stations. **Vertical backwards** integration occurs when a company moves backwards down the chain of production and acquires one of its suppliers (for example, a food manufacturing firm taking over an agricultural producer).

Motives for vertical integration include:

- **Protection** By controlling its outlets and/or suppliers, the firm is in a more protected position.
- **Control** The firm now has closer control over quality, delivery and levels of supply, as well as greater control of its market.
- **Profits** The profits of the previous supplier/outlet now belong to the firm, allowing greater flexibility on pricing and profit margins.
- **Products** Although the firms produce similar products, there will be some product differentiation. Examples include truck and car companies amalgamating (e.g. Leyland with what is now Rover), and also car manufacturers in different segments of the same market (e.g. BMW acquiring Rover for its small car and Land Rover segments).

Lateral integration

Also known as **conglomerate** or **diversified** integration, this occurs when firms in different industries amalgamate (see Table 3.3). There may be some link between the firms' products, or the conglomerate may own quite diverse companies.

Table 3.3 *Segmental analyses, THORN EMI*

	1996 Turnover £m	1996 Operating profit £m	1995 Turnover £m	1995 Operating profit £m
By class of business				
EMI Music	2,705.1	365.2	2,189.0	294.9
THORN	1,537.4	187.2	1,589.4	152.4
HMV	771.2	19.6	503.2	14.0
By origin				
UK	1,218.3	160.1	1,371.3	103.9
Rest of Europe	1,403.3	193.9	1,207.0	157.3
North America	1,464.6	132.9	1,293.0	132.0
Asia Pacific	843.2	73.9	525.0	53.4
Other	126.2	14.2	111.0	8.8

Source: THORN EMI plc

The main advantage claimed for lateral integration is diversification. Risk becomes spread over different markets and failure in any one market does not automatically lead to the company collapsing. Companies which were in a saturated or declining market are no longer limited by that market. An example is British-American Tobacco (BAT) diversifying to counter its contracting market for smokers' products.

Arguments against integration

1. **Reduced competitiveness** The growth which results from integration can cause diseconomies of scale (see page 85).

2. **Reduced competition** This is an important motive for many amalgamations, but it leads to less consumer choice as a result of product rationalisation and potentially higher prices.

3. **Asset stripping** All forms of integration have expected financial benefits for the participants. Some amalgamations have resulted in the acquiring company closing the firm bought, and selling off its assets.

4. **Over-borrowing** The 'leveraged buyouts' (LBOs) of the 1980s were based on high levels of borrowing by some companies which were acquiring others. The increase in interest (repayment) rates left many of these companies struggling to meet their debts to external lenders.

Deintegration

A company – often a conglomerate – might decide to reduce the scope of its activities. The main reason is financial: either to raise finance through the sale of a subsidiary, or to cut costs through the drive for greater efficiency and improved communication channels. Deintegration occurs through:

- **Divestment** Selling a subsidiary (which could result in a management buy-out: see page 69), for example Sears' decision to withdraw from the menswear market, by divesting Fosters.

- **Demerger** Dividing an existing company into two or more new groups or divisions.

Major divestments

After the diversifications of the 1970s and early 1980s BP found – like other companies which followed a similar course – that it experienced mixed success in managing its 'new' businesses. Towards the end of the decade, in a change of strategy, the company decided to concentrate on its core, hydrocarbon-based activities. To that end, it began a series of divestments.

In early 1988, BP sold its subsidiary, Scicon, and so withdrew from the computing services industry. After developing its minerals interests successfully during the 1980s, the company sold most of the business to RTZ in 1989 and disposed of the balance during the next few years. Similarly, most of BP Coal was sold in 1989 and 1990. The company did not begin to sell its nutrition interests until 1992, but by the middle of that year the divestment programme was well advanced.

Source: The British Petroleum Company plc

3.2   EFFECTS OF GROWTH

INTERNAL ECONOMIES OF SCALE

These are created when a firm's **unit cost of production falls as output and its scale of operations increase**. An increase in the size of a firm brings with it the opportunity for larger-scale production and lower unit costs. The increased volume of production need not increase fixed costs (see page 183) and so the average cost per unit can fall. Other economies can also be made as a result of the firm's increased size as it benefits from increasing returns to scale.

Economies of increased dimensions   These arise from an increase in physical size: for example, supertankers, with a carrying capacity some twenty times as much as that of a traditional tanker, more than offset their greater (three or fourfold) cost of manufacture to an oil company.

Financial economies   Larger firms are assumed to be more stable financially and therefore find it easier to obtain loan capital. They are able to negotiate lower interest rates on these loans. Larger companies such as PLCs also have more, and less expensive, sources of finance available to them.

Managerial economies   The growth in a firm's size can make possible the employment of specialist managers, who bring with them greater levels of expertise. The principle of **division of labour** operates and leads to greater efficiency in specialist areas such as marketing, finance, production and personnel.

Marketing economies   Larger firms can afford the services of specialist marketing firms, such as advertising agencies. A wider range of promotion and advertising is possible: the greater costs here are likely to be spread over a much larger turnover, reducing the unit cost of promotion. Packaging, market research and other marketing costs are shared across higher production levels.

Purchasing economies   A larger firm is able to take advantage of bulk-buying discounts which reduce unit material costs. It can also negotiate more favourable credit terms and delivery schedules than can a smaller competitor.

Risk-bearing economies   Firms often grow larger by increasing their product range. This diversification spreads business risk over a number of products and markets.

Technical economies   A larger firm can afford research and development costs which might result in improved products and great savings from technological breakthroughs. It is only the larger firms which can meet the major research costs required in industries such as defence and pharmaceuticals.

In large companies the division of labour principle operates on the shop floor, where trained specialists use specialised equipment. Mass production and handling techniques also reduce unit manufacturing and storage costs. The use of technologically advanced equipment only becomes cost effective where the large costs of such equipment can be spread over mass production.

EXTERNAL ECONOMIES OF SCALE

These arise from a growth in the size of the industry: all firms in the industry benefit from these economies. External economies are most likely to be found where the industry is **concentrated** in a particular area. Historical examples include the manufacture of china in the Potteries, and shipbuilding in North East England: nowadays London operates as a major provider of financial services, and some towns such as Telford support a concentration of 'high-tech' manufacturing industries.

- **Training**   The workforce improves its levels of skill and training through local colleges supplying industry-specific courses. Some areas therefore developed specialist skills, such as the West Midlands (heavy engineering) and South Wales (mining).

- **Support**   Local firms which provide support services (such as buying the industry's waste output or providing specialist insurance or components) set up in or move to the area.

- **Information**   Trade associations develop and provide additional information and support services.

- **Reputation**   Areas can gain good reputations through specialising (e.g. Potteries china and Sheffield steel).

DISECONOMIES OF SCALE

There are practical limits to the amount of growth which can take place. Beyond a certain point, a firm will find that its **unit costs start increasing**, as it suffers from diseconomies of scale. These diseconomies arise for a number of reasons. The larger the firm, the more levels there are through which communication has to flow, leading to greater bureaucracy ('red tape'). This results in:

- Worker dissatisfaction and poor labour relations, which in turn cause:
  - low morale
  - higher absenteeism
  - actions such as overtime bans.
- The chain of command lengthening, and decisions becoming slower to implement which:
  - reduces efficiency
  - raises costs
  - means that the firm is slower to react to changing market conditions.
- Increasing overheads, due to the need to sustain more complex systems and processes.
- More difficult coordination of the firm's activities as they become spread across more markets and countries.

Higher unit costs and falling returns to scale are found. Problems caused by diseconomies of scale might cause a large conglomerate to demerge or divest, to make its size more manageable.

Growth which takes place too quickly can also cause problems. Many firms experience liquidity difficulties: a shortage of working capital (see page 152) to support new orders leads to overtrading, where the firm cannot meet its debts, even though it may be making substantial paper profits. A second problem arises when the firm cannot expand its productive capacity quickly enough: customers become disappointed and withdraw their orders. Thirdly, the firm's administrative and communication systems may not be efficient enough to cope with the expansion of work: this slows down the support operations and again causes customer dissatisfaction.

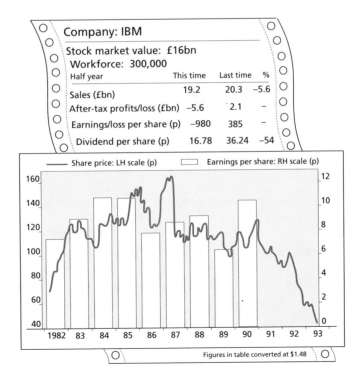

Fig. 3.2 IBM, July 1993

Source: *The Guardian*

As an example of the problems of size, the computer giant IBM was forced to restructure dramatically in the early 1990s as its traditional computer mainframe and mini market declined with the expansion of the PC hardware and software market. In 1993 IBM reported a three-month pre-tax write-off of $8.9 billion, based on a loss of $8 billion, with a loss of 35,000 jobs worldwide. This was largely due to a fall in hardware sales of 13 per cent. Part of its problem appeared to be its size in an increasingly competitive environment, made worse by the effects of international recession. IBM had remained based in the mainframe market, and its centralised bureaucracy appeared too large and slow to compete with the speed of response of its smaller competitors.

We must remember that the best – the optimum – size for a firm will vary over time. Technological developments will continue to change the relationship between labour and capital: as an example, the use of cashpoints and other technology-based services in the 'high street' banks has replaced labour and led to lower employment and the rationalisation of branches. The conclusion is that the most cost-effective size for the firm will also change over time.

3.3 MULTINATIONAL CORPORATIONS

A multinational corporation operates internationally, although its ownership is based in a single country. Ownership may be in the form of a **holding company**, which 'holds' or controls the different subsidiaries. Many of the best-known firms are multinationals: Shell, Ford and IBM, for example.

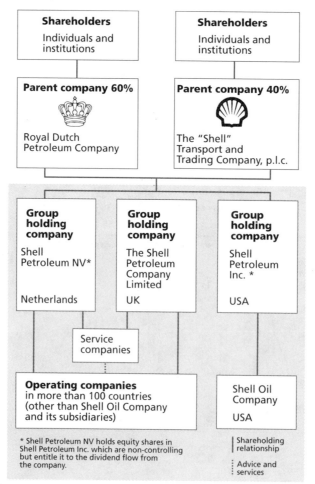

Fig.3.3 Structure of the Royal Dutch/Shell Group of Companies 1994

Source: Royal Dutch/Shell Group of Companies

The importance of multinationals lies in their significant economic contribution. They contribute about one-third of total world production and the larger multinationals generate output and turnover levels which exceed the gross national products (GNPs) of many countries.

Multinationals have increased in number because they gain from the following benefits:

❶ Cheaper labour or materials found in different countries   General Motors relocated plants from the USA to Mexico; footwear/sportswear multinationals such as Nike also gain labour-cost benefits from manufacturing in the Far East (some analysts have suggested that costs can be saved to such an extent that the labour-cost element of a sports shoe retailing at $80 can be as low as 12 cents).

❷ Entering tariff-protected markets   One way round the EU's Common External Tariff is to set up production in one of its countries. Overseas firms such as Nissan, Toyota, Epson, Tatung and Ricoh have located in the UK and now form part of the 'home' economy.

Table 3.4 *Turnover by destination*

	1995 £m	1994 £m
United Kingdom	1,803	1,747
Rest of Europe	664	530
Australasia	531	481
North America	658	652
Asia – Pacific	479	401
Other	227	162
	4,362	3,973

Source: BICC plc

❸ Avoiding legislation in the home country   Legislation or other restrictions (e.g. those on monopolies and mergers in the UK and the EU) can be avoided by the multinational basing some of its operations in a different country.

Benefits of multinationals

Advocates of a free market system and 'market forces' argue that multinationals are subject to the same basic laws of supply and demand as any other business form. A host economy gains many benefits from allowing multinationals to operate.

- Unemployment is reduced. Multinationals are major employers of labour and can help alleviate unemployment blackspots (e.g. Nissan in the North East of England). In addition, ancillary firms such as component manufacturers and suppliers of canteen and cleaning services grow in the local area and provide additional employment.

- Other factors of production are employed more fully and used more efficiently through the competition generated by the multinational.

- Advanced technology is introduced. Examples in the UK include Honda's work with Rover, and technology-based multinationals such as Epson (printers), Tatung (TVs), Toyota (vehicles) and Sony (entertainment systems), bringing ideas and expertise into our economy. Training in more advanced techniques and skills also develops in the local area.

- Modern work practices are introduced. Many multinationals have work practices which highlight teamwork, shared goals, and employee participation in decision-making. They might also operate no-redundancy policies (e.g. some of the Far Eastern multinationals based in the UK).

- There is greater choice and higher income. Consumers benefit from wider product choice and the economy gains through the multinational's activities, both at home (employment rises, tax revenue is generated and greater expertise improves economic competitiveness), and by exporting (balance of payments benefits).

Problems of multinationals

The policies of a multinational may not always benefit the country in which it is based, causing a series of tensions as a result of the economic power it wields.

- The multinational concentrates on its own interests rather than those of the host country:
  - it may decide at short notice to move production out of the country, causing unemployment and other economic problems to the areas affected, and hitting the host country's balance of payments and level of economic growth;
  - it can adjust its costs between its various subsidiaries to gain maximum benefits from one country's lower taxation requirements;
  - it has the power to move its reserves between different countries, gaining financial advantage but causing currency fluctuations.
- The multinational can also use its economic power in ways which are socially undesirable. Accusations of bribery, corruption and financial irregularity have been levelled against some multinationals, and exploitation of cheap labour and raw materials can take place with only limited concern for the environment or the long-term stability and growth of the countries affected.

3.4 THE SURVIVAL OF SMALL FIRMS

Definitions of what constitutes a 'small' company have been made. Under Companies Act legislation, small companies meet two of three conditions:

- annual turnover below £2,800,000;
- balance sheet total assets under £1,400,000
- fewer than 50 employees on average.

A firm satisfying these criteria in two consecutive financial years only has to file an abridged balance sheet with the Companies Registration Office. It does not have to reveal details of profitability or turnover.

The principle of economies of scale suggests that small firms should be driven out of the market, as a result of their higher unit costs. Other common weaknesses include:

- reliance on a single product for survival;
- lack of business expertise;
- limited financial resources to withstand competition and recession and to employ specialists.

How small firms survive

There are a number of reasons why small firms continue to survive.

1 Supplying a local or limited market:

- supplying personal services, such as hairdressing and plumbing;
- operating in a particular segment of the market, e.g. domestic building extensions and improvements;
- providing convenience (the 'corner shop');

- concentrating on specialist or luxury items with limited demand, such as specialist firms for coin and stamp collectors;
- working in areas where growth is naturally limited, such as the markets for personal services.

2 The policy of the owners:

- a lack of ambition;
- desire to remain in charge;
- the wish to avoid risk.

3 Vertical disintegration:

- where larger companies subcontract out to small firms, because they find it unprofitable to do certain work themselves.

4 The attraction of entrepreneurship:

- small firms are established by people who want to be their own boss;
- they allow those who dislike working for a large firm the opportunity to work for themselves.

Small firms have a number of typical strengths which help them to survive. They are quicker to respond to market forces, communication between management and shop floor is efficient, and labour relations are usually good.

The growth of the small-firms sector has been encouraged by government policies in the 1980s and 1990s, in an attempt to stimulate the economy and reduce unemployment. The main developments have been in the areas of:

- **reducing bureaucracy**: a reduction in the statistical and other information required by government authorities;
- **providing advice**: for example, through the DTI's Enterprise Initiative, which provides assistance in areas such as marketing and information technology;
- **taxation policy**: lowering corporation tax levels for small firms, and establishing a turnover threshold for VAT registration;
- **finance**: for example, the Business Expansion Scheme, which gave tax relief on investment, and the Enterprise Allowance Scheme giving new business owners a £40 weekly allowance in the first year of operation.

Chapter roundup

Chapter 3 has concentrated on why and how firms grow. It has explained the general cost-related benefits of growth and given examples of both internal and external economies of scale. The chapter has outlined the main methods of growth and the nature and importance of the two size 'extremes': multinational corporations and small firms.

Illustrative questions

1 Name **two** ways (other than number of employees) of assessing the size of a business organisation. (2)

2 Explain what is meant by 'economies of scale' and how these might be useful to vehicle manufacturers. (5)

Cambridge

Tutorial note

Question 1 asks you to 'name', so two short statements only are needed. Question 2 is almost two questions in one (be careful with questions asking you to explain something 'and' something else). The split of marks is probably two for the explanation and three for applying your comments to vehicle manufacturers.

Suggested answer

1   Amount of capital employed; size of market share.

2   'Economies of scale' refers to the unit cost savings which are made as firms grow in size. Although total costs will increase, these are proportionately lower than the increase in output (fixed costs do not increase automatically as output increases) which results in lower unit costs. Economies may be internal to the firm (e.g. bulk-buying discounts lowering the price of materials) or external (e.g. improved provision of local training).

An example of an internal economy of scale from which a vehicle manufacturer might benefit is the purchasing economy mentioned above. Other likely economies include financial economies (lower interest rates on loans for new machinery), marketing economies (spreading the cost of advertising over higher output could make national TV advertising of the vehicles cost effective), managerial economies (specialists could be employed in researching new vehicle designs, more efficient engines, etc.), and technical economies (shopfloor employees using specialist machinery and equipment as a result of division of labour).

3 (a) Why might a firm give a false impression if it uses 'number of employees' as the only indicator of its size?

(b) Give **two** reasons why a healthy small-firm sector is important to the UK economy.

Tutorial note

Part (a) asks you to evaluate the given indicator of size: your answer should include some examples of firms and industries. Part (b) requires a straightforward recall of key facts; your answer should include any two of the points below.

Suggested answer

(a) The 'number of employees' is only one of a range of indicators used to measure the size of a firm. It may give a misleading indication of size for these reasons:

(i) Some industries (e.g. chemicals) are capital-intensive and others (e.g. tourism) are labour-intensive; firms which are the same size when measured in, say, capital employed or turnover can have greatly differing employee levels.

(ii) Within an industry, the level of technology varies: a firm replacing labour with capital might be growing, yet have a falling number of employees.

(iii) 'Employees' needs defining: one firm might include only productive and direct support (office) employees, whereas another could count part-time staff, cleaners, etc. There can be a lack of consistency in whom to include.

(iv) Some industries (e.g. agriculture) face large seasonal fluctuations in their workforce: when does the count take place?

(b) The small-firm sector remains important because it:

(i) contributes to the UK's balance of payments by exporting;

(ii) often provides service support to large firms.

(Also: it can adapt and respond quickly to changing conditions; it provides competition; it provides employment; it fills gaps in the economy where larger firms do not operate; it often acts as a 'seed-bed' of ideas and developments. These could form alternative reasons, or in some cases be used to support the above reasons.)

4 (a) Explain how a country's economy gains when a multinational corporation establishes a base in that country. (10)

   (b) Identify and explain **three** reasons why the multinational might be treated with suspicion by the host country's government. (10)

Tutorial note

The question is in two distinct parts: 'pro' and 'con', from the point of view of the country. General questions such as this one are often answered more effectively if you can include real-life illustrations.

Suggested answer

(a) Multinational corporations produce and/or sell their goods internationally. Their presence in any country can bring substantial economic benefits. A multinational is a major employer of labour and user of other economic resources. These resources may be underemployed in advanced economies (e.g. unemployment levels in the EU illustrate underuse of economic resources); if the corporation is located in a developing country, that country may not be in a position to otherwise develop and use its resources. Multinationals can import efficient work practices, advanced technology and general expertise in business operations into a country, leading to that country's economy becoming increasingly competitive as 'satellite' businesses grow around the operations of the multinational. Good examples of this are some of the work practices (e.g. 'Just-in-Time' production methods, and quality initiatives such as TQM, introduced to the UK economy by multinationals). Overall, a country's levels of production can increase in volume and efficiency (higher productivity), its taxation revenue increases, and its balance of payments benefits through the multinational exporting its products.

(b) One reason why the host might be suspicious of the multinational is that it may well displace home-based competitors. The net effect on employment and revenues might be negligible. Secondly, multinational corporations are notoriously 'footloose', being willing and able to move their manufacturing bases from country to country depending on such factors as local/national tax levels, and workforce skill levels. There is no guarantee that the multinational, once established, will remain: examples include the removal of some manufacturing bases from the US and Western Europe to Pacific Basin countries having lower labour costs. Multinationals are not responsible to Western governments and are willing to move their resources between different countries according to their own criteria. Thirdly, the multinational might operate on a short-term, exploitative basis, for example in developing countries, extracting resources and having little regard to local social concerns or welfare. Examples include the exploitation of the environment in some South American countries.

(Other, linked, reasons include political interference, exploitation of cheap labour, and the movement of profits out of the host country.)

Practice questions

1 What is the difference between horizontal and vertical integration? (2)

Pitfalls

Many candidates mistakenly relate these terms to communication systems. Two simple definitions only are required.

Key points

Horizontal: firms at the same stage of production amalgamate. Vertical: a firm takes over a supplier (vertical backwards) or a buyer (vertical forwards).

2 (a) What are the benefits and problems associated with a merger between a UK-based manufacturer and a similar-sized competitor? (10)

(b) What are the additional factors if the competitor is based in the European Union? (10)

Pitfalls

You can assume from the question that the firms are in the same industry ('...competitor'). A possible problem with part (b) is that you might simply repeat the points made in (a): this is bad exam practice, since the question clearly states that 'additional factors' are required.

Key points

Possible benefits: economies of scale (described), greater market share, reduced competition, defensive motive (easier to fight off future takeover bids).

Possible problems: employee problems (creating and handling redundancies, worse labour relations, low morale), duplication of systems, need to rationalise, there may still be gaps in product ranges, cost considerations, breaking legislation on mergers.

Additional factors: possible transport problems, communication problems, different (taxation etc.) policies of the host governments, language (need for retraining, change of recruitment policy) and cultural influences, breaking EU directives on mergers.

CHAPTER 4

EXTERNAL INFLUENCES ON ORGANISATIONS

Units in this chapter

Chapter objectives

All organisations are affected by the environment within which they operate. This chapter analyses how firms are affected by the actions of external agencies other than those (customers and suppliers) with whom they trade. It examines how central government – often regarded as the main external influence – regulates and encourages business. The role of other bodies such as pressure groups is explained, and technological influences on the organisation are considered.

The key topics and concepts covered in this chapter are:

● government economic objectives;
● national and international incentives to encourage enterprise;
● regional policy;
● employee and consumer protection;
● competition policy;
● pressure groups;
● technological influences.

4.1   GOVERNMENT INVOLVEMENT

Firms are influenced by the policies of local government, national government and international organisations such as the European Union. The main governmental and other influences on firms are shown in Fig. 4.1.

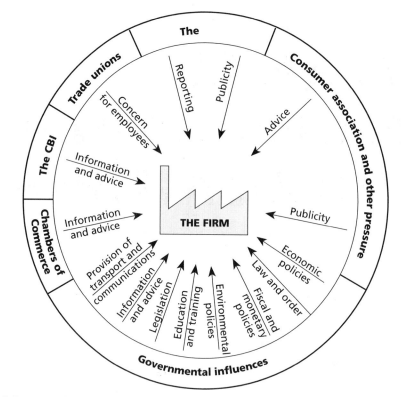

Fig. 4.1 Influences on firms

REASONS FOR INVOLVEMENT

Local and central government, together with the European Union, influence a firm's decisions regarding its:

- **location:** e.g. granting planning permission, creating the Single Market;
- **workforce:** e.g. passing employee protection and health/safety legislation, allowing free movement of labour in the EU;
- **trade links:** e.g. removing tariff barriers, giving help through the Export Credit Guarantee Department and British Overseas Trade Board;
- **expansion:** e.g. passing monopolies and mergers legislation;
- **income:** e.g. altering taxation policies regulating the level of demand;
- **finance:** e.g. influencing interest rate levels.

Central government becomes involved because it wants to influence the country's economy. It has a number of key economic objectives.

Controlling inflation

Inflation is defined as a persistent tendency for prices to rise over time. Recent Conservative governments have made the control of inflation their main priority.

Inflation affects the behaviour of firms. Long-term planning becomes difficult; profit margins are squeezed if a firm cannot pass price increases on (and if it does, its prices can become uncompetitive); the increase in interest rates during inflationary periods hits firms with high debt borrowing and encourages them to pay larger dividends (which reduces their funds); and exporters could find the increase in their prices through inflation makes them uncompetitive internationally.

Inflation also:

- hits people such as pensioners who are on fixed incomes (though indexing of pensions counters this);

- distorts economic behaviour: high inflation might encourage saving and reduces spending, often on consumer durables, whereas low inflation tends to encourage spending and fuels output and recovery;
- brings about a lack of confidence in the currency and a possible collapse (through hyperinflation) of economic activity.

In a recent example from the civil war in the former Yugoslavia, Serbia started issuing million-dinar denomination notes, followed two weeks later by five-million dinar notes and another six weeks later by 50-million dinar notes. The rate of inflation, once calculated annually, began to be calculated on a daily basis, the daily rate reaching 50 per cent in July 1993.

Causes of inflation *Demand-pull* inflation occurs when aggregate demand in the economy as a whole exceeds aggregate supply. Governments attempt to control demand through:

- **Monetary policy** controlling credit by reducing its availability or increasing its cost.
- **Fiscal policy** increasing direct taxation (income tax) or indirect taxation (VAT) to reduce spending power, or cutting government spending to contract demand.

Cost-push inflation occurs on the supply side of the economy. Costs of production increase, perhaps due to pay rises not being supported by productivity increases, or through costs of imported raw materials rising due to the pound falling on the foreign exchange market. These cost increases 'push' prices up.

Measuring inflation A common measure of inflation is the retail price index (RPI). The prices of a representative sample of purchases made by households are weighted in importance and recorded. The index is calculated against a base year. Other measures of inflation include the 'factory gate' indicator of the price of firms' inputs. The RPI itself can also be adjusted by excluding elements such as mortgage interest payments.

Table 4.1 *Measures of UK inflation*

	Retail prices. increase (%)	Average earnings Increase (%)
1981	11.9	12.8
1986	3.4	7.9
1991	5.9	8.0

Source: ONS

Full employment

A common criticism of Conservative government economic policies from 1979 into the 1990s was the apparent lack of concern over high unemployment levels, through concentrating on the control of inflation. Unemployment creates major social costs and also wastes economic resources. There are several types of unemployment:

- **Structural**: where industries face structural decline through lack of competitiveness (e.g. the old staple industries): this has badly affected regions such as Lancashire (textiles) and South Wales (coal), and continues with the trend towards deindustrialisation.
- **Frictional**: caused by the time-lag between moving from one job to another: this is closely linked to labour's **geographical immobility** (e.g. where a person will not move to another job in a different area, because of social links or higher housing costs) and its **occupational immobility** (a lack of skill to do the jobs available).
- **Casual (or seasonal)**: found in tourism, agriculture and other seasonal industries.
- **Technological** (a form of structural): arising from increased automation when capital replaces labour.
- **Cyclical**: when there is a general lack of demand in the economy.

Fig. 4.2 indicates the areas in the economy hit hardest by job losses in recent years.

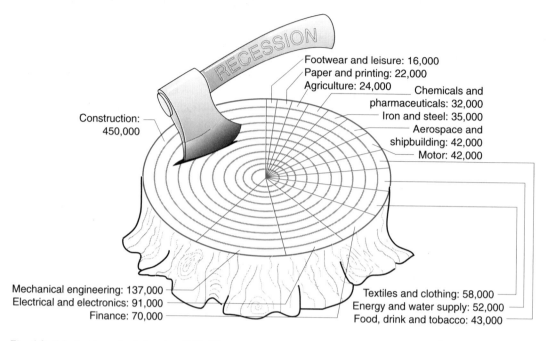

Footwear and leisure: 16,000
Paper and printing: 22,000
Agriculture: 24,000
Chemicals and pharmaceuticals: 32,000
Iron and steel: 35,000
Aerospace and shipbuilding: 42,000
Motor: 42,000

Construction: 450,000

Mechanical engineering: 137,000
Electrical and electronics: 91,000
Finance: 70,000

Textiles and clothing: 58,000
Energy and water supply: 52,000
Food, drink and tobacco: 43,000

Fig. 4.2 Jobs lost in major industries, 1989–93

Source: ONS

Employment policies   Recent Conservative government policy concentrated on controlling the power that organised unions have when bargaining for wage increases. It was based on the belief that excessive wage demands price workers out of the job market. Relative levels of pay and benefits may also be adjusted: reducing welfare benefits makes low-wage jobs more attractive. The belief that financial incentives work 'at the top end' has resulted in lower personal tax levels in an attempt to encourage greater enterprise.

Alternative policies concentrate on the demand side of the economy: the government can encourage demand through its fiscal and monetary policies, for example by reducing taxation. Regional policy (see page 98) also takes account of localised high levels of unemployment.

Specific policies to help the unemployed include providing advisory services, such as Restart interviews, job search seminars, job clubs, JIGs (job interview guarantees), and the establishment of TECs and the training schemes described later. In the 1993 budget, for example, £125 million (net cost) was invested in a package of measures which included:

● **Learning for Work**   30,000 places for the unemployed on vocationally relevant schemes.

● **Community Action**   60,000 places for voluntary community work, for an extra £10 on top of benefit.

● **Business Start-up Scheme**   10,000 additional places.

Stable balance of payments

Chapter 1 explained that a country's balance of payments record indicates its ability to earn its keep in the international community. A persistent deficit causes a drain on a country's foreign reserves and creates the need to borrow. Even a long-term surplus can cause problems for a government, for example by encouraging 'demand-pull' inflation.

GOVERNMENT ASSISTANCE

The roles of the UK government are to control and to help business. Control is primarily through legislation, fiscal and other policies which directly affect firms. The government helps firms in a number of ways.

Providing information and advice

The Office for National Statistics (ONS) is the government agency responsible for compiling many of the UK's economic and social statistics. Firms use this information to analyse market and other trends. ONS publications include

1. **The 'Blue Book':** this details the income and expenditure in the national accounts.

2. **Regional Trends:** this includes information on regional population and income movements.

3. **Social Trends:** this contains annual summaries of statistical information on population, employment, income and wealth.

4. **Annual Abstract of Statistics** and **Monthly Digest of Statistics:** these summarise the whole of the UK economy, including wages and prices, population, expenditure and output.

5. **Economic Trends:** this illustrates the monthly changes in the economy.

The Department of Trade and Industry (**DTI**) provides help for UK businesses. In 1988 it launched its Enterprise Initiative, a self-help package of advice, assistance and guidance.

- The Enterprise Initiative provides consultancy help for most firms with fewer than 500 employees. The DTI subsidises the cost of a consultancy project lasting between five and fifteen days.

- The 'Managing in the '90s' programme provides information on integrated management approaches, e.g. in design and manufacturing.

- The MPI (manufacturing, planning and implementing) programme provides grants to help firms of up to 500 employees introduce modern manufacturing systems.

- Other schemes include information about technological developments, grant support for new ideas, help in forging education–industry links, and special assistance for firms in Assisted Areas and Urban Programme areas.

The Small Firms Service (in London) and Training and Enterprise Councils (**TECs**) provide advice for small and medium-sized firms. TECs (LECs – Local Enterprise Companies – in Scotland) are business-led local companies contracting to take charge of training in their area.

Assistance to exporters

The DTI also provides help for exporters. Its Export Market Information Centre offers a self-help facility including statistics and overseas trade directories, and its Export Marketing Research Scheme (EMRS) provides free advice on export market research.

Exporting to Europe is supported through:

- the DTI's Business in Europe Branch (BEB) which gives information on individual markets and advice on import regulations, taxes and other special requirements;

- its 'Spearhead' database which contains summaries of Single Market measures and other aspects such as collaborative EU research and development programmes and EU measures on health and safety.

Fig. 4.3 illustrates other elements of the DTI's 'Business in Europe' programme.

Through the DTI/Foreign and Commonwealth Office Overseas Trade Service, assistance is available to help all companies export. This includes consultancy advice on marketing strategy, and help in finding an overseas representative. For firms with fewer than 500 employees the DTI's Enterprise Initiative offers subsidised access to independent private sector expertise, to help develop an export marketing strategy.

The **British Overseas Trade Board**:

- supplies information on export opportunities through its Market Prospects Service;

- helps potential exporters with overseas market research through its Export Market Research Scheme;

- operates a Trade Fairs Overseas Scheme for exporters.

BUSINESS IN EUROPE

DTI's Business in Europe programme includes:
- information on the single market;
- advice and assistance on overcoming barriers to trade;
- information on individual markets and opportunities;
- expertise from private sector export advisors;
- task forces and other promotional activities;
- signposting to sources of detailed advice;
- a range of publications.

BUSINESS IN EUROPE HOTLINE
01179 444888

Our Business in Europe Hotline is open 24 hours a day, 7 days a week. It can put you in touch with a wealth of information and advice about trading in Europe. It can provide you with:
- government contacts for specific sectors or areas of EC legislation;
- signposting to private sector sources of advice;
- free literature.

Remember the number ☎ 01179 444888 ☎ phone today!

Fig. 4.3 Business in Europe

Source: DTI

The Export Credit Guarantee Department (**ECGD**) of the Department of Trade has an annual turnover of over £2 billion for its services of guaranteeing payment to banks providing export finance, supporting export finance at favourable interest rates, and insuring against non-payment on export contracts. An exporter pays a premium to the ECGD, which then assesses the status of the overseas firm and the payment record of the country, and normally agrees to meet bad debts. ECGD cover is available for exports of capital goods and projects to the EU, where credit terms of two years or longer are involved.

Financial, training and employment schemes

The UK government has developed a range of financial incentives to encourage people to create new firms or expand existing ones.

- The Business Expansion Scheme allows tax relief of up to £40,000 a year to investors in small firms.
- The Enterprise Allowance Scheme pays unemployed people a sum of money to start up new businesses.
- The Loan Guarantee Scheme encourages banks to lend to smaller (often riskier) firms by guaranteeing 70 per cent (85 per cent in Inner City Task Force areas) of the loan.

Firms which create employment may be eligible for government grants and tax relief. Regional Investment Grants (15 per cent of costs up to a maximum grant of £15,000) are available to small firms in Development Areas or other areas designated by the EU. Regional Innovation Grants (50 per cent of costs up to a maximum grant of £25,000) are available for small firms in Assisted Areas, Inner City Areas and other areas designated by the EU.

UK-based training schemes have included **Employment Training** (ET) and **Youth Training** (YT). The government has set NTETs (National Training and Education Targets) in order to improve the quality of training in the UK.

Providing a regional policy

Regions which relied on old staple industries such as textiles, shipbuilding and coal have been hit badly by structural unemployment. Current policy is to identify areas of greatest need and to provide direct or indirect financial support, such as the Regional Investment and Innovation

Grants, described earlier. The government has also targeted many inner-city and redevelopment areas as Enterprise Zones: financial benefits to entrepreneurs establishing business in these areas have included tax incentives and rent subsidies.

The DTI has a number of regional offices offering advice, and local chambers of commerce support business in their own area. Fig. 4.4 indicates the range of work undertaken by the Birmingham Chamber of Commerce.

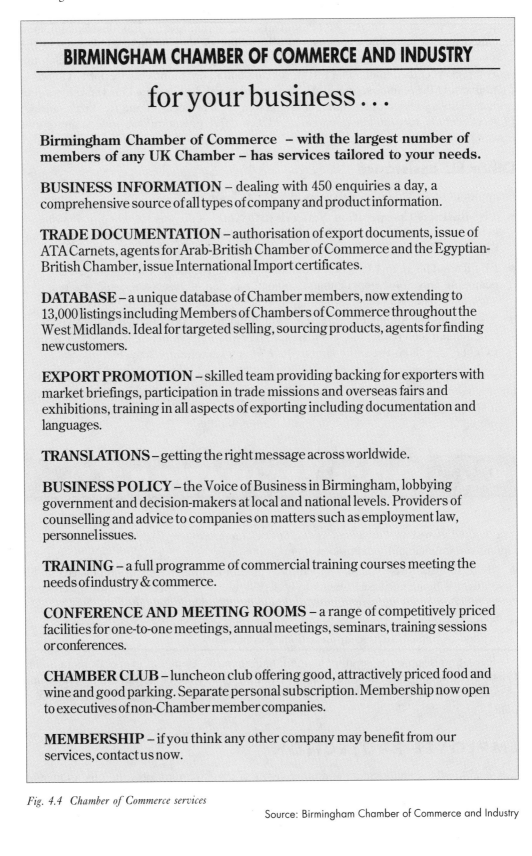

BIRMINGHAM CHAMBER OF COMMERCE AND INDUSTRY

for your business...

Birmingham Chamber of Commerce – with the largest number of members of any UK Chamber – has services tailored to your needs.

BUSINESS INFORMATION – dealing with 450 enquiries a day, a comprehensive source of all types of company and product information.

TRADE DOCUMENTATION – authorisation of export documents, issue of ATA Carnets, agents for Arab-British Chamber of Commerce and the Egyptian-British Chamber, issue International Import certificates.

DATABASE – a unique database of Chamber members, now extending to 13,000 listings including Members of Chambers of Commerce throughout the West Midlands. Ideal for targeted selling, sourcing products, agents for finding new customers.

EXPORT PROMOTION – skilled team providing backing for exporters with market briefings, participation in trade missions and overseas fairs and exhibitions, training in all aspects of exporting including documentation and languages.

TRANSLATIONS – getting the right message across worldwide.

BUSINESS POLICY – the Voice of Business in Birmingham, lobbying government and decision-makers at local and national levels. Providers of counselling and advice to companies on matters such as employment law, personnel issues.

TRAINING – a full programme of commercial training courses meeting the needs of industry & commerce.

CONFERENCE AND MEETING ROOMS – a range of competitively priced facilities for one-to-one meetings, annual meetings, seminars, training sessions or conferences.

CHAMBER CLUB – luncheon club offering good, attractively priced food and wine and good parking. Separate personal subscription. Membership now open to executives of non-Chamber member companies.

MEMBERSHIP – if you think any other company may benefit from our services, contact us now.

Fig. 4.4 Chamber of Commerce services

Source: Birmingham Chamber of Commerce and Industry

SUPPORT FROM THE EUROPEAN UNION

The EU supports national government initiatives in a variety of ways. It provides both direct and indirect support to the UK.

Regional assistance

The European Union offers financial assistance to the regions. The Union's Structural Funds support investment in infrastructure, industry and agriculture in less developed Union regions. Funding for 1993 was agreed at £10 billion. A part of these funds goes to the European Regional Development Fund (ERDF), set up in 1975, which helps develop the poorest regions of the Union. The ERDF controls and issues funds under priority Objective 2 ('Converting the regions seriously affected by industrial decline'): in 1993 the UK was the main beneficiary under this heading and received 38.2 per cent of the funding available. Projects include road-building, energy, and the development of tourism, training and consultancy.

Other EU assistance

Examples of other Union initiatives include the following:

● **The Business Co-operation Network (BC-Net)** This was launched in 1988 to help small and medium-sized firms make contact with business in other EU countries for the purpose of financial, technical or commercial partnership.

● **PETRA** This is an EU action programme for the vocational training of young people. It provides the opportunity to spend a period of grant-supported study or work experience abroad.

● **The European Social Fund (ESF)** This fund financially supports vocational training and job creation. In 1989 the UK received over 18 per cent of the 3.5 billion ECU (£2.3 billion) fund: the largest share of any Community state.

International mobility of labour is also encouraged by the Community. Barriers to mobility for regulated professions have been removed and work continues on establishing comparisons between national qualifications for groups such as skilled workers.

4.2   LEGAL REGULATION

The United Kingdom Parliament is responsible for passing legislation. In the European Union, the Council and Commission:

● **Make Regulations** These apply directly in all member states and do not have to be confirmed by national parliaments to be legally binding. If there is a conflict between an EU Regulation and existing national law, the Regulation prevails.

● **Issue Directives** These are binding on member states, but leave the precise method of implementation up to national governments.

EU legislation is subject to scrutiny by the UK Parliament. Copies of proposals go to Select Committees in both Houses of Parliament, and may be considered and debated. The major areas of business legislation include employee protection, consumer protection and competition policy.

EMPLOYEE PROTECTION

The health, safety, employment and other rights of employees are protected by a range of UK and European Union law. Fig. 4.5 summarises the position of a worker employed under a contract of employment.

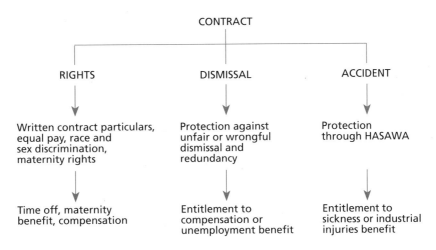

Fig 4.5 Contract of employment

The Health and Safety at Work Act (HASAWA) 1974

Under HASAWA, employers must take all reasonable care to ensure the safety of their employees. They must provide appropriate training and instruction on health and safety matters, and are obliged to provide safe:

- working environments;
- plant and systems of work;
- entry and exit arrangements;
- working processes (e.g. the safe use, handling, storage and transport of dangerous materials).

The obligations of employees under HASAWA are:

- to co-operate with their employer on health and safety matters;
- to take reasonable care of themselves and others at work;
- not to interfere with anything provided for their safety;
- to report defects in workplace equipment and processes.

Enforcement of HASAWA is carried out by the Health and Safety Executive (HSE), which is divided into various inspectorates, such as the Factory Inspectorate. Inspectors have extensive powers, including the right to enter premises and to require persons to answer any questions they think fit to ask. Breach of HASAWA results, depending on its seriousness, in:

- a verbal warning;
- the issue of an improvement notice, giving the employer time to carry out the improvement required;
- prosecution, usually in the case of accidents or continuous breaches of the law.

European Union health and safety protection

Member states have adopted measures to ensure that the Single Market does not lead to trade in unsafe goods. Common product safety standards have been introduced, including Directives on toy safety, safe machinery and personal protective equipment, food safety, and gas appliances. The Single European Act contains Articles which directly and indirectly affect firms' health and safety policies.

Article 118A has brought about specific health and safety provisions. The Safety Framework Directive outlines the responsibilities of employers and employees for encouraging workplace health and safety improvements. It also provides a legal framework within which further Directives give more detailed specific requirements.

- **Workplace requirements:** such as fire safety, lighting and ventilation, and structural stability.

- **Work equipment**: dealing with health and safety requirements for machinery and equipment.
- **Visual display units**: covering design features of VDU work stations.
- **Temporary workers**: providing measures to improve their safety at work.
- **Manual handling of heavy loads**: employers must, where possible, provide mechanical assistance for handling heavy loads.
- **Safety signs**: these will be harmonised at the workplace.

Other provisions cover personal protective equipment, carcinogens, asbestos, and work by pregnant women. The HSE enforces these provisions in the UK, employers facing fines up to £20,000 and six months' imprisonment for non-compliance.

Health and safety matters are also indirectly influenced by the 'product safety' **Article 100A** which removes trade barriers, and **Article 130** which contains provisions on environmental matters.

EMPLOYMENT PROTECTION

A range of employment protection legislation exists.

The Employment Protection (Consolidation) Act (EPCA) 1978

The EPCA protects workers employed under a contract of service against unfair dismissal by their employer.

- **To qualify for protection an employee must work at least sixteen hours per week for two years, or eight hours per week for five years.**
- **Dismissal can be:**
  - **through the employer terminating the contract;**
  - **through a fixed-term contract being completed;**
  - **constructive (where the employee resigns due to the conduct of the employer).**
- **The employer can dismiss an employee on the grounds of:**
  - **incompetence;**
  - **gross or serious misconduct (e.g. assault, refusing to obey instructions, persistent lateness, dishonesty);**
  - **the post becoming redundant.**
- **Remedies for unfair dismissal include:**
  - **reinstatement, if the employee wishes;**
  - **re-engagement in a comparable job;**
  - **compensation**

The EPCA requires employers to give written particulars of the contract of employment to employees within three months of starting employment. Fig. 4.6 summarises the details which must be included.

CONTRACT OF EMPLOYMENT

Names of parties
Date employment commenced
Job title
Pay: rate, calculation, intervals
Hours worked
Holidays and holiday pay
Sickness and sick pay
Pension rights
Length of notice

Fig. 4.6 Details in the contract of employment

European Union protection in this area includes Directives which restrict the working week to forty-eight hours. This has been the source of much debate in the UK, but

- the forty-eight-hour rule is only scheduled to operate from the year 2003;
- most occupations where longer hours are traditionally worked are excluded; and
- employees are still free to work in excess of forty-eight hours if they wish, but the employer cannot force the employee to do so.

The EU's Acquired Rights Directive 1977 led to **TUPE** (the Transfer of Undertakings (Protection of Employment)) Regulations 1981. The purpose of TUPE is to protect employment rights when the employees' organisation is taken over by a new employer.

Discrimination

The **Race Relations Act 1976** made it unlawful for employers to discriminate on the grounds of race, nationality and ethnic origin.

The **Sex Discrimination Acts 1975 and 1986** have made it unlawful for employers to discriminate on the grounds of gender when they advertise a job, recruit staff and set retirement dates. Some exceptions exist, such as in the employment of domestic servants.

The **Equal Pay Act 1970** requires employers to pay men and women doing the same job, or work of 'equivalent value' equal rates of pay.

CONSUMER PROTECTION

Consumers enter **contracts** when buying goods or services. To support the basic law of contract, UK governments and the EU have passed a range of consumer protection legislation.

UK legislation

The **Sale of Goods Act 1979** consolidated earlier legislation. Its provisions refer to goods but not services. Under the Act, goods must be

- **fit for their intended purpose**: the seller is liable if inaccurate advice concerning the product's use is given to the buyer;
- **of merchantable quality**: the goods must be capable of doing, in normal use, what they were designed to do;
- **as described**: goods sold by description must match this description.

Sellers cannot exclude liability under the 1979 Act, and any additional benefits given by the seller do not affect the buyer's statutory rights under the Act. Protection under the Act was extended to services, for example holidays and hairdressing, by the **1982 Supply of Goods and Services Act**.

The **Unsolicited Goods and Services Act 1971** prevents firms from delivering unordered items and then requesting payment for them. Unsolicited goods can be kept by the recipient if the sending company, following notice from the recipient, fails to collect the goods within thirty days.

Under the **Trade Descriptions Acts 1968 and 1972**, it is a criminal offence to give false descriptions of goods (price, materials, size, weight, etc.).

The **Consumer Credit Act 1974** and the **Financial Services Act 1986** control firms or people lending money or offering financial services. The annual percentage rate of interest (APR) must be stated in advertisements and documents, and credit brokers must be licensed.

The **Consumer Protection Act 1987** makes the supply of unsafe goods (e.g. electrical items and children's clothing) an offence under the Act. Manufacturers can be held responsible for damage or injury arising from the use of their products.

The **Food and Drugs Act 1955** protects the consumer by making the sale of unfit food a criminal offence.

The **Weights and Measures Acts (to 1985)** require quantities to be stated on goods, and manufacturers selling underweight goods commit an offence under the Acts.

UK organisations for consumer protection

The Office of Fair Trading (OFT), set up by the 1973 Fair Trading Act, helps protect consumers. It encourages trade associations to set up voluntary codes of practice; it prosecutes traders breaking the law; it advises on the need for new consumer legislation; and it issues information and publications.

Local enforcement of consumer legislation takes place through councils.

- Trading Standards departments handle complaints on weights and measures and trade descriptions
- Environmental Health departments deal with food quality and hygiene

Pressure groups also influence UK firms in the area of consumer protection (see page 107).

European Union influences

The European Commission has issued Directives designed to establish common levels of protection throughout the EU. Under the General Product Safety Directive (in force in the UK from June 1994), producers, importers and distributors have to supply safe consumer products. There are other specific directives on consumer protection.

- **The Consumer Credit Directive protects consumers in the same way as the UK's Consumer Credit Act. An amendment in 1990 established a common method of calculating the APR.**
- **The Dangerous Imitations Directive bans food imitation products which might fool consumers into thinking they were food.**
- **The Dangerous Preparations Directive enforces child-resistant packaging and danger warnings for household chemicals.**
- **The Doorstep Selling Directive allows a week's cooling-off period for certain contracts entered into at the customer's home or workplace.**
- **The Gas Appliance Directive establishes minimum safety standards for gas appliances.**
- **The Misleading Advertising Directive protects consumers and firms against the effects of misleading advertisements.**
- **The Package Travel Directive sets minimum standards of protection for consumers taking package holidays.**
- **Price Indication Directives require firms to display selling prices (and in some cases, unit prices) of products.**
- **The Toy Safety Directive harmonises toy safety standards across the Community.**

A major area of EU consumer protection is legislation on food, and a framework for harmonising food laws is in place. These 'framework' Directives cover food additives, materials in contact with food, food and nutrition labelling, and control of quick-frozen and irradiated food.

Other general Directives are under consideration, for example on unfair contract terms and distance (e.g. television) selling.

COMPETITION POLICY

European Union policy seeks to ensure that trade between member states is based on free and fair competition.

- **Article 85(1)** prohibits agreements between firms which might prevent, restrict or distort trade in the common market. Examples include agreements to fix prices, share markets or discriminate against third parties.

This Article applies only where there would be an appreciable effect on EU competition: agreements between small and medium-sized firms (with an aggregate annual turnover of below ECU 200 million and a market share below 5 per cent) are normally outside its scope. Breach of Article 85(1) makes the parties liable to fines by the Commission and injunctions from injured third parties.

- **Article 86** stops a firm or firms from abusing a dominant market position (but not from establishing such a position). Such abuses include predatory pricing and limiting production.

- **Article 90** extends Articles 85 and 86 to measures taken by member states affecting the operation of public firms.

Control of monopolies and mergers

The EU's **Merger Control Regulation** came into force in 1990.

- It considers mergers 'with a Community dimension' – where the businesses have an aggregate worldwide turnover of ECU 5 billion or aggregate EU turnover (of two of the firms) of 250 million ECU each.

- Mergers which lead to or strengthen a dominant market position and impede competition in the Single Market are prohibited.

Mergers with a Community dimension must be notified to the European Commission and suspended for at least three weeks. The Commission examines the consequences of the merger.

The use of subsidies by member states for their industry is also controlled by the EU. The purpose is to prevent competition and free trade becoming distorted, and government subsidies may be disallowed by the Commission.

In the United Kingdom, the government:

- investigates mergers through the Monopolies and Mergers Commission (MMC);

- regulates privatised companies – for example through Oftel (BT) and Ofgas (British Gas).

- used the 1980 Competition Act to extend the powers of the OFT (see page 104) in investigating unfair trading practices and activities which might lead to local or national monopolies.

Pricing and distribution

Firms are normally free under European Union competition law to charge different prices for their goods in different parts of the EU. They can also charge different prices to different customers. The exceptions are where prices fixed by agreement contravene Article 85, and where differential pricing amounts to an abuse of market position under Article 86.

Exclusive distribution and sole agency agreements amount to restriction of competition and as such, if large enough, would fall within the scope of Article 85(1) and be banned.

Legislation against misleading pricing exists for goods sold in the UK, under the Trade Descriptions Act. This law is extended to prices of services and facilities by the Consumer Protection Act 1987.

4.3 SOCIAL INFLUENCES

Most modern-day organisations show great awareness of their image and the relationship they have with the community and the environment. Fig. 4.7 illustrates how two organisations see their role in this context.

MARKS & SPENCER

Each year Marks and Spencer receives some 10,000 appeals for support. In addition to channelling funds to charities and community organisations, we provide management expertise and encourage our staff to become involved.

The programme covers community development and environmental programmes; health and care projects; and, arts and heritage initiatives. We focus support on those projects which help young and elderly people, those with special needs and vulnerable members of the community. For 1995/6, the total community involvement budget was £8.5m, of which donations amounted to £4.9m. There are 35 staff on full-time secondment and a further 200 are involved part-time, at a cost of £2.4m. A further £500,000 was raised through charity fashion shows and selling of charity Christmas cards. The majority of Marks and Spencer donations are small, often less than £5,000, but this seed-corn money can make a real difference.

As founder members of Business in the Community, we encourage other companies to play an active part in their communities. One of the most effective ways of achieving this is the use of programmes such as 'Seeing is Believing', which enable business leaders to experience community issues at first hand.

Sainsbury's

We have enhanced our community programme, both nationally and locally in the communities in which our stores trade, in a variety of ways. Corporate contributions to charitable and community causes in the UK totalled £2 million. These included donations to direct appeals and contributions to the funding of voluntary organisations and to town centre improvement schemes.

In addition, substantial sums were raised through store door collections and fund-raising campaigns. Foremost amongst these was the Children in Need campaign for which staff and customers at Sainsbury's and Savacentre raised over £370,000. In America, Shaw's associates successfully raised nearly $500,000 for the United Way Campaign.

The Sainsbury's Penny Back scheme raised over £600,000 for local charities. Schoolbags, which also encourages the re-use of carrier bags, was launched in September. Vouchers collected by our customers can be redeemed by schools against school equipment. Over 14,000 schools are currently registered.

Side By Side local volunteering
Most importantly, our stores have continued to build supportive links with their local communities drawing on the enthusiasm and energy of our staff.

This year we piloted a new community scheme called Side By Side at 25 Sainsbury's supermarkets.

Fig. 4.7 Awareness of social influences

Sources: Marks and Spencer plc and J Sainsbury plc Annual Reports, 1996

CONSUMER ORGANISATIONS

These operate in addition to the central and local government agencies for consumer protection. Some are independent: others receive government and/or industry-based financial support. These are some of the more important organisations.

- **The Advertising Standards Authority (ASA)**   Financed by the advertising industry, it oversees much of the advertising in the UK. Its voluntary British Code of Advertising Practice summarises the expectations of the industry regarding advertisements, which should be 'legal, decent, honest and truthful'. Its work is influenced by the European Union (eg the Misleading Advertising Directive) and UK legislation (the Trade Descriptions Act).

- **The Consumers Association**   Best known for its 'Which?' series of magazines, it campaigns for consumer rights and researches into the quality and standards of consumer products and services.

- **The British Standards Institution (BSI)**   This organisation sets standards for a wide variety of goods and services. It is best known for its 'Kitemark', which indicates that the item conforms to British Standards. The BSI has established standards which can be applied to work routines (e.g. BS 5750), and has been involved in developing common standards in the Single Market.

The BSI operates THE – Technical Help to Exporters – which provides advice on European requirements on matters such as safety, environmental protection and technical standards.

- **Citizens Advice Bureaux (CAB)** This organisation receives some financial support from the government, but is independent and also relies on voluntary support. Its officers help people with a range of consumer problems.

- **Consumer councils and regulating agencies** Privatised firms are regulated by authorised agencies such as Ofgas and Oftel. These agencies are empowered by law to ensure that the privatised firm meets its obligations: they ensure that the code of practice is being followed, and examine price increases or other proposals that are made. Independent advice can also be obtained from a local advisory committee such as the Telecommunications Advisory Committee (for BT).

  Nationalised industries are partly controlled by their Users' Councils, which also represent consumer interests.

Pressure groups

A 'pressure group' is an organised group of people with similar interests, who attempt to influence others (notably governments and/or industries). They range in size from large international organisations such as Greenpeace and Amnesty International, to small community groups concerned only with local matters.

One way to classify these groups is to divide them as follows:

- **Sector groups**, which represent a particular section of the (business) community – e.g.:
  - Association of British Chambers of Commerce
  - British Medical Association (medical practitioners)
  - Confederation of British Industry (employers)
  - Royal Automobile Club (vehicle owners).

- **Cause groups**, which seek to promote a particular cause – e.g.:
  - ASH (Action on Smoking and Health)
  - CND (Campaign for Nuclear Disarmament)
  - FOREST (Freedom Of the Right to Enjoy Smoking Tobacco)
  - League Against Cruel Sports.

The work of a pressure group may directly involve business: for example, trade unions act as pressure groups on behalf of their members. Other examples are the AA and the RAC, which influence vehicle manufacturers on motoring matters such as safety and security devices.

The media can also influence firms' policies. Television and other 'campaigning' programmes such as 'Watchdog' and 'The Cook Report' reflect consumer interests and concerns with firms' products or their actions in the market-place.

Pressure groups may seek to influence particular firms or particular industries. Their success in so doing depends on the level of:

- financial support;

- public support;

- government support;

- organisational ability of the group's leaders.

ROLE OF THE EUROPEAN UNION

The Single European Act (SEA) established the Single Market. The Union acknowledges the need to monitor competition and control firms through its Directives. The SEA also brought in rules on the environment. Environmental protection requirements influence a range of EU policies, and many Directives and Regulations on environmental matters are in force. At present there is an action programme (the fifth) for environmental legislation, which is due to run until the year 2000.

Current EU Directives cover areas such as:

- water and air pollution;
- control of dangerous chemicals;
- nature protection;
- common emission standards for industries;
- noise standards (e.g. for aircraft, lawn-mowers and motor cycles).

4.4 TECHNOLOGICAL INFLUENCES

Many of the technological developments which have taken place over the last decade are mentioned in Chapters 5–8, which are devoted to the main functions of a typical firm. The effect of technology in the context of a changing environment is also discussed in Chapter 10. The major technological revolution is based on the microchip: this allows quick access to, and storage, retrieval and manipulation of, data and information (data being 'unorganised' information).

The new technologies influence firms in many ways: some examples are given below.

Location of business

The EU's Single Market financial and other 'passports' acknowledge that modern technology allows firms to operate in markets where they do not have a physical presence: advances in telecommunications make this possible. In the UK, for example, 'First Direct' is a division of the Midland Bank offering cheque account and other personal banking services to customers exclusively by phone.

Production

CAD/CAM (computer-aided design/manufacture) and similar packages are widely used by firms in:

- **Designing products** Computer graphics, modelling and simulation allow designs to be altered immediately through light-pens or touch-sensitive screens.
- **Making products** Robots and other forms of automation are increasingly being used, bringing the firm advantages such as consistency of the operation and of the end product, and thus improved quality control

Selling

Electronic funds transfer (**EFT**) has revolutionised banking, allowing sales and transfer of funds to take place instantaneously. In retailing, bar-code readers are widely used by the larger stores. For example, Marks and Spencer invested £250 million to update its point-of-sale technology: it uses electronic point-of-sale (**EPOS**) tills which transfer sales data to a central computer, which in turn calculates stock needed by the store and transmits delivery instructions to suppliers. **HHTs** (hand-held terminals) are used by staff to identify stock sizes and varieties available. The advantages to a retailer such as Marks and Spencer include:

- simplicity – cheque and credit card procedures are more straightforward;
- reduced administrative costs;
- reduced queueing time, leading to higher consumer satisfaction;
- better security, through reduced cash-handling;
- lower stockholding costs;
- reduced supply cycles (for Marks and Spencer, down from a ten-day cycle for food, to two or three days).

THE FIRM

The use of computers and other technology can affect the firm's structure, and its methods of operation and communication. The computer brings with it advantages of speed, accuracy, capacity and reliability to the firm. Routine or logical tasks such as production control are easily computerised, and computer packages are available to carry out a range of business functions: for example, an integrated software package might include:

● specialist software for accounts, invoicing, stock control and payroll;
● desk-top publishing (DTP), for letterheads and other customer-designed printed work;
● a database, used for personnel and other records;
● a word processing package for written communication and personalised circular letters;
● a spreadsheet, for financial and other numerical calculations.

Computerised systems in a firm can also affect its structure, because centralisation is not as important when the speed and flow of communications improves. Computerisation also brings with it departmental reorganisation, to accommodate the new systems. New forms of training are undertaken because employees require new skills: some skills become redundant – most commonly, those of unskilled or semi-skilled workers and middle managers.

Chapter roundup

The content of this chapter is based on the fact that a firm cannot operate in isolation from its environment. This is acknowledged elsewhere (e.g. Chapter 2 covers the Memorandum of Association), but the major influences are contained here. You should now be able to explain how the actions of the UK government and European Union both assist firms and also help to control them. The chapter has also examined the other key external influences – legal, social and technological – on firms.

Illustrative questions

1 Name **three** external groups to whom a firm has a responsibility. (3)

2 How do pressure groups which work for the benefit of consumers achieve their aims?
(6)
SEB

Tutorial Note

Question 1 requires basic statements, though you must not fall into the trap of mentioning internal groups. Question 2 gives little guidance on the depth of answer: two well-explained methods, or three which are more briefly outlined, should be enough for full marks.

Suggested answers

1   Customers; suppliers; shareholders.

2   Methods include:
    (a) Lobbying government (via MPs, petitions, etc.) and companies: this can be effective, since direct contact is made.

(b) Legal action through the courts, e.g. to make a company follow health and safety or equal opportunities legislation.

(c) Establishing formal groups to co-ordinate the various forms of action: examples include ASH and CAMRA.

(d) Publicity seeking through demonstrations, press releases and collecting signatures for petitions.

3 (a) Explain clearly the meaning of the term **information**, and describe the main types of information which may be available to a firm. (8)

(b) How would you assess the **reliability and value** of the types of information you have described in (a)? (10)

(c) Why has the application of information technology become so important to business success? (7)

SEB

Tutorial note

In part (a), refer to information in the general context of business: see Chapter 7 for more information. I have used specific illustrations of IT in my outline answer to part (c).

Suggested answer

(a) The term 'information' refers to organised data; it is what is communicated between individuals. These communications may take place in a firm through the use of oral, written or technological means. Oral information is transmitted, for example, at meetings and through telephone conversations. Popular forms of written communication include business letters and memoranda, and faxes (which rely on electronic means of transmission). Perhaps the most important development for information transmission is the computer, for example in the use of LANs, e-mail and the Internet. Another way of classifying types of information available to a firm is to consider internal and external sources, both numerical and text-based. Internally generated information includes sales statistics, budget information, and output figures. External information, again both text and numerical, is obtained from sources such as the published accounts of competitors, and governmental and EU sources.

(b) The reliability and value of the information in (a) depends on the nature of the source and whether the information is recorded accurately and comprehensively. Government and EU statistics, for example, are summarised and general in scope, but largely accurate and objective. Minutes of meetings and written notes of telephone conversations, on the other hand, are less reliable summaries of information, though probably more specific to the information needs of the firm.

(c) The application of information technology is a major contributor to the success of modern firms. Specific applications such as word processing, spreadsheets, databases, and dedicated software such as sales and purchase ledger packages, help the firm improve its efficiency. (The use of IT also includes transmission by telephone and fax, and electronic computer communications). In general, the use of IT allows the firm to receive, store, manipulate and transmit data and information accurately, in high volumes and at high speeds.

4 Explain how a continuously high level of unemployment affects:
(a) firms;
(b) a region of the UK.

Tutorial note

A danger here is that you might over-concentrate on the social effects of unemployment and ignore the more direct business effects. I have listed the main points and bracketed against each one how it might be developed.

Suggested answer

(a) Heavy unemployment could influence the demand for a firm's product and therefore its pricing policy (depending on the type of product, its price elasticity, the degree of market competition and the firm's current profit margins). It might contract the product range (rationalise production to reduce costs, but at a danger of competitors coming into the market to plug the gap) or reduce the product quality (cost saving, but possible customer dissatisfaction). It will have to review its overall marketing strategy (analyse the 'mix': see Chapter 7; also explore possibility of new markets, perhaps overseas, where demand is still buoyant). Other actions the firm could take include a review of costs (research and development activities are often 'mothballed', but this is inadvisable where existing products are advanced in the product life cycle: see Chapter 7) including labour costs (cut labour force, negotiate with unions, improve productivity, wage freeze).

(b) As unemployment increases, income in the region falls and so does spending, reducing current demand levels. Output in turn will fall, increasing unemployment (the 'multiplier' effect). The local infrastructure is also likely to decline. The region could also suffer from a diminished reputation in the eyes of the business community, as skilled workers tend to move away and social problems cause bad publicity. Government action might be taken (e.g. regional policy in general, EU funding).

Practice questions

1 Explain briefly how a change of government policy on VAT could affect UK firms. (2)

2 How can high interest rates result in lower consumer spending? (5)

3 How can strict data protection laws benefit individuals? (6)

Pitfalls

Question 1 requires a brief answer only (relating to one policy) whereas questions 2 and 3 are more demanding. In answering 2, you can concentrate on either the effect on savings or the effect on credit.

Key points

1 A change in VAT policy affects a firm's costs and the demand for its products.

2 Saving now more attractive, and so increases at the expense of spending; higher credit charges lead to reduced demand for goods (durables/white goods) usually bought on credit; rise in mortgage rates reduces real disposable income.

3 Protects personal privacy; protection against inaccurate information being held/ circulated/used against the individual; protects against manipulation by those accessing personal records/detailed personal profiles.

4 (a) How might a firm attempt to become more competitive through the use of information technology? (13)

   (b) Discuss whether it is possible to gain a long-term competitive advantage by these means. (12)

SEB

Pitfalls

The question is quite clear in asking for long-term competitive advantages, but you should also refer to shorter-term gains in your answer.

Key points

(a) Use of information technology should lead to greater efficiency in recording, storing, manipulating and transmitting information. Specific examples include electronic customer databases and accounts leading to tighter credit control; use of spreadsheets to calculate cash flow.

(b) Short-term advantage is gained through greater efficiency. This could lead to competitors going out of business, thereby bringing longer-term gains (greater market share), but long-term competitive advantages normally occur through more competitive products rather than through more efficient support services such as IT.

5 Explain why the UK government operates a 'Regional Policy'. (8)

Pitfalls

This is quite a wide-ranging question for only 8 marks. Your answer should therefore concentrate on two or three main reasons.

Key points

Generally, to help ensure an element of 'balance' throughout the country.
Specifically: to counter the problems of structural and other forms of unemployment affecting the regions; to try to ensure more equal standards of living throughout the country; to ensure networks/infrastructure operate efficiently across the regions; for political purposes (e.g. to court popularity in a particular region).

6 "The 1990s is the 'green' decade." Explain how organisations might be influenced by any increased awareness of environmental matters. (20)

Pitfalls

The problem here is to ensure that your answer stays focused on business aspects. One way that you can do this is to identify a series of business functions – accounts, personnel and so on – and to use these as headings in structuring the answer. The temptation is to discuss environmental issues in general, thereby failing to relate the issues to the work of a firm. The points that I have listed are possible areas of impact: you may well identify many different, but equally valid, ones.

Key points

Finance: investment in 'environmentally friendly' equipment, possible cash flow problems.
Personnel: employee training, greater employee awareness, increased public relations responsibility.
Marketing: influencing advertising/selling policy, need to create consumer awareness of changes, alterations in packaging policy.
Production: lower economies of scale, products less standardised in nature, increased production costs, more expensive quality control, manufacturing with new materials, discontinuing some processes and ingredients (e.g. CFCs), adds to research and development costs.
Other: facing fines for pollution/other offences.

HUMAN RESOURCES

Units in this chapter

Chapter objectives

All firms depend for their success on a well-trained and contented workforce. This chapter examines the role of the personnel function in modern firms, in the context of the main theories on motivation and leadership. It explains how firms obtain staff and – having employed them – how and why these staff are developed. The chapter ends by describing the role of organisations such as trade unions, and analyses the nature and importance of labour relations to firms.

The key topics and concepts covered in this chapter are:
- human resource management;
- rewards for work;
- motivation;
- leadership;
- manpower planning;
- recruitment, selection, training and appraisal;
- industrial relations;
- collective bargaining;
- disputes and reconciliation.

5.1 HUMAN RESOURCE MANAGEMENT

Employers seek to ensure that employees are happy in their work and that they achieve job satisfaction. The personnel, or human resource management (**HRM**) function exists in all firms, either as one of the roles undertaken by a general manager in a small business or in the form of a separate department in a large company.

Outlined below are the main policy areas which firms use to create a satisfied and involved workforce. They reflect the key HRM functions of recruitment and selection; training, development and appraisal; staff welfare; and industrial relations.

Policy	Reasons
Manpower planning	To identify and meet shortfalls of labour and to review employees' current skills and situation; to help them achieve their potential.
Recruitment and selection	To ensure company objectives are met; to bring in new ideas; to appoint employees who are suitably qualified and experienced.
Training and development	To allow new employees to settle quickly; to help employees develop and make additional contribution to the work of the firm.
Appraisal	To allow employees to achieve their potential; to support and counsel employees in their attempts to achieve personal goals.
Welfare	To help employees satisfy their personal needs.
Consultation and negotiation	To communicate key company policies; to motivate employees through involvement; to anticipate and identify employee concerns; to allow employees to contribute to decisions (e.g. on pay and conditions) which affect them.

The Personnel Department has the responsibility of implementing these policies. The effectiveness of its work and influence can be assessed by carrying out a personnel audit. The purpose of the audit is to check that HRM and other management procedures and systems are operating successfully. Common areas for an audit investigation are summarised in Fig. 5.1.

Audit Checklist

Personnel policies ☐
Communication procedures ☐
Remuneration ☐
Labour relations ☐
Personnel records ☐
Training policies ☐

Fig. 5.1 Areas for investigation by a personnel audit

5.2 MOTIVATION AND HUMAN NEEDS

MOTIVATION

When we examine motivation in a business context, we study why people behave the way they do at work. When an employee is given a task to do and it is not carried out satisfactorily, this failure may well be due to a lack of motivation, rather than a lack of ability.

Influences on motivation

Different theorists have different ideas on what makes a job 'satisfying'. These are the main factors which influence the motivation of employees:

- pay levels;
- working hours;
- working environment;
- existence of fringe benefits;
- recognition of the importance of the work by others;
- nature of the tasks undertaken at work;
- degree of job security;
- promotion prospects;
- management styles;
- organisational culture.

Problems of poor motivation

Employees who are poorly motivated often score badly on at least one of these factors: an undemanding job, unpleasant working conditions and low pay, which are all common causes of poor motivation.

A lack of motivation – either limited to one area or department, or spread throughout the firm – causes employee dissatisfaction. This results in higher labour turnover, increased incidents of absenteeism and/or sickness, poor timekeeping, and more disputes between both formal and informal groups within the firm.

Approaches to overcoming poor motivation

Motivation problems are not easily overcome. Organisations therefore try to avoid them arising in the first place. Fig. 5.2 illustrates the policy of one major employer.

To provide a clean, safe, healthy and enjoyable working environment.

To provide training and development for all employees to enable them to achieve the highest level of skills possible.

To provide career opportunities which allow employees to develop to their full potential.

To provide challenging and rewarding work.

To pay for performance.

Fig. 5.2 Policy statement extract: concern for employees

Source: McDonald's

Approaches to overcoming poor motivation include:

- changing **leadership styles** – for example, moving towards a more democratic style;
- establishing **teamwork** to develop a team spirit and a sense of common purpose;
- improving the quantity and quality of **communication**, e.g. by reviewing the effectiveness of noticeboards, or through introducing a company newsletter;
- reviewing levels and methods of **payment**, possibly offering incentive payments or additional fringe benefits, and comparing financial rewards with those of similar organisations;
- introducing greater employee **involvement**, e.g. through setting up a suggestion scheme, quality circles, and other formal and informal groups;

- allowing **job rotation** and developing **job enrichment**;
- setting up **training** and **staff development** schemes.

The results of the personnel audit provide additional information for the firm's management to evaluate its policies.

THEORIES ON MOTIVATION AND JOB SATISFACTION

Motivation theory is concerned with the goals which people set, and the methods they use to achieve these goals. Many of the theorists in this area have also contributed thoughts on the suitability of organisational structures and management or leadership roles: the main ideas are summarised below.

CLASSICAL THEORY

The ideas of F. W. Taylor and Henri Fayol illustrate the Classical School's approach to motivation and organisation theory. This approach involves studying organisational behaviour by examining the nature of the work done.

One application of motivation theory is based on creating a job from a number of specific tasks. Many individual jobs are still created using the scientific management principles of **F. W. Taylor**, who developed his ideas around the turn of the century. He was concerned with how jobs could be separated into their constituent elements. This aspect of his work resulted in the development of work study and method study principles (see page 197). Taylor believed that high pay acted as the prime motivator, and ignored morale and other influences which are emphasised by the Human Relations theorists (below).

Henri Fayol identified a range of functions which he believed were common to all managers:

- **planning** (selecting objectives);
- **organising** (resources);
- **staffing** (recruitment and welfare policies);
- **directing** (helping subordinates achieve objectives);
- **co-ordinating** (taking corrective action where necessary);
- **reporting** (communicating efficiently);
- **budgeting** (financial planning and forecasting).

Fayol's work on organisational structures emphasised the value of specialisation, the division of labour, and control. His analysis of management functions and organisational structures identified areas for study, such as the nature of an organisation's span of control.

The work of the classical theorists in the context of motivation theory is regarded as being limited and has been modified by theorists representing other schools of thought. Assumptions underlying the classical approach are that:

1 individuals always act in the organisation's interests;

2 they are rational in their actions;

3 they are motivated primarily by money.

The work of these classical theorists is still of value today, e.g. in Taylor's contribution to work study and Fayol's analysis of hierarchical structures.

HUMAN RELATIONS AND CONTENT THEORIES

These theories concentrate on **people's needs**, rather than on the job of work being done: the emphasis is on individual and group interaction in the workplace. Human Relations theorists define an organisation in terms of its social environment, and analyse how it could be altered to accommodate the needs of both individuals and groups.

Attempts are made to measure:

- how groups work together;
- individual needs;
- the effect of different forms of supervision on employees.

Different management styles are relevant here: one group of workers may wish to make contributions in a democratic management environment, whereas another group may prefer to work in the context of close authoritarian control.

Elton Mayo

Mayo researched into groups at the Hawthorne works of the Western Electric Company between 1927 and 1932. He made a number of changes to the working conditions of Hawthorne employees, discovering that output rose even when conditions worsened. His conclusions were that the employees being observed:

- had formed a tightly-knit group;
- enjoyed the attention being paid to them;
- increased their self-esteem;
- as a result increased their output.

His conclusions regarding the importance of morale influenced others in their research into motivation at work.

Abraham Maslow

Maslow formulated a 'hierarchy of needs' in the 1940s (see Figure 5.3). He identified five levels in the hierarchy:

1 **Basic**   Physiological requirements for survival; at work these include food, drink, ventilation, rest breaks, and payment.

2 **Safety**   Protection from danger; a safe working environment through health and safety provisions, and a safe (i.e. secure) job.

3 **Social**   Friendship; the companionship of fellow employees, and sports/social clubs and events.

4 **Esteem**   Ego needs; recognition of 'a good job done' at work, promotion.

5 **Self-actualisation**   Personal ambition and self-fulfilment; complete job satisfaction.

Fig. 5.3 Maslow's hierarchy of needs

At any given time, one group of these needs is dominant. The needs in this group must be met before the individual can proceed to the next group. In a work context, employees must be provided with the opportunity to fulfil these needs.

This hierarchy does not operate in such a mechanical way, in practice: for instance, many people may be motivated by higher-order needs before their lower-order ones have been fully satisfied. These needs (notably the higher-order ones) can also be fulfilled by personal activities outside work.

Maslow's ideas illustrate the importance of work to individuals, and they help in explaining some of the social costs of high unemployment levels in societies which stress the importance of being employed.

Frederick Herzberg

Herzberg analysed needs under two headings: **motivators**, which broadly relate both to work content and to Maslow's higher-order needs; and **hygiene factors**, which relate to the working environment and to Maslow's lower-order needs.

Motivators	Hygiene factors
● achievement	● company policies
● recognition	● supervision
● responsibility	● status
● the work itself	● security
● promotion or advancement	● interpersonal relationships
	● money
	● working conditions

He developed a framework to distinguish between motivators and hygiene factors. Although hygiene factors should be present – motivation falls if they are ignored or neglected – they do not by themselves motivate employees.

Herzberg's theory suggests that managers must provide motivators in the form of satisfying jobs (eg through job rotation and job enrichment schemes), and at the same time ensure that the negative hygiene factors do not detract from the work being done.

Douglas McGregor

McGregor identified two opposing attitudes towards the formal organisation of workers. He referred to the negative attitude as **Theory X** and to the positive attitude as **Theory Y**. Theory X links to the earlier work of the classical theorists such as Taylor, and emphasises the role of money as the main motivating factor. Theory Y recognises (like Herzberg) the importance of Maslow's higher-order needs in motivating employees.

Theory X management assumes:	Theory Y management assumes:
● People inherently dislike work and will try to avoid it if possible.	● Expending effort at work is as natural as play or rest, and the average person does not dislike work.
● Because of this, they must be coerced, controlled, directed and threatened in order to get sufficient effort towards achieving the organisation's objectives.	● Employees can exercise their own control and direction, and are rewarded through their efforts made towards achieving the organisation's objectives.
● The average person wants to be controlled and directed, has little ambition, and seeks to avoid responsibility.	● The average person learns to both accept and seek responsibility, its avoidance coming from experience only.

Advocates of Theory X support an authoritarian form of organisational structure; supporters of Theory Y argue that the main limiting factors in an organisation are management's ability and willingness in channelling employee potential. Problems arise when employees who expect Theory Y management are subjected to Theory X approaches, and vice versa: symptoms associated with low motivation (e.g. absenteeism and high labour turnover) will develop.

PROCESS THEORIES

Process theories of motivation analyse how employees make decisions and their thinking behind these decisions.

V. H. Vroom's Expectancy Equation is based on the belief that the strength of a person's motivation to act in a particular way depends on two factors: how attractive the outcome is, and the level of expectation that the action will produce the hoped-for outcome.

$$F = E \times V$$

where F is the motivation to act in a particular way;

E is the expectation that the action will be followed by the outcome;

V is the value (attraction) of that outcome.

On the basis of this theory, managers should analyse the motives of employees and provide them with goals which are achievable and realistic.

J. S. Adams suggested that employee motivation is influenced by perceptions of inequity, which exist where employees believe the rewards they receive for work are not equivalent to the rewards of others. Management roles should therefore include comparative analysis between their firm and others, and high levels of communication and consultation with employees.

MANAGEMENT FUNCTIONS

Henri Fayol's work proved valuable in identifying the roles of management. Nowadays these are normally summarised as four key functions.

❶ **Planning**   This is seen as the first function of management. It is associated with setting corporate objectives and establishing plans to achieve these objectives. Specific examples include setting cashflow and other budgets, and manpower planning.

❷ **Organising**   Once objectives have been set, the role of the manager is to establish an organisation which allows these objectives to be achieved. Specific examples include organising the different factors of production, and setting up line and staff organisation structures.

❸ **Controlling**   The third function of a manager is to exercise control. This is carried out in a variety of ways: examples include controlling financial resources and other assets, and comparing the firm's actual performance to its budget.

❹ **Directing**   Managers are required to co-ordinate staff and direct their work, for example through the process of delegation. Directing is the function most closely associated with motivating staff.

MANAGEMENT AND MOTIVATION

The strength and effectiveness of a manager's motivation is influenced by two linked factors: the management style adopted, and the culture of the organisation.

Management styles

The quality of individual and group performance at work is influenced by factors such as the skills, training and attributes of the personnel, and the tasks which they have to carry out. A major influence on performance is the style of leadership or management adopted.

Democratic management   The manager guides and advises, but allows the group as a whole to make decisions. This style is associated more with the Human Relations theorists, notably McGregor's Theory Y approach. It is found in organisations which have efficient and open communication procedures, limited chains of command and routine delegation. Examples include many small firms where the emphasis is on communication and employee involvement.

Autocratic management   The manager might allow group involvement and suggestions, but makes the final decision. Concentrating decisions in the hands of senior management encourages a 'top-down', centralised structure influenced by the work of classical theorists and McGregor's Theory X. Examples include state-operated services such as the police and armed forces.

Laissez-faire **management**   The *laissez-faire* ('let it be') manager chooses not to interfere in the work of the group. This form of management can operate successfully if there are cohesive groups which are prepared to work together to achieve common objectives. It is, however, an approach which is usually regarded as unsuitable, because the manager is avoiding the specific functions of controlling and directing.

Another way of analysing management styles is to identify the extreme situations. Management in an organisation might be seen in terms of the following dimensions:

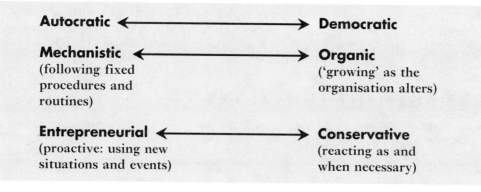

The 'best' style of management will depend on factors such as the:
- level of management training;
- preferences of individual managers;
- degree of awareness of the different styles;
- culture of the organisation (see below);
- organisation's size and complexity;
- stage of the organisation's evolution.

Organisational cultures

A culture is created from various beliefs, ideals, norms and values. Each organisation has a culture, in much the same way that we represent different cultures. Its culture is expressed in the way that the people who make up the organisation act. This culture can also be seen in the organisation's rules, procedures, structures and systems.

R. Harrison has suggested four distinct organisational cultures:

❶ Power culture
  - mainly associated with small entrepreneurial organisations;
  - relies on a central source of power;
  - has relatively few rules and procedures.

2 **Role culture**
  - found in organisations structured by function and specialism;
  - relies heavily on rules and procedures.

3 **Task culture**
  - associated with matrix and project-based structures;
  - decentralised and flexible (team-based) organisations.

4 **Person culture**
  - typical of small professional organisations with minimal structures.

A culture which is unsuitable for a firm and its employees (eg where a merger or privatisation has occurred) will result in low motivational levels and conflict between management and employees. The work of McGregor highlights the potential problems when a group of employees has one set of beliefs or expectations, and managers have a different set. If employees have Theory X expectations and their managers expect Theory Y attitudes, the resultant delegation and involvement is likely to produce poor quality output and misdirection of effort. Managers who use Theory X approaches with groups who wish to operate on a Theory Y basis will find that output and morale will again be adversely affected.

5.3 EMPLOYING PEOPLE

MANPOWER PLANNING

A key function of HRM is to ensure there is the **right number** of employees of the **right quality** in the **right place** at the **right time**. Manpower planning seeks to ensure that:

- manpower requirements in the corporate plan are identified and carried out;
- manpower levels guarantee that production takes place;
- manpower quality leads to improved productivity;
- manpower costs which are controllable meet the budget targets.

Manpower planning requires managers to assess staffing needs for a number of years (normally up to five years) ahead. The medium- and long-term plans are continuous or 'rolling' in nature, being updated annually. The plan is often based on a 'STEP' analysis of the external influences on the firm:

- Social influences: e.g. increased numbers of women wishing to return to employment.
- Technological influences: e.g. new production processes requiring new skills.
- Economic influences: e.g. free movement of labour in the EU.
- Political influences: e.g. government training schemes.

Imbalance in numbers

A firm's manpower plan could identify one of two situations, where supply and demand for labour are not in equilibrium. The plan might identify shortages in one area and surpluses in another.

If the firm's labour supply exceeds demand, policies include:

- voluntary or (if necessary) compulsory redundancy;
- redeployment with retraining;
- encouraging early retirement;
- allowing 'natural wastage'.

If the firm's demand for labour exceeds supply, policies include:

- additional (e.g. national) advertising;

- retraining programmes;
- acknowledging labour as a limiting factor in forecasting;
- improving competitiveness in the labour market (e.g. through pay and other incentives).

INFLUENCES ON THE MANPOWER PLAN

Labour turnover

An important source of information for, and influence on, the manpower plan is the level of the firm's labour turnover (**LTO**). A certain level of LTO benefits firms through introducing new staff with new ideas. A firm with a high level of LTO faces

- low morale (although this may in any case be an existing symptom in such a firm);
- increased costs of recruitment, training and overtime (the existing staff trying to maintain production levels);
- lower production.

Industries such as fast-food traditionally have high levels of LTO: for example in 1993, only 25 per cent of McDonald's staff had over two years' service.

LTO is usually calculated on an annual basis using the formula

$$LTO = \frac{\text{Number of leavers in the year*}}{\text{Average number employed in the year}} \times 100$$

* This figure is adjusted to take account of unavoidable reasons (e.g. death, pregnancy, marriage).

Further information is provided from the **Stability Index**:

$$\frac{\text{Number of staff with at least one year's service}}{\text{Number of staff employed one year ago}} \times 100$$

Retention profiles are a third indicator of turnover patterns. Staff are grouped according to the year they joined: the annual percentage of those in each yearly group who leave can be calculated.

Demographic factors

The total supply of labour is affected by changes in the working population. The following demographic factors influence a manpower plan.

The effects of migration The UK has a history of both net immigration and net emigration: in recent years, more people have left the UK than have entered it. The effect on skill levels is probably more important than the total numbers involved. The Conservative government in the 1980s greatly reduced the top rates of income tax, one justification being an attempt to discourage entrepreneurs from leaving the country.

The continuing removal of barriers to the free movement of labour in the European Union (see Table 1.4 on page 49) will be a major influence on migration levels and therefore on recruitment and manpower planning.

An ageing population The average age of the UK population is increasing (see Fig. 5.4). Effects of this on firms and individuals include changing demand levels for age-related goods and services, and pressure from the state for additional tax and other contributions to support the ageing population.

Young people are forming a smaller proportion of the population. In 1971 there were 15.8 million people in the UK aged under eighteen, but this had fallen by 1996 to 13.6 million.

A firm's manpower plan might respond by, for example, reviewing and extending age ranges employed.

Geographical distribution of the workforce The Industrial Revolution led to the movement of population from country to city. Recent changes have involved the movement from inner city areas to the suburbs. A search for lower costs (e.g. rent), and improvements in communications and infrastructure have led to many businesses locating away from traditional city bases, to areas such as the 'M4 corridor'. This becomes increasingly possible as firms become less dependent on large labour forces and therefore less reliant on the geographical distribution of labour.

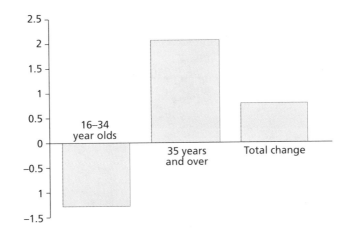

Fig. 5.4 Projected change in the British labour market, 1991–2001 (millions)

Source: Department for Education and Employment

Sex structure There are just over one million more women than men in the UK: this has only a limited effect on the labour market, as much of this apparent surplus is represented by women over the age of retirement.

Other demographic factors include national and/or local:

- skill surpluses or shortages;
- unemployment levels;
- school leaver totals;
- policies on retirement.

New working patterns

Manpower plans have to be amended to account for changes in working patterns. The traditional view of employment is of a full-time permanent contract with a single employer. Whilst this still applies to many firms and employees, increasing numbers are being employed under new working patterns. The labour market is more flexible nowadays, with two workers in five outside permanent employment. The benefits to a firm include lower total labour costs and a more flexible workforce. Trade union representation and negotiating power are also reduced. The following are the main new working patterns.

Part-time work Although part-time seasonal work is traditional in the agriculture and tourism industries, part-time work has grown in importance in the rest of the economy. Firms such as the Burton Group and British Home Stores have converted many full-time posts into part-time ones: up to two-thirds of the staff of Sears plc are now part-time.

One UK worker in four is now a part-timer. Many 'women returners' are employed on a part-time basis: in 1994 only 7 per cent of men, but 49 per cent of women in employment, were part-time workers. People employed for less than sixteen hours a week do not enjoy the same employment-related rights (e.g. for redundancy payments) as full-time staff, employers can avoid paying NI contributions to low-paid part-time workers, and the existence of more part-timers and weaker unions has made it easier for firms to shed staff.

Flexible hours The number of workers on 'flexitime' has increased: a core time band (e.g. between 10 a.m. and 4 p.m.) is established when all employees must be present, with the rest of their weekly hours being flexible to suit individuals themselves.

Shift work Continuous twenty-four-hour operation is appropriate for many industries (e.g. the flow-production section of the chemicals industry). Employees may rotate shifts or may be based on 'permanent nights'. Although hourly labour costs will rise (through extra payment for working unsocial hours), the increased production helps account for fixed costs, and so unit costs still decrease.

Table 5.1 shows people who were working shifts and other unsocial hours in 1992. The trend towards more Sunday working is likely to increase with the increase in commercial activities taking place at the weekend and the recent legislation allowing Sunday trading.

Table 5.1 *People engaged in shift and other unsocial hours work, Spring 1992*

	Percentage of employed
Saturday working	14.3
Sunday working	1.5
Full weekend working	10.0
Shift work	14.9
Night work	5.7

Source: Department for Education and Employment

Job sharing Two or more employees may decide to share a full-time post, with the employer's agreement. One benefit to the firm is the likelihood of increased cover at times of sickness or absence.

Fixed contracts A firm might recruit staff on a short-term contract, perhaps to carry out a project. This is often found in the construction industry and is now used in many other areas, for example in recruiting certain managers and senior staff. Benefits to the firm include greater control over labour costs, the opportunity to bring in 'new blood', and a highly motivated employee where the 'carrot' of a renewed contract exists. Firms may also employ people on a consultancy basis to complete a project. In such cases the person is self-employed and the consultancy will be terminated once the project is completed.

Task-based operation Employees are given tasks to do, such as redecorating an office or constructing a wall. If these tasks are finished before the set time, the employees are free to leave work. This can act as a substantial motivator, although the firm's quality control procedures must be capable of identifying substandard work.

RECRUITMENT

Recruitment involves assessing the nature of a post and advertising for a suitable candidate. Successful recruitment depends on how well the personnel function carries out the following tasks.

Job analysis

The Personnel Department relies on the specialist department having the vacancy to draw up details of the work involved in the post. This **job description** acts as one information source for the job advertisement. Information for the job description is collected from various sources, including the present post-holder, observation, questionnaires, previous performance appraisals, and training manuals.

The role of the **job specification (or person specification)** is to identify the personal qualities expected of a suitable candidate. It provides additional information required in the job advertisement.

Job description contains:	Job specification contains:
• the post title and location;	• experience required;
• a summary of the task;	• educational qualifications required;
• an outline of the work environment;	• physical characteristics;
• expected performance standards;	• personality factors;
• details of employment conditions.	• any special aptitudes.

Recruiting staff

The job description and job specification are used to identify appropriate sources of recruitment. Sources outside the firm include:

- advertising in:
  - local papers
  - national press
  - specialist publications;
- Job Centres and careers offices;
- commercial employment agencies;
- informal networks;
- schools and higher education contacts;
- executive search agencies ('head-hunters').

The choice of source depends on its **cost, coverage** and **suitability** for the post. Semi-skilled shopfloor workers are likely to be recruited locally, using sources such as local papers and Job Centres: senior executives are more likely to be recruited nationally or even internationally through head-hunting and national press advertising.

An alternative source is to **recruit internally** through promotion, redeployment, or appointing a trainee (e.g. the Modern Apprenticeship scheme). Notice-boards and house magazines are popular sources for advertising the post.

Internal recruitment has the advantages that the candidate is already known to the firm, and will be familiar with work routines. It also improves staff morale and motivation, and it is less expensive. Internal recruitment does limit the firm's choice, however, and does not result in new ideas being introduced into the firm.

SELECTION

Application forms and curriculum vitae (CVs) received are the sources used for shortlisting candidates. An application form is the more popular document because it gives consistent information (all candidates complete the same subheadings), it ensures that candidates do not omit essential information, and it reduces the chance of discrimination. The personnel department will take into account relevant anti-discriminatory legislation (see page 103) affecting recruitment and selection methods.

Following shortlisting, applicants are subject to further selection procedures. The choice of procedure depends on its perceived suitability for the post under consideration, its cost, and the time available.

Interview

This is the most popular selection method. It may be formal or informal, and can be conducted on a one-to-one or group basis.

The interview allows the interviewer to assess the candidate's:

● oral communication skills;

● physical appearance (e.g. where customer liaison is part of the job);

● personal attributes, such as confidence.

The interviewee can assess:

● physical working conditions;

● future prospects;

● the working atmosphere.

An interview offers the advantage to both candidate and interviewer of being a two-way process. However, the interview is not a reliable form of selection: it is often subjective, and there is not a perfect correlation between the ability to interview well and the ability to do the job well.

Other selection procedures

These include:

● **Aptitude tests and simulations** These test the candidate's skills and ability to carry out the duties of the post.

● **Achievement tests** These have the advantage of testing whether candidates still possess the skill for which they have qualifications.

● **Personality tests** These attempt to measure the candidate's personality 'type' (gregarious, introverted, etc.) and suitability for the culture of the organisation.

● **Intelligence tests** These 'IQ' tests seek to check the candidate's general reasoning and mental abilities.

Appointment and termination

Once the successful applicant has been offered and has accepted the post, a contract of employment (see page 102) is drawn up. Termination of this appointment can take place by:

● resignation;

● redundancy – the post ceases to exist, due to factors such as changed work practices or production methods;

● dismissal – fair (e.g. for incompetence), unfair or constructive;

● a fixed-term contract expiring.

5.4 DEVELOPING PEOPLE

TRAINING

The purpose of training is to impart knowledge, skills and techniques to individuals, so that they can carry out their work more efficiently. Fig. 5.5 shows the relative levels of training undertaken by various industries.

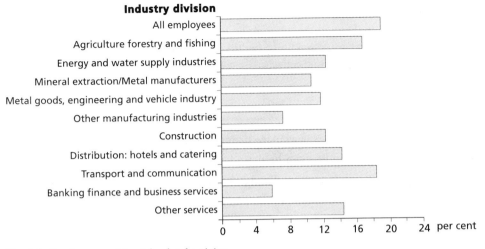

Industry division

Fig. 5.5 *Employees receiving job-related training*

Source: Department of Employment Labour Force Survey

The Personnel Department has two key training-related functions: to identify individual and group **training needs**, and to arrange suitable **training to meet these needs**.

Induction

Induction involves the new employee being introduced to the organisation, and the organisation to the new employee.

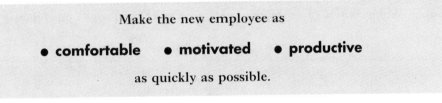

Make the new employee as

● **comfortable**   ● **motivated**   ● **productive**

as quickly as possible.

A typical induction programme includes the following features:
● information on the organisation's history and current situation (structure, products etc.);
● a guided tour of the organisation;
● introduction to colleagues;
● meetings with formal groups (e.g. trade unions);
● identification of personal needs (e.g. training).

Internal training

Also known as 'on-the-job' training, this is the most common form provided by firms. The employees learn as they work, the instructor being the post-holder. Training tends to be limited to particular skills and procedures, using the firm's technical and work manuals as sources of information.

The advantages of internal training are that it is:
● easy to organise;
● adaptable to meet the work needs of trainer and trainee;
● relatively inexpensive;
● job-specific and not general.

It can, however, disrupt work; the trainer might not possess specialist training skills and may be a poor communicator; bad work practices are passed on; and new approaches and methods are not introduced into the firm.

External training

'Off-the-job' training can involve employees attending local colleges and studying for various qualifications. External training methods include lectures, demonstrations, simulations, group activities such as role play, and self-study packages. The advantages of external training are that:

● specialist trainers are employed;

● training can be intensive;

● training takes place away from workplace distractions;

● more general theories and ideas can be considered.

External training can suffer from being isolated from the practicalities of work; it is expensive; and it removes the trainee from the workplace and therefore from production.

Evaluating training

Any training programme should be evaluated to determine whether it has produced the anticipated development in employees. The Personnel Department can select from a range of possible evaluation methods:

● pre-tests and interviews and (following training) post-tests and post-training interviews;

● questionnaire completion by the participants;

● performance appraisal;

● in-course assessment.

The evaluation of the organisation's training programmes is the end result of a process which starts with the creation of a manpower plan. Figure 5.6 summarises this process.

Fig. 5.6 Evaluating the effectiveness of a training programme

Performance appraisal

The personnel function includes performance appraisal. This seeks to

● improve **present performance** levels by identifying individual strengths and weaknesses;

● improve **future performance** by identifying individual potential for development and/or promotion;

- obtain information for **reviewing pay levels**;
- establish written performance records which can be used in the **appraisal process**.

STAFF APPRAISAL SCHEME

Name of Appraisee: .... Name of Appraiser: ....

PRIORITY KEY PERFORMANCE AREAS

PERFORMANCE OBJECTIVES   TARGETS AGREED   METHOD OF MEASUREMENT

Agreed: .... *Appraiser*   Agreed: .... *Appraisee*

Date: ....   Date: ....

Fig. 5.7 Document from a company staff appraisal scheme

The methods of performance appraisal vary. Management by objectives (**MBO**) is widely used to appraise management performance: agreed targets are established and the manager's performance is measured against these targets. Other employees may have their performance compared to a rating scale which summarises performance as a series of levels, e.g. from 'outstanding' to 'unsatisfactory'. Performance appraisal is normally supported by an appraisal interview.

Appraisal is not always effective: employees may mistrust or misunderstand it and therefore distort information provided, and appraisers may lack skill or commitment in carrying out the appraisal process.

REMUNERATION

Payment of wages and salaries is one element in the 'reward management' function of HRM. The Personnel Department implements various policies to attract and retain staff. Decisions on remuneration and other rewards are influenced by the organisation's answers to a number of questions.

- **Rates of pay**   Should the firm base its rates above, at or below other (national, local and competitor) rates?

- **Pay structures**   Is pay linked to the job, age, length of service, or the results of job evaluation (see below)?

- **Merit rises**   Are these to be incorporated into the pay structure? Is credit given for additional qualifications or experience?

- **Differentials**   Should these be maintained?

- **External influences**   How much attention is paid to factors such as the cost of living and RPI, and government advice? Should there be an automatic annual pay rise? Is relevant legislation on pay being followed?

- **Benefits**   How do non-wage benefits, such as the number of days' holiday, influence pay?

Job evaluation is often used to group different jobs together into one of a series of pay bands. A job's elements are identified, each element being given a 'complexity value'. These values are summated and the job can then be placed in the appropriate pay band.

Payment systems

Piece rates These incentive schemes pay employees in direct relation to their output. Work study techniques are used to identify a standard output and this determines the pay rate per unit produced. Employees are thus encouraged financially to make items as quickly as possible: this increases productivity, but this benefit can be offset by increases in the cost of quality control. The differentials in pay can also cause morale and motivation problems, where piece-rate systems operate.

Time rates Employees are paid on the basis of time: per day, week or month. Time worked over the agreed hours may be subject to overtime payments at a higher hourly rate (salaried staff might receive time off in lieu, rather than additional payment).

Time rates have the advantages that they are easy to calculate and the total wage bill (excluding overtime) is known in advance.

Merit rating is sometimes linked to time rates: merit pay is received if an individual produces work of greater quantity or higher quality than the norm. Merit awards are usually linked to performance appraisal.

Measured day rates These are based on incentives being incorporated into a time-rate system. Production standards for a job are fixed using job evaluation procedures, and a standard output is established. An employee's output for a previous period is recorded. The employee's actual efficiency can then be compared to the standard level of efficiency: if actual is higher than standard, the employee receives an additional hourly rate based on the percentage by which the actual has exceeded standard output.

Measured day rate systems are sometimes used in mass production industries. They rely for their success on employee trust, union co-operation, and accurate measurement of performance.

Other rewards Profit-sharing and share ownership schemes may be operated. These motivate employees by making them (feel) part of the success of the organisation. Profit-sharing and other employee-based schemes exist in about three-quarters of all UK public companies.

Employee ownership

The BP share schemes are evidence of the importance we attach to our employees being stakeholders in the company. Eligible employees in the UK were invited in May to participate once again in the share schemes. At the end of 1992, 25,400 current and former employees in the UK were participating in these schemes.

In 1992, we established share schemes in BP companies in Austria, Germany, Japan, Malaysia, Singapore, southern Africa and the USA, bringing to 14 the number of countries where we operate share schemes for employees.

Fig. 5.8 Employees as stakeholders

Source: The British Petroleum Company plc

Fringe benefits are widely found. They include:

- a company car;
- free or subsidised meals;
- products at cost price;
- subsidised travel;
- lower interest rates on loans and mortgages;
- private health and/or education.

5.5 INDUSTRIAL RELATIONS

The terms 'labour relations', 'employee relations' and 'industrial relations' refer to the relationship between employers and employees. Employers have historically been in a much stronger position – the 'master and servant' relationship, for example – which led to the growth of organised labour. Employers have realised the value of formal organisation and have responded by establishing their own associations.

TRADE UNIONS

A trade union is an organisation of workers which has been established to represent their interests.

Union membership grew to a peak of 12 million in the early 1980s, but had fallen back to below 8 million by 1993. Only 30 per cent of the workforce in 1994 was in a union, compared with 53 per cent in 1979. This trend towards a reduction in total union membership has been accompanied by union reorganisation and mergers: for example, the joining together of NALGO, NUPE and COHSE to create UNISON, the largest union in the United Kingdom with 1.5 million members. Nowadays some two-thirds of total union membership in the United Kingdom belongs to the ten largest unions. Small unions still survive, however: for example, craft unions such as the Military and Orchestral Musical Instrument Makers Trade Society (which had a membership of 48 in 1993).

Why have we merged?

The continued attacks on public services, the reorganisations and cut backs in the essential industries, all underline the vital need for an effective trade union, if jobs, pay and conditions are to be maintained or improved. Planned new laws threaten our trade union organisation. New-style local bargaining means that, increasingly, branch officers and regional officials are replacing national negotiators in reaching deals on pay and conditions. The need to be strong has never been more important.

Members in all three unions voted overwhelmingly in a secret ballot last November for merger – more than 80% of those voting said yes to the formation of the new union. Uniting three strong unions in UNISON gives us the extra unity, negotiating strength and resources which we need to represent our members effectively in the future.

Fig. 5.9 Reasons for the creation of UNISON

Source: UNISON

Union structure

Trade unions are normally structured as shown in Fig. 5.10.

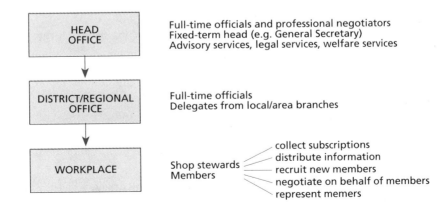

Fig. 5.10 Trade union structure

Union types

There are four recognised types of trade union.

① **Craft unions**   The first to be established, they consist of groups of skilled workers carrying out the same craft, for example the National Union of Journalists (25,000 members, 1993).

② **Industrial unions**   These contain most of the employees in a particular industry (such as USDAW, the main union in retailing: 310,000 members, 1993).

③ **General unions**   These are large and often contain high proportions of unskilled and semi-skilled workers from different industries, for example the Transport and General Workers' Union (1,030,000 members, 1993).

④ **White-collar unions**   These non-manual unions have been the most recent to develop: examples include the teaching and banking unions, such as the NUT (the National Union of Teachers: 160,000 members, 1993).

Union rights

UK legislation up to 1980 concentrated on protecting unions; since 1980 the emphasis has shifted to protecting the individual union member. Trade unions and their members have rights under several main items of legislation:

● The **Trade Union and Labour Relations Act 1974** defines a union and a trade dispute.

● The **Employment Acts 1980, 1982, 1988 and 1990**
  – require secret ballots to be held to get approval to take strike action, and for elections to union posts;
  – allow a member to prevent the union from strike action if no ballot has been held;
  – protect members from disciplinary action if they refuse to take part in a strike;
  – make 'closed shops' (see page 133) and all forms of secondary action illegal;
  – allow damages to be awarded against union members who are not involved in a dispute but who take secondary action.

● The **Trade Union Act 1984** makes a union liable for damages if it has not carried out a secret ballot to get approval from its members for strike action.

● The **Trade Union Reform and Employment Rights Act 1992** makes it unlawful for employers to collect union dues without the written consent of workers.

Union aims

A trade union seeks to improve the working life of its members.
  To do this it:

● **advises, represents and protects** members:
  – it advises on procedures following industrial accidents, represents employees at industrial tribunals, and gives general legal advice
  – it ensures that members receive sick pay and other benefits to which they are entitled
  – it helps protect against redundancy, unfair dismissal, disciplinary action, discrimination, etc.;

● **negotiates** with employers for:
  – improved pay and working conditions
  – improved pension and retirement arrangements
  – greater job satisfaction and better job security;

● **seeks to influence** others:
  – as a pressure group influencing employers and governments on legislation and other matters
  – regarding improved social objectives, such as full employment and better social security.

Union benefits

Membership of a trade union brings a number of benefits to its members (see Figs. 5.11 and 5.12).

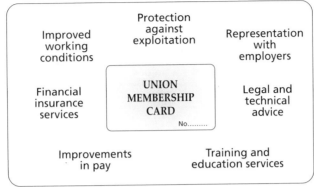

Fig. 5.11 Benefits of union membership

Many employers recognise the benefits that unions bring, and gain themselves from only having to negotiate with a single body. Some industries had union membership agreements requiring all employees to join a union – a '**closed shop**' agreement – but the **1988 Employment Act** made it unlawful to dismiss an employee who refuses to join a union. (Employers are now free to also recruit workers who are not union members.)

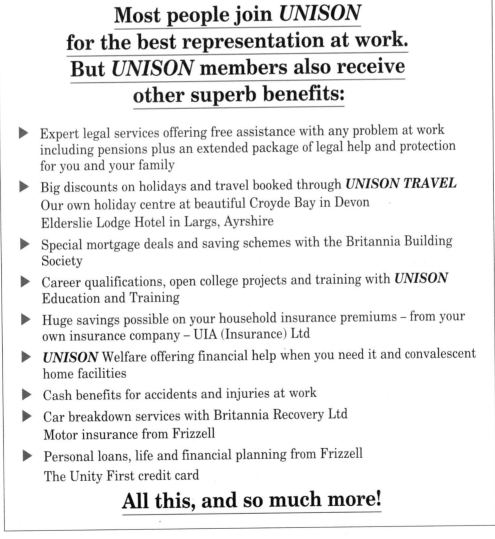

Fig. 5.12 UNISON benefits

Source: UNISON

The Trades Union Congress (TUC)

Since unions have similar goals and mutual concerns, it is in their joint interests to come together and agree common policies and approaches. The TUC as a central body acts as the collective voice of its affiliated unions. It promotes the general aims of the trade union movement and – like individual unions – operates as a pressure group to influence government policies affecting union members. It has members on government bodies such as the Health and Safety Commission. Total TUC membership, following the creation of UNISON in July 1993, stood at 7.3 million, consisting of 69 unions.

Trades councils act as the local equivalents of the TUC. These councils are voluntary local and regional union groupings.

EMPLOYER ORGANISATIONS

The Confederation of British Industry (CBI)   The CBI is the employers' equivalent of the TUC. It represents a cross-section of the UK economy, being composed of companies, trade associations and employers' associations. It negotiates with the TUC and the government and undertakes activities such as its quarterly surveys of business confidence.

Other employers' associations   Local chambers of commerce (see page 99) act in the interests of the local business community, providing advice and assistance.

Various trade associations exist to promote their joint interest. Examples include the National Farmers Union (NFU), the Society of Motor Manufacturers and Traders, the Engineering Employers' Federation (EEF) and the Road Haulage Association (RHA).

A recent example of trade association activity occurred in 1993, when the RHA defended the increase in lorry size allowed into the United Kingdom (from 38-ton to 44-ton lorries). Its arguments were presented on the grounds of economies of increased dimensions (see page 84), against the criticism by groups concerned about possible damage to the environment.

The Institute of Directors is a body formed from interested directors of UK companies. Its views on economic policy and other company-related matters are represented to the government.

COLLECTIVE BARGAINING

Most pay rises and changes to working conditions have resulted from collective bargaining. Many union members regard this as the most important function of their union. Under a system of collective bargaining, union representatives negotiate a pay rise or changes in conditions with the employer. These negotiations may take place locally, regionally or nationally.

The two main methods of collective bargaining are

❶ **integrative** bargaining, where both sides seek to negotiate a pay and productivity deal;

❷ **distributive** bargaining, where each side negotiates from its exclusive viewpoint.

A modern development is the acceptance of **no-strike deals**, which normally ban industrial action until procedures such as binding arbitration have been followed: in return for such an agreement, the union receives sole bargaining rights with the employer.

INDUSTRIAL DISPUTES

Collective bargaining is not bound to succeed: union demands may be regarded by employers as excessive, or employers may try to impose changes to pay and conditions which the union finds unacceptable.

Strike action

A strike involves union members in withdrawing their labour. This is discouraged by UK legislation, although the prevailing European view appears to regard withdrawal of labour as a fundamental human right. Strikes tend to be viewed by union members as a strategy of last resort and have declined greatly in frequency, falling from a national rate of 195 days lost per thousand employees in 1981 to 13 per thousand employees by 1994.

Under the legislation of the 1980s, any strike has to be approved through a secret ballot of union members. If the ballot approves strike action, members are allowed to engage in peaceful picketing (no more than six members at any work entrance). Strike action has a number of effects.

To the striker:

- loss of income
- potential loss of job

BUT

- possible long-term improvement in pay and conditions

To the employer:

- loss of – output
  – sales
  – cash-flow
  – reputation
  – customers
  – worker goodwill

BUT

- reduction in – wages
  – stock levels
- winning results in a position of greater power

The losses to the economy as a whole include:

- unemployed factors of production;
- lost – output
  – exports
  – consumer choice;
- reduced tax revenue (income and corporation tax);
- increased imports and overseas involvement in the economy.

Other methods used in disputes

Overtime bans   These occur when the union instructs its members not to work overtime, in order to reduce production and put pressure on the employer. Overtime bans are often used in industries which rely heavily on overtime to maintain production levels.

Working to rule   Union members follow the firm's rulebook to the letter, which slows production and has the same basic effect as an overtime ban.

Go-slow   Members carry out their work as slowly as permissible under the rulebook, again to reduce output.

Sit-ins   Members occupy the employer's premises: this strategy is sometimes used when there is a threat of closure.

RESOLVING THE DISPUTE

After a dispute has started, it may be resolved by the actions of one or both parties: the employers may offer improved terms, or the union may accept what is 'on the table' due to pressure from its members.

Advisory Conciliation and Arbitration Service (ACAS)

If deadlock persists, the employers or unions can call in the Advisory, Conciliation and Arbitration Service. The equivalent body for Northern Ireland is the Labour Relations Agency (LRA). **ACAS** was established in 1975 to improve industrial relations. It is independent of both parties, and it offers a range of services:

- **Conciliation**   An ACAS or LRA official discusses the dispute with both parties to find areas of common ground which might form the basis for further negotiations by the parties.
- **Mediation**   The ACAS or LRA official suggests a solution to the dispute, which is then considered by both parties.
- **Arbitration**   Both parties must agree to arbitration, where ACAS or the LRA provides an independent arbitrator to listen to the arguments and arrive at a decision which then binds the parties. If 'pendulum' arbitration is used, the arbitrator makes a straight choice between the two positions (pendulum arbitration discourages unrealistic bargaining positions).

Other services include the publication of guidelines and codes of practice on industrial relations.

Industrial tribunals

These hear claims brought under employment legislation, for example on unfair dismissal or discrimination. A tribunal consists of a legally qualified chairman and two lay members drawn from the business world. Appeals on decisions made by these tribunals are heard at Employment Appeal Tribunals.

Chapter roundup

Chapter 5 has concentrated on the relationship between employer and employee. The quality of this relationship is influenced by the level of workforce motivation. After studying this chapter you should be able to explain how the personnel function implements the firm's manpower plan, how it recruits and trains staff, and the nature of industrial relations and collective bargaining.

Illustrative questions

1   Give **two** reasons why firms invest in training for their employees.   (2)

AEB

2   (a) State **three** symptoms of badly motivated employees.   (3)
   (b) How might poor motivation be improved?   (4)

Tutorial note

Brief answers are required to these questions. Question 1 tests your recall of training, and a 'textbook' answer is required for question 2.

Suggested answers

1   Firms invest in training to (a) increase employee productivity and (b) increase employee motivation.

2   (a) Three common symptoms are poor attendance records, bad timekeeping, and an increased number of disputes.
   (b) Remedies could include improved communication and consultation (with individuals and unions), job rotation and enrichment (to improve motivation and morale), and reviews of pay and/or working conditions. The work of Human Relations theorists such as Mayo suggests that this increased concern for employee welfare will produce positive benefits.

3   Read the following passage and then answer the questions that follow.

"The Welsh economic landscape has undergone significant change over the last ten years. A substantial inflow of investment, much from overseas, has offset a decline in the old primary industries such as coal and steel. It provides a springboard for industry to take advantage of improved economic conditions. The structure of the economy has changed dramatically and is now concentrated in areas such as electronics, motor vehicles and component manufacture, light industry and financial and business services.

Whilst the nature of industry has changed dramatically, communities remain intact and a major challenge facing people in Wales is to adapt to meet the changing environment.

Banking is vital to support the business aspirations for the emerging and more traditional businesses and it is no accident that in 1993 the Midland Bank decided to move its most experienced managers back into the branch network. It was felt that their greater experience would be of benefit to all businesses in the community.

The future is undoubtedly high-tech and companies are faced with the need to re-train their staff, e.g. in-house training or employing external agencies."

(a)   Outline **two** problems that face the workforce, when changes like those described in the above passage occur.   (4)

(b)   What do you understand by the term in-house training (paragraph 4) and what are its advantages to the firm?   (6)

(c)   To what extent do you consider it to be more beneficial, for a firm to pay higher wages to attract skilled workers than to re-train existing workers?   (8)

WJEC

Tutorial note

The questions are a mix of the general and the specific. Note that answer (a) should focus on the employees, whereas in answers (b) and (c) you write about the firm. Be careful in (b): although you are describing in-house training of employees, the advantages you identify refer to the firm and not the employees.

Suggested answer

(a)   One problem facing the workforce is the likely need to retrain. The passage mentions the decline in traditional extractive and heavy engineering industries, and the growth in light industry, electronics, etc. The skills required to work in these industries are different, and therefore the workforce can anticipate a degree of re-skilling to meet the new needs.
    A second problem is that the workforce will probably find that there is greater competition for the given jobs. Many of the newer industries are more capital-intensive, with less demand for labour as a factor of production. It is likely, therefore, that – with younger people also coming on to the job market – the demand for jobs may exceed their supply.

(b)   'In-house training' refers to training carried out on the firm's premises (normally by its own trained employees). It is also known as 'on-the-job' training; essentially internal, with employees learning by doing the work (usually supervised). In-house training has a number of advantages for the firm: it tends to be less costly than 'off-the-job' training; it is tailored precisely to the needs of the firm (it has 'specificity'), and it can easily and quickly be updated or altered as necessary.

(c)   Retraining existing workers can improve their motivation and therefore their loyalty and productivity, whereas employing skilled workers from outside can have a detrimental effect on the existing employees who resent the lack of opportunity for themselves. (This assumes that the existing workforce has sufficient ability and motivation to retrain.) Linked to this point is the possibility that industrial relations will worsen as a result of the firm ignoring the wishes of its existing employees. There is also a cost consideration: the firm has to balance the costs of recruitment and selection (plus induction training) with those of retraining. Looking outside the firm, there will be an effect on the local community: for example, there is a possible loss of lower-skilled workers' jobs, with a consequent effect on the image of the firm in the eyes of its local community.

4   'BEST EMPLOYER 1994'

'North Bucks Engine Castings Ltd. has won this year's Home Counties Advertiser Best Employer award. The firm employs 370 full-time workers and 80 part-time workers. Despite the impact of two major recessions and a shortening of the order books from 1989 to 1993, the firm has successfully maintained its no
5   redundancy policy.

    Lucy Moore, the Director of Human Resources at North Bucks, introduced annual appraisal schemes for all employees, starting with managers, and is a strong supporter of internal promotion. In 1985 she negotiated a Single Union deal with the Amalgamated Union of Engineering and Electrical Workers,
10   already the dominant union in the firm. Increased flexibility in work practices have been the result of management offering profit-related bonuses, increased job security and enhanced pension rights.

    The firm is proud of its record in the field of industrial safety. The use of Quality Circles has contributed to success here; the meetings place emphasis
15   upon the quality of the working environment. Each employee spends one hour a week in such meetings. The firm feels the consequent major improvements in productivity and quality are well worth the effort.'

(a) Evaluate the possible advantages for North Bucks Engine Castings Ltd. of employing the current mixture of full-time and part-time employees.   (10)

(b) Evaluate the extent to which the working practices of North Bucks Engine Castings Ltd. reflect motivational theories.   (9)

(c) Analyse the advantages and disadvantages to the employees of the firm's Single Union policy.   (6)

London Examinations

Tutorial note

Each part of the question is open-ended; you have to judge the number of advantages (etc) by the relative marks given to each part. Part (b) is quite difficult, since you have to identify the nature of the firm's working practices and then link them to particular theorists: Maslow, McGregor and Herzberg are obvious ones.

Suggested answer

(a) The advantages to the firm from employing full-time workers include greater continuity (thus reduced costs, e.g. of induction training) and known stability; the overall experience and skill levels are also known, which assists the firm in its future planning; full-time staff often have greater commitment and loyalty than part-time staff, which should increase productivity; there can be lower personnel-based costs compared with employing part-time staff; and channels of communication are more efficient where full-time employees are involved.

    The advantages of employing part-time workers are essentially greater flexibility for the firm: management finds it easier to monitor hours worked and therefore control labour costs, and has flexibility in using differing skill levels (greater freedom to employ the type of skills required for a particular situation). Also, the firm might face lower wage costs (e.g. lower hourly rate) and fewer legal formalities with part-time employees.

    The company can therefore employ an appropriate 'mix' of full-time and part-time employees, to suit its short-term and long-term goals.

(b) The passage states that the company 'has successfully maintained its no redundancy policy' (lines 4–5) which improves morale and motivation (Maslow – feeling of worth; Herzberg – motivators such as recognition and responsibility, and hygiene factor of security). It has 'annual appraisal schemes' (line 7) (Mayo – interest in employees stimulates production; Herzberg – hygiene factor). Factors such as 'internal promotion' (line 8, illustrates Maslow's esteem and self-actualisation needs, and Herzberg's motivators), 'Increased flexibility in work' (line 10, relevant to McGregor's Theory Y workers, exercising their own control and direction), 'profit-related bonuses, increased job security' (lines 11–12, referring to Maslow's lower-order basic needs), all indicate an interest in employees. Finally, the reference to industrial safety and meetings (line 13 on, illustrations of Maslow's basic safety need and McGregor's hygiene factor of working conditions) confirms that the firm takes account of the work of motivation theorists.

(c) The advantages to employees include having a recognised single union by management, thereby making negotiations more efficient. Also, demarcation disputes should not arise for employees. Finally, there will be an element of consistency with a single negotiating and organising voice. Disadvantages include the lack of recognition for members of other unions, and the possibility that the local branch will become subject to control by a particular group of employees with their own interests, denying representation to others.

Practice questions

1 What is the difference between a **job description** and a **job (or person) specification**? (4)

2 Identify **four** reasons why firms carry out staff appraisal. (4)

Pitfalls

Both questions require brief answers only. Many candidates get confused between the two terms in question 1: the word 'person' is the clue.

Key points

1 Description: duties of the job. Specification: qualities of the person.
2 Identify suitable candidates for promotion; identify training needs; identify overall strengths and weaknesses of staff; use in connection with performance-related pay schemes.

3 Top managers receive large incomes. Why is their role vital to the success of firms? (7)

Pitfalls

This is a very general question, limited only by the mark allocation. The expected answer requires either two or three points to be fully developed, or seven listed (or a combination). You have to limit your points to 'top' management and therefore your answer should refer to the functions of the chairman and major directors.

Key points

(a) To provide leadership for the company: e.g. representing it in its relationships with the outside world, at meetings with the media or shareholders, etc., also internally when liaising with unions or employees.

(b) To provide motivation for internal and external groups (e.g. employees and shareholders respectively), through effective leadership and communication of their vision of the company's future.

(c) To set the company's overall strategic plan, which is then translated into strategic objectives: these in turn are developed in detail and passed down the chain of command, helping to reinforce motivation and to develop and improve both communication and co-ordination.

4 (a) Briefly explain what you understand by the terms autocratic and democratic styles of leadership. (6)

(b) 'Profit-sharing schemes are the best way of motivating employees.' Critically discuss this statement. (14)

WJEC

Pitfalls

It is important to spend most of your time on (b). The request to 'critically discuss' requires you to state arguments for and against, and make judgements. Notice the use of the phrase 'the best' which you can use in your answer (e.g. to help construct your conclusion).

Key points

(a) Autocratic: manager keeps tight control over decision-making process; associated with 'top-down' management.

Democratic: manager allows subordinates greater say in matters, though may still make final decision; chain of command likely to be more limited in scope, delegation likely to take place to a greater extent.

(b) Profit-sharing schemes bring feeling of greater involvement, owning a share of the firm's success and having a direct benefit (profit) from direct involvement (work). However, like all other financial rewards, these schemes are of limited motivational value only; theorists such as Maslow and Herzberg identified the importance of non-financial factors in motivating employees. To call it 'the best' is inaccurate, if only because different employees are 'best' motivated by different things.

5 This question is about Human Resources. You will be expected to include knowledge relevant to this aspect of business studies in your answers.

Read the passage below and answer the questions that follow it.

'The National Health Service is the biggest single employer in the UK. Until the government's recent reforms, the pay of the majority of its employees was set at a national level. However, since the introduction of trust status and the workings of the internal market many hospitals now face greater commercial pressures. The costs of such hospitals have to be controlled and management has to look at ways of improving efficiency. One way of achieving the latter would be to increase productivity. The government believes that this can be done by moving towards performance related pay, negotiated at a local level.'

(a) State how labour productivity is measured, and suggest the implications for manpower planning requirements of an increase in labour productivity. (4)

(b) State the key factors that a Personnel Manager in the private sector would take into consideration when devising a performance related pay scheme. (4)

(c) What difficulties would have to be overcome when trying to introduce a performance related pay scheme into the National Health Service? (8)

'The writings of Frederick Taylor are used by some observers to argue that performance related pay schemes which are implemented properly will lead to a well motivated workforce. This is not the view of other people. For example, an article entitled "Productivity and Pay", written by Martin Wolf, which appeared in the *Financial Times* on 15 August 1994, stated that the "consensus that pay should be linked to productivity is... a damaging mistake... Employers should pay people as market conditions dictate. 'Market plus motivation' is the right slogan, not 'more productivity, higher pay' ".

(d) By referring to other motivational theories with which you are familiar, list and explain **four** factors which Martin Wolf may have been considering when he wrote his article. Why may these factors be as important as pay when it comes to motivating people in the National Health Service? (24)

London Examinations

Pitfalls

The Examiner's Report stated that 'Few candidates were able to state how labour productivity is measured...' and, for (b), 'Instead of referring to such things as job descriptions, target setting, appraisal etc many answers referred to the National Health Service... a large number of candidates failed to score any marks in this question'.

Key points

(a) Labour productivity: output per employee. Increased productivity will result in pay claims; it may also lead to redundancies (fewer employees need to produce the same level of output). Likely negotiations with trade unions.

(b) Job held by appraisees (job descriptions referred to); organisational goals (to help set targets for appraisees); likely costs of such a scheme; need to train (and cost of training of) the appraisers; publicising the scheme; liaison with relevant unions.

(c) Problem of measuring output (common to 'service' occupations); resistance to change (new scheme); cost of such a scheme; problem of implementing it across the NHS; problem of applying it fairly to all parts of the NHS.

(d) Need/desire for job enrichment (e.g. identified by Herzberg's motivators); esteem and self-actualisation (Maslow's higher-order needs); wish to be involved and take responsibility (McGregor's Theory Y management); safety and social needs (Maslow's lower-order needs). Each relevant to NHS employees: many deal directly with people and are motivated by this direct involvement in caring.

6 Explain:

(a) the main functions of a personnel manager (10)

(b) how the human resource function seeks to maximise the efficiency of a firm's workforce. (10)

Pitfalls

The number of 'functions' is not specified: five well-developed ones should be enough.

Key points

(a) Obtaining staff (recruitment and selection); organising staff training (induction, on-the-job, off-the-job); organising staff records; appraising staff performance; liaison with other internal/external organisations (e.g. unions); involvement in staff leaving (e.g. dismissal, redundancy).

(b) Motivation (see theorists); involvement; support; leadership; developing teamwork.

FINANCE AND ACCOUNTING

Units in this chapter

6.1 *Financial accounting*
6.2 *Ratio analysis*
6.3 *Management accounting*

Chapter Objectives

This chapter explains the rules used by accountants in recording financial transactions, and how these records are used to calculate profit or loss. It also describes the use of other final accounts information to create balance sheets and cash flow statements. Once the financial data are recorded and categorised, they can be analysed, and this chapter shows how this analysis takes place. Much accounting is historical: projections into the future must also be made, and the chapter outlines the budgetary control and standard costing procedures used for forecasting and control purposes.

Major financial decisions on matters such as capital investment and sources of finance are dealt with in Chapter 10, and these units link closely with that chapter.

The key topics and concepts covered in this chapter are:

● accounting conventions;
● profit and loss;
● expenses, revenues, assets and liabilities;
● ratio analysis;
● liquidity and profitability;
● budgeting and budgetary control;
● standard costing.

6.1 FINANCIAL ACCOUNTING

The role of the accounting function in an organisation is to

● **Obtain**
● **Record**   **financial**
● **Analyse**   **information**
● **Present**

Information is obtained from various source documents; accounts are used in recording this information; accounting ratios provide information for analysis; and final accounts, cashflow statements, budgets and forecasts illustrate the different forms in which the financial information is presented.

ACCOUNTING CONCEPTS

Accounting practices have evolved over hundreds of years. The key procedures and 'rules' now used in the United Kingdom have been incorporated into **SSAPs** (Statements of Standard Accounting Practice), and **FRSs** (Financial Reporting Standards) set by representatives of the professional accountancy bodies. SSAP 2 – *Disclosure of accounting policies* – refers to the first four concepts below as 'fundamental accounting concepts'. They are included in the **1985 Companies Act**, which also adds the fifth one in the list.

All these concepts ensure that accountants follow generally recognised procedures. Harmonisation of accounting procedures has also taken place within the European Union.

1 **Accruals**   Expenses and income must be matched to the period to which they refer: for example, if goods are sold in December 1996 and payment is received in January 1997 (the next financial year), the sale increases 1996's profit, even though no cash had been received by the end of that year.

2 **Consistency**   Accountants do not change methods used (e.g. the way fixed assets are depreciated) unless there is good reason to make a change: this allows accurate comparisons to be made from one period to the next.

3 **Going Concern**   The firm is assumed to continue indefinitely: assets are therefore valued at cost, and not at their market resale price.

4 **Prudence**   Where accountants have a choice of figures to use, they select those which tend to understate profit: and profits are never anticipated, in accordance with the Realisation concept (below).

5 **Separate Valuation**   Each separate asset or liability in its class should be valued individually: if a company has twenty separate stock items, for example, each item should be valued to obtain the total stock value for the balance sheet.

Other important concepts are:

- **Business Entity**   The owner's financial dealings are kept separate from those of the firm.
- **Materiality**   Accountants balance the value of the information gained with the cost of obtaining it.
- **Money Measurement**   Accountants only concern themselves with items which have a measurable financial value: the 'value' of a good management team or an excellent workforce is therefore not shown directly in the business accounts.
- **Realisation**   Profit is not recorded as being realised (made) until legal title to the goods passes, ie they are sold.

Source documents

Accounts are created and updated from source documents, as shown below.

Document		Accounts updated
Sales invoice	⟶	sales debtor
Purchase invoice	⟶	purchases creditor
Credit note	⟶	debtor sales returns
Cheque received	⟶	debtor bank
Cheque paid	⟶	creditor or expense bank

VARIETIES OF ACCOUNTS

Assets   Asset accounts record details of the items owned by a business. Assets are grouped under two headings:

❶ Fixed assets: long-lasting assets, such as premises, equipment and machinery used by the firm in its operations

❷ Current assets: assets such as stocks, debtors (credit customers) and cash, which fluctuate regularly and are directly used to make profit.

Liabilities   Liability accounts record details of amounts owing by a firm. The main liability is **capital**, which shows the value of the investment in the business by the owner(s). Capital is treated as a liability because it is owed by the firm to the owner(s): this is an application of the Business Entity concept.

Other liabilities are either:

● **long-term**, such as debentures and other loans which are not due to be repaid for at least one year; or

● **current**, payable within twelve months and which fluctuate in value regularly, such as creditors (suppliers of goods on credit) or a bank overdraft.

Expenses   Expense accounts record costs incurred by the firm. Examples include rent, salaries and wages, advertising, insurance and purchases of stationery and raw materials.

Income   Income or 'revenue' accounts record the results of the firm's trading. The sales account is the principal revenue account.

Reserves and provisions   A company's directors normally decide not to distribute all profits after tax in the form of dividends. This helps retain cash in the company. To do this, the directors use accounts known as reserves: examples include:

● fixed asset replacement reserve

● general reserve

● profit and loss appropriation account (the total of undistributed profit).

These are 'revenue' reserves because they are created from the company's revenue (trading) activities. 'Capital' reserves are created from capital movements: for example, a share premium account records the value of total share premium, where new shares have been issued at a price above their nominal (face) value.

Provisions are created where a firm has expenses but the amount of the expense is not known with any certainty. A well-known example of the use of provisions is the provision for depreciation account. Fixed assets depreciate – ie fall in value over their useful life – but the precise annual amount of depreciation can only be estimated. An estimated annual charge (the provision) is made against profits, so that each year's profit bears its share of the total cost of depreciation. If this were not done, one year's profit – the profit for the year in which the asset was sold – would bear the full cost and comparisons between it and other annual profits would be unfair.

Capital and revenue expenditure

Asset and expense accounts record purchases made in business. These purchases are analysed separately under two headings.

Capital expenditure	Revenue expenditure
● the firm buys or improves its fixed assets	● the firm pays everyday running expenses
● e.g. buying vehicles or extending premises	● e.g. paying wages, rent or selling expenses
● shown in the balance sheet	● shown in the trading, and profit and loss accounts

THE DOUBLE-ENTRY SYSTEM AND THE TRIAL BALANCE

Financial transactions have a twofold effect in the accounts. This involves receiving and giving value (e.g. money or goods).

> An account **receiving** value is **debited**
> (an entry on its left-hand side or in its left-hand column)
>
> An account **giving** value is **credited**
> (an entry on its right-hand side or in its right-hand column)

The following typical accounting transactions illustrate how a double-entry system operates.

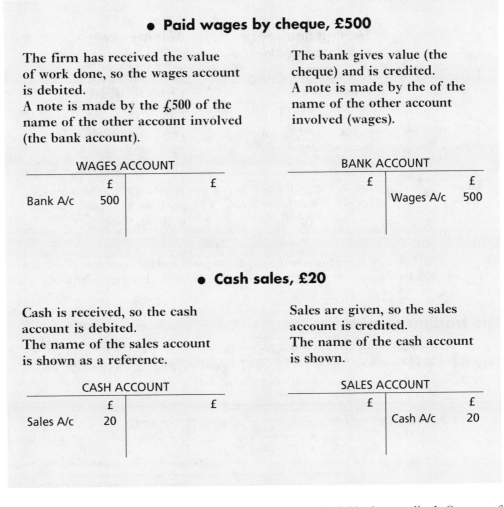

• Paid wages by cheque, £500

The firm has received the value of work done, so the wages account is debited.
A note is made by the £500 of the name of the other account involved (the bank account).

The bank gives value (the cheque) and is credited.
A note is made by the of the name of the other account involved (wages).

WAGES ACCOUNT			
	£		£
Bank A/c	500		

BANK ACCOUNT			
	£		£
		Wages A/c	500

• Cash sales, £20

Cash is received, so the cash account is debited.
The name of the sales account is shown as a reference.

Sales are given, so the sales account is credited.
The name of the cash account is shown.

CASH ACCOUNT			
	£		£
Sales A/c	20		

SALES ACCOUNT			
	£		£
		Cash A/c	20

Alternative methods exist to identify whether an account is debited or credited. One set of rules states that

● Expense accounts are debited and income (revenue) accounts are credited.

● An asset account is debited if the transaction increases the value of the asset, and credited if it reduces the asset value (and vice versa with liability accounts).

Where a double-entry system is followed, its accuracy is checked by the **trial balance**. This is a list of individual account balances to check arithmetical accuracy: it is based on the double-entry principle that for every debit entry there is an equivalent credit entry. The trial balance can be used as a source for constructing the firm's final accounts.

THE LEDGER AND ITS DIVISION

The term 'ledger' refers to a collection of accounts. For control purposes, the ledger is normally divided into the

- **Cash book:** for cash and bank accounts, isolating money to be controlled by a cashier.

- **Sales Ledger:** debtor accounts are grouped together, allowing more effective credit control to take place.

- **Purchases Ledger:** this is a grouping of creditor accounts to enable the firm to control its own total debts.

- **General Ledger:** containing the remaining accounts.

THE FINAL ACCOUNTS

	Trading and profit & loss accounts	**Balance sheet**
Purpose:	to act as an income statement and to calculate net profit	to summarise the firm's financial position
Information base:	expense and revenue accounts (revenue expenditure)	asset and liability accounts (capital expenditure)
Heading:	'for the period ending...' (profit is made over a period of time)	'as at...' (the financial position at a particular point in time)

The term 'final accounts' refers to a firm's trading, and profit and loss accounts and its balance sheet (although the latter is not strictly an account). These final accounts have important differences.

The trading account

The purpose of the trading account is to calculate **gross profit**. The two figures from which gross (i.e. trading) profit is derived are sales and cost of goods sold, which is also known as cost of sales. Its basic construction is shown in Fig. 6.1.

A. Lee Trading Account for year ending 31 December	£ (000)	£ (000)
Sales		400
Less Cost of sales:		
Opening stock	55	
Purchases	290	
	345	
Closing stock	(45)	
		300
Gross profit		**100**

Fig. 6.1 Trading account

Firms which make the goods they sell also construct a **manufacturing account** to record costs of manufacture. This account precedes the trading account and lists costs under two headings.

- **Prime costs:** direct production costs:
  - direct labour (e.g. machine operator's piece-rate wage)
  - direct materials (raw materials used to make the product).
- **Factory overheads:** indirect production costs:
  - supervisory wages
  - depreciation on factory machinery.

The profit and loss account

The purpose of the profit and loss account is to calculate **net profit**. Net profit is the excess of the firm's gross profit plus any other revenues (such as rent received from subletting premises) over its expenses. Fig. 6.2 illustrates a typical profit and loss account.

A. Lee Profit and Loss account for year ending 31 December	£ (000)	£ (000)
Gross profit		100
Less expenses:		
Administration	32	
Selling and distribution	16	
Financial	12	
		60
Net profit		**40**

Fig. 6.2 Profit and loss account

Appropriation A sole trader's net profit does not require appropriation (sharing out), because the sole trader is its only recipient. Partnerships and companies must appropriate their profit. The appropriation of a partnership profit is influenced by:

- the amount of capital invested by each partner;
- the amount of work each partner undertakes in the partnership.

A 'sleeping' (inactive) partner would receive a greater share of the net profit available for appropriation under the first category, but none of the profit under the second one.

A company's net profit presents the directors with the same decision that people have to make regarding their own income: how much to spend, and how much to save. The 'spending' element of appropriation includes corporation tax and share dividends. The directors realise the higher the dividends they award, the more contented the shareholders will be: but more cash resources have to be committed to this payment, which can leave the company short of money. Note that the payment of dividends is not an expense to the company: it is not taken from gross profit and does not appear in the profit and loss account. This payment is out of (taxed) net profit and is an appropriation of that profit.

Limited company appropriation accounts contain

- net profit for the year (before tax);
- Corporation tax deducted from this profit;
- remaining balance of last year's profit (held as a reserve);
- voluntary appropriations:
  - interim (paid) and proposed (unpaid) dividends
  - transfers to reserves;

● closing balance of undistributed profit, held as a reserve until next year's appropriation.

The balance sheet

A. Lee   Balance sheet as at 31 December

	£ (000)	£ (000)	£ (000)
	Cost	Depreciation	Net
Fixed assets			
Land and buildings	100	–	100
Plant and equipment	24	6	18
Vehicles	5	3	2
	129	9	120
Current assets			
Stocks		45	
Debtors		25	
Bank and cash		20	
		90	
Current liabilities			
Creditors	20		
Accrued expenses	10		
		30	
Net current assets			60
Net assets			180
Capital			
Opening balance			140
Net profit for year			40
			180

Fig. 6.3 Balance sheet

The purpose of the balance sheet (see Figs. 6.4 and 6.5) is to show the firm's **financial position** – what it owns and what it owes – at a stated point in time. It lists assets and liabilities under their appropriate headings.

Modern balance sheet layouts show the firm's net current assets, or **working capital**. Working capital is the difference between current assets and current liabilities. It is one of the most important figures for a business, because it indicates its **liquidity**, i.e. its ability to meet short-term debts. Working capital is explained fully in Unit 6.2.

Funds flow and cash flow statements

The importance of adequate liquidity is that it allows the firm to survive. The profit and loss account and balance sheet give only limited information on liquidity, since this is not their primary purpose. They are also historical by nature, looking back at the company's past liquidity performance, rather than forecasting future liquidity levels and requirements. Firms therefore undertake funds flow and cash flow forecasting.

Funds flow statements   These statements are also historical, but are used as a basis for constructing future cash and other forecasts. They analyse where the firm's funds come from – the sources – and where they go to – the applications. The firm's working capital increases if its total sources for the period exceed total applications: its working capital falls in periods where applications exceed sources.

Cash flow statements   These must now be presented by companies, rather than source and application statements (funds flow). Cash flow statements concentrate more fully on cash inflows and outflows. Fig. 6.5 illustrates a cash flow statement.

Group Financial Record

for the years ended 31 March

	1996 £m 52 weeks	1995 £m 52 weeks
PROFIT AND LOSS ACCOUNT		
Turnover		
General	4,090.4	3,889.0
Foods	2,847.5	2,682.0
Financial Activities	178.9	135.7
Direct export sales outside the Group	114.8	99.8
Total turnover (excluding sales taxes)	7,231.6	6,806.5
Retailing – continuing	7,030.3	6,645.0
– discontinued	22.4	25.8
Financial Activities	178.9	135.7
Operating profit:		
United Kingdom	885.4	847.4
Europe (excluding UK)	20.0	20.7
Rest of the World	34.8	28.4
Total operating profit	940.2	896.5
Retailing – continuing	881.0	848.8
– discontinued	(2.2)	(1.2)
Financial Activities	61.4	48.9
Loss on disposal of discontinued operations	(25.0)	–
Fundamental restructuring	–	–
Loss on disposal of property and other fixed assets	(4.2)	(5.4)
Net interest income	54.8	33.2
Profit before taxation	965.8	924.3
Retailing – continuing	930.5	876.9
– discontinued	(27.9)	(2.3)
Financial Activities	63.2	49.7
Taxation on ordinary activities	(312.0)	(299.5)
Minority interests	(1.2)	(1.0)
Profit attributable to shareholders	652.6	623.8
Dividends	(320.9)	(288.2)
Undistributed surplus	331.7	335.6
BALANCE SHEET		
Tangible fixed assets	3,428.4	3,297.0
Investments	46.0	43.3
Current assets	2,875.5	2,365.8
Total assets	6,349.9	5,706.1
Creditors due within one year	(1674.9)	1,363.8)
Total assets less current liabilities	4,675.0	4,342.3
Creditors due after more than one year	(497.8)	(568.7)
Provisions for liabilities and charges	(35.0)	(37.9)
Net assets	4,142.2	3,735.7

Fig. 6.4 Final accounts

Source: Marks and Spencer plc

| | 1996
52 weeks | 1995
52 weeks |
|---|---|---|
| CASH FLOW | | |
| Net cash inflow from operating activities | **808.8** | 908.8 |
| Net cash outflow from returns on investments and servicing of finance | **(215.5)** | (218.3) |
| Tax paid | **(297.0)** | (273.4) |
| Net cash outflow from investing activities | **(325.3)** | (397.4) |
| **Net cash (outflow)/inflow before financing and treasury activities** | **(29.0)** | 19.7 |
| Net cash inflow/(outflow) from financing and treasury activities | **23.3** | (108.2) |
| **(Decrease)/increase in cash and cash equivalents** | **(5.7)** | (88.5) |
| **Increase in net funds** | **4.4** | 48.6 |

Fig. 6.5 Cash flow statement

Source: Marks and Spencer plc

Additional company statements

A company's Annual Report consists of the profit statement (trading and profit and loss accounts details summarised to meet the disclosure requirements of the Companies Acts), the balance sheet, and the cash flow statement. The 'Notes to the Accounts' section provides additional information concerning the various items in the final accounts. An Annual Report also contains the following information.

Chairman's Statement This provides an overview of the company's past performance and its present situation. It may be supported by a special strategic review by the Chairman or other official (e.g. a chief executive), or a review based on the different activities or divisions of the company.

Directors' Report This includes more specific information on the past year's performance, for example:

- principal activities of the business;
- results and dividends;
- fixed assets and investments;
- research and development policies;
- the directors' service contracts;
- political and/or charitable donations made;
- employment policies.

An extract from a Directors' (and Auditors') Report is given on page 216.

Statement of accounting policies This outlines the main accounting policies adopted, for example on the basis for consolidation of group accounts (for a conglomerate) and on the methods of asset valuation.

Report of the auditors This is required by law and requires the auditors to state – if relevant – that the accounts give a 'true and fair view' of the company's financial performance and standing.

Large PLCs may support the above statements by others, for example a summary statement of overall performance, and/or a profile (where relevant) of the group activities. Statistical information may also be produced to support relevant accounts and statements.

6.2   RATIO ANALYSIS

The profit and loss account and balance sheet provide information on an organisation's financial position. These statements are interpreted by calculating ratios and using the results to compare the organisation's current performance against:

- that of its **competitors**, to establish its relative competitiveness;
- its own **performance in previous years**, to identify any trends.

Interested parties

Both internal and external groups are concerned with the financial performance.

Group	Interest area	Main reasons for interest
Management	Liquidity Profitability Asset efficiency Investment	Re-election of directors; share dividend levels; financial reward; survival of the firm.
Employees	Liquidity Profitability	Job prospects; pay claims; reward (e.g. if in profit-sharing scheme)
Lenders	Liquidity	Assessment of ability to meet debts owed to them.
Investors	Profitability Liquidity Asset efficiency Investment	(Short-term) dividends and share values; (long-term) share values; security of investment.
Government	Profitability Liquidity	Taxation income; economic objectives (e.g. full employment).

PROFITABILITY

A firm's profitability is a measure of its **total profit compared to the resources used** in making that profit.

Profitability ratios

1 **Return on capital employed (ROCE)**

Calculation:
$$\frac{\text{Net profit}}{\text{Capital employed}} \times 100$$

Purpose: to assess the profitability of the investment by calculating its percentage return.

This can then be compared with other investment rates of return to indicate whether it is worth the owner(s) retaining their investment in the business. In the case of A. Lee's business, £140,000 capital employed has generated £40,000 net profit, giving a ROCE of 28.6 per cent.

2 **Net profit margin**

Calculation:
$$\frac{\text{Net profit}}{\text{Sales}} \times 100$$

Purpose: to show the percentage of turnover represented by net profit (i.e. how many pence out of every £1 sold is net profit).

The net profit margin will fall if the gross profit margin has fallen (see below), or if the firm's other expenses (expressed as a percentage of sales) have risen. Lee's business currently has a net profit margin of 10 per cent (£40,000 as a percentage of £400,000): every £1 of sales made results in 10p net profit.

③ Gross profit margin

Calculation:
$$\frac{\textbf{Gross profit}}{\textbf{Sales}} \times \textbf{100}$$

Purpose: to show the percentage of turnover represented by gross profit.

This percentage may fall because the firm is not passing on increases in its own cost of sales. Alternatively, it may have deliberately cut the price of its goods (thereby cutting into this margin) to remain competitive: this is a common approach during economic recessions. Lee's business shows a current gross profit margin of 25 per cent (£100,000 on sales of £400,000).

The term **mark-up** is used when gross and net profit figures are expressed as a percentage on the cost figure, which is 'marked up' to give the selling price. **Margin** is used when the profit figure is expressed as a percentage of sales.

The relationship between the gross and net profit margins can be shown using information from Lee's business (see Fig. 6.6). The gross profit margin is 25 per cent, therefore the firm's cost of sales are 75 per cent (75p in the £). The net profit margin is 10 per cent and so the firm's expenses represent 15 per cent (the difference between the two profit margins) of sales. The trading, and profit and loss accounts can be reconstructed with percentages replacing money.

A. Lee Summarised trading and profit and loss accounts	%	%
Sales		100
Less: Cost of sales		75
Gross profit		25
Less expenses:		
Administration	8	
Selling and distribution	4	
Financial	3	
		15
Net profit		10

Fig. 6.6 Relationship of the margins

LIQUIDITY

An organisation's liquidity identifies its **ability to meet its debts**. Extremely profitable firms can still fail, due to financial resources becoming overstretched. Cash resources are put under pressure, for example by a firm extending credit to its customers to encourage sales, but receiving a much shorter credit period on its own purchases.

Working capital

Working capital = current assets – current liabilities

Current assets ⟶ Cash and 'near-cash' (e.g. amounts owed by debtors which will shortly become cash).

Current liabilities ⟶ Short-term debts owed by the firm which have to be paid soon in cash.

This is displayed in the balance sheet. The calculation of working capital is carried out to assess the firm's ability to meet its short-term debts.

The operating cycle This term is used to describe the connection between cash movements and working capital. The operating cycle provides a clear indicator to the accountant of how the firm's production cycle, and credit periods allowed (to customers) and taken (from suppliers), affect cashflow. Fig. 6.7 shows the operating cycle.

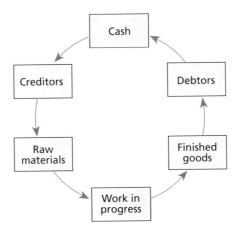

Fig. 6.7 The operating cycle

Liquidity ratios

① **The current ratio**

> Calculation: **current assets (CA) to current liabilities (CL)**

Purpose: to identify the firm's liquidity position.

If current liabilities exceed current assets, the firm may have difficulty in meeting its debts. Short-term borrowing to pay off creditors increases current liabilities and also costs the firm interest on the amount borrowed. If the firm sells assets to help meet debts, it risks loss of production and future expansion. A ratio of 2:1 is often used as a rule-of-thumb measure, though this varies between different industries.

Too high a current ratio indicates that the firm is inefficient: working capital tied up in current assets suggests that its liquid assets are not being used productively.

Lee's balance sheet shows a current ratio of 90:30, i.e. 3:1

② **The liquid ratio** This is also known as the 'acid test' or 'quick assets' ratio.

> Calculation: **current assets – stock to current liabilities**

Purpose: to see how easily the firm can meet its short-term debts without having to sell any stock. Stock is regarded as the least liquid of the current assets.

This is a more cautious assessment, influenced by the Prudence concept. The rule-of-thumb ratio here is 1:1. Lee's acid test is 45:30, i.e. 1.5:1

③ **Debtors' collection period**

> Calculation: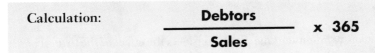

Purpose: to show the length of time (number of days) on average that it takes debtors to pay the firm. This ratio measures how efficiently the business collects its debts. Lee's collection period is $(25 \times 365)/400 = 22.8$ days.

❹ Creditors' collection period

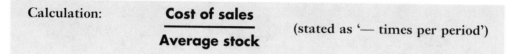

Calculation: $$\frac{\text{Creditors}}{\text{Purchases}} \times 365$$

Purpose: to calculate the average length of credit the firm receives from its suppliers. Lee receives $(20 \times 365)/290 = 25.2$ days.

ASSET EFFICIENCY

Managers wish to assess how efficiently the various assets of the firm are being utilised.

Asset efficiency ratios

❶ Rate of stock turnover

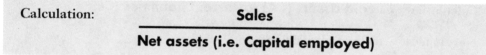

Calculation: $$\frac{\text{Cost of sales}}{\text{Average stock}}$$ (stated as '— times per period')

Purpose: to calculate how often in a period the firm 'turns over' (sells) its stock.

This ratio is also known as 'stockturn'. If the stockturn ratio is falling, the firm is taking longer to sell its stock: reasons include holding higher stock levels, or falling demand for the firm's products. Lee's stockturn is $300/50 =$ six times per annum, ie once every two months.

❷ Asset turnover

Calculation: $$\frac{\text{Sales}}{\text{Net assets (i.e. Capital employed)}}$$

Purpose: to assess the value of sales generated by the net assets (which represent the capital employed in the business).

To utilise assets more efficiently, managers will seek to increase sales volume, which in turn increases this ratio.

There is a relationship between this ratio and two others:

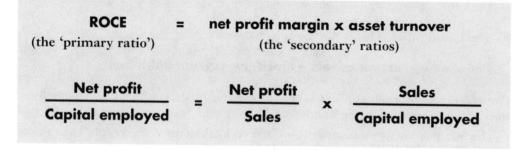

ROCE = net profit margin x asset turnover
(the 'primary ratio')   (the 'secondary' ratios)

$$\frac{\text{Net profit}}{\text{Capital employed}} = \frac{\text{Net profit}}{\text{Sales}} \times \frac{\text{Sales}}{\text{Capital employed}}$$

In Lee's case: $28.6 = 10 \times 2.86$

INVESTMENT

There are two groups of investment ratios. One group considers the effect of the firm's choice of capital; the other group concentrates on stock market investment analyses.

Gearing

1 Gearing ratio

Calculation:	**Prior charge capital** (long-term loans and preference share capital)
	Total long-term capital

Purpose: to compare how much long-term capital is provided by investors who are entitled to a return (interest and preference share dividend) before ordinary shareholders can receive a dividend.

Gearing is the first of two analyses based on the relationship between the different types of capital. Companies with more than 50 per cent prior charge capital are called 'high-geared'; those with less than 50 per cent 'low-geared'. An acceptable level of gearing varies between companies and countries (for example, Japanese companies tend to be more highly geared than UK companies). Higher gearing is also more acceptable in larger companies.

Gearing becomes important when additional capital is required. If the company is already highly geared it may find difficulty to obtain a further loan. A company may seek the advantages associated with high gearing (debt capital):

- it is cheaper
  - the return is fixed and therefore reduces in real terms with inflation
  - lenders are happier with a lower return because their investment is more secure
  - interest payments benefit from tax relief (dividends do not);
- control is retained (debt capital confers no voting rights).

The danger remains, however, that the company is in danger if it fails to earn enough to cover interest payments.

2 Interest cover

Calculation:	**Profit before interest and tax**
	Interest paid

Purpose: to see how much profit is absorbed by interest charges.

This ratio falls as interest payments increase: this would indicate that there is less profit for other purposes such as dividend payments. A ratio of little more than 1 shows that the company only just makes a profit after paying interest, and is therefore a risky investment. The minimum safe ratio is often stated as being 3:1.

3 Earnings per share (EPS)

Calculation:	**Profit after tax and interest**
	Number of ordinary shares

Purpose: to calculate the return on each ordinary share.

This is the first of the ratios linking to shares and the stock market. It shows the profit in terms of pence per share.

4 Price/earnings (P/E) ratio

Calculation:	**Market price per share**
	Earnings per share

Purpose: to compare current market value with EPS.

The P/E ratio shows the level of investor confidence in the company. It varies between companies because it is influenced by market expectations of company growth rate, and the industry within which the company operates.

⑤ Dividend yield

Calculation:

$$\frac{\textbf{Dividend per share}}{\textbf{Market price per share}}$$

Purpose: to relate dividends to the market price of the shares to give a truer indication of the return on investment.

⑥ Dividend cover

Calculation:

$$\frac{\textbf{Profit after interest, tax and preference dividend}}{\textbf{Ordinary dividend}}$$

Purpose: to indicate the likelihood that the company can continue paying the current level of ordinary share dividend.

KEY PERFORMANCE MEASURES		1996 52 weeks	1995 52 weeks	1994 53 weeks	1993 52 weeks	1992 52 weeks
Gross margin	$\frac{\text{Gross profit}}{\text{Turnover}}$	34.8%	35.1%	35.0%	34.7%	33.7%
Net margin	$\frac{\text{Operating profit}}{\text{Turnover}}$	13.1%	13.2%	13.1%	12.3%	11.7%
Profitability	$\frac{\text{Profit before tax}}{\text{Turnover}}$	13.8%	13.7%	13.1%	12.5%	11.4%
Earnings per share	$\frac{\text{Standard earnings}}{\text{Weighted average ordinary shares in issue}}$	23.3p	22.4p	20.9p	18.0p	13.5p
Dividend per share		11.4p	10.3p	9.2p	8.1p	7.1p
Dividend cover	$\frac{\text{Profit attributable to shareholders}}{\text{Dividends}}$	2.0	2.2	2.3	2.2	1.9
Return on equity	$\frac{\text{Profit after tax and minority interests}}{\text{Average shareholders' funds}}$	17.4%	17.8%	18.5%	17.8%	17.1%
Capital expenditure		£303.3m	£366.9m	£343.5m	£250.8m	£305.4m

Fig 6.8 Financial ratios: five year summary

Source: Marks and Spencer plc

6.3 MANAGEMENT ACCOUNTING

Managers require information in order to make sound financial judgements. Management accounting contributes some of this information. It consists of elements from financial accounting (such as the final accounts and their accompanying ratios), and the techniques of investment appraisal and cost accounting.

Financial accounting deals with **external influences** on the firm – notably debtors, creditors and shareholders – and gives an overall financial view of the business. The role of the management accountant is to provide an **internal analysis** of the firm's operations. To do this, the management accountant relies largely on cost accounting techniques.

COST ACCOUNTING

This includes 'the establishment of budgets, standard costs and actual costs of operations, processes, activities or products; and the analysis of variances, profitability or social use of funds' (Chartered Institute of Management Accountants, 1991). Cost accounting aims to answer questions such as:

- How profitable are the different products?
- What values do we place on stocks?
- What are the likely future costs of goods or operations?

Cost classification

Chapter 8 explains the different cost bases found in business (see page 202). Cost accounting distinguishes between

- **Direct costs**: those expenses which can be identified precisely with a product or a process.
- **Indirect costs**: those expenses (overheads) incurred in production but which cannot be traced directly to a product or process.

Direct costs are analysed into **materials, labour and expenses**. A car manufacturer has sheet steel and engine parts as direct materials, assembly-line operatives as direct labour, and the cost of transporting product-specific items (such as the engine parts) as direct expenses. Indirect costs for this manufacturer will include general supervisors' wages, and factory rent.

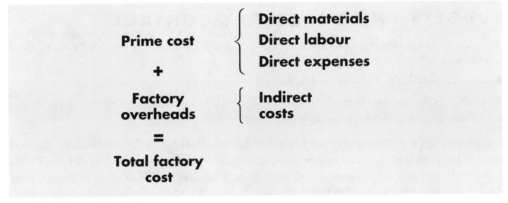

Fig. 6.9 *Elements of total factory cost*

These cost elements appear in the firm's manufacturing account. To the total factory cost will be added the 'office' costs which appear in the profit and loss account. These costs are classified under the following headings.

Administration	Financial	Selling and distribution
e.g. office staff salaries, office stationery.	e.g. discounts allowed to credit customers.	e.g. sales staff salaries, advertising, delivery costs.

Absorption costing

This is one of two key methods used in cost accounting (marginal costing, the other method, is outlined in Chapters 7 and 8: see pages 184 and 202). Absorption costing is based on classifying costs as direct or indirect. It attempts to charge the firm's indirect costs to its products or processes.

Allocation and apportionment Some overheads can be allocated completely to **cost centres** (areas of the firm such as a production or service department which are used to 'collect' costs). Other overheads have to be apportioned (shared) between the cost centres as fairly as possible.

Overheads which are apportioned include the following.

Overhead	Method of apportionment
● factory depreciation	apportioned between departments on the basis of their floor area
● rent	floor area
● heating	floor area, or volume
● insurance	book value of the assets
● canteen	number of employees

Reasons for absorption costing The reasons for carrying out absorption costing include:

- **Pricing decisions** Many firms calculate the full production cost and then add a mark-up percentage to obtain the selling price.
- **Comparing profitability** Managers seek to compare the relative profitability of different product lines.
- **Stock valuation** For the balance sheet and profit calculation (stock valuation is explained on page 205).

The weakness of this costing method is that apportionment is a **subjective method** of distributing costs. Different decisions regarding apportionment produce different total cost figures for the products.

BUDGETS AND BUDGETARY CONTROL

A budget is a plan expressed in money which relates to a defined time period. Budgets allow activities to be

- **co-ordinated:** through the master budget;
- **controlled:** by comparing actual performance with budgeted;
- **communicated:** through involving all staff in their creation.

Budget creation in smaller businesses is quick and informal. In larger firms it becomes a formal process through the work of **budget committees** – who oversee budget creation and co-ordinate the completed budgets – and the use of a **budget manual**, a written record of procedures and individual responsibilities.

Budgets are prepared for each major function or activity of the firm. Fig. 6.10 summarises the main budgets, in their approximate order of creation.

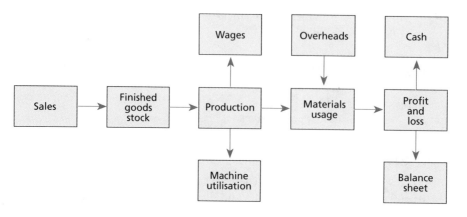

Fig. 6.10 The main budgets

The principal budget factor This is also called the 'limiting budget factor' and represents the item which limits the firm's activities. The most common principal budget factor is the level of demand for the products: other examples include the amount of skilled labour available, machine capacity, and raw material availability.

Budget preparation

A budgeted profit and loss account is prepared from a range of functional budgets, which include the following.

Sales budget Sales units and total value are calculated on the basis of past sales levels, current market research, and an estimate of the expected competition.

Production budget This is based on the sales budget, adjusted for the budgeted change in stock (from the finished goods stock budget).

Production resources budgets Budgeted production is analysed into requirements for:
● materials – the materials usage budget;
● labour – the wages budget;
● machine operating hours – the machine utilisation budget.

Overhead budgets Assessment of the total production overhead, selling overhead, administration overhead and research and development overhead takes place. Each of these overhead categories has its own budget.

Cash and other budgets The above budgets are incorporated into the budgeted profit and loss account. The main additional budget is the cash budget. This is prepared to summarise anticipated cash receipts and payments over the budget period. Cash receipts are based on the sales budget, adjusting it to account for the expected credit periods allowed to debtors. Other receipts such as the budgeted sale of fixed assets or an expected capital issue are also included.

Budgeted outflows of cash can be identified from other budgets, which are again adjusted for any credit periods involved. These include payments for labour (from the wages budget), materials (materials usage and production budgets) and other expenses (e.g. the various overhead budgets). Capital expenditure is also included (see the fixed assets budget below). The firm can see from its budgeted cashflow whether it will have surplus funds for investment, or a shortage of funds: in the latter case it can plan its borrowing requirements.

Additional budgets include
● **Working capital budget**: budgeted changes in debtors and creditors (cash and stock budgets already exist).
● **Fixed assets budget**: for new assets needed in the budget period.

The budgeted balance sheet can now be drawn up which forms, with the cash and profit and loss budgets, part of the firm's **master budget**.

Budgetary control

Once budgets have been established and implemented, managers can compare the **actual performance** of their department or function with its **budgeted performance**. Control takes place through the principle of **management by exception**.

Variance analysis 'Management by exception' is based on comparing expected with actual. In budgeting this means:

● **comparing actual performance with budgeted performance**
● **calculating any differences**
● **establishing reasons for these differences**

Differences are called 'variances', which can be:
● **favourable** – e.g. where actual sales exceed budgeted or where a particular cost comes in under budget;

● **adverse** (unfavourable) – actual sales do not reach budgeted targets, or an actual cost exceeds its budgeted level.

As an example, a favourable sales variance overall might consist of both a favourable volume variance (more are sold than had been planned) and an adverse price variance (the actual selling price is lower than budget – which partly explains the favourable volume variance).

Some variances are due to factors which are **controllable** by the manager. In the example above, the sales manager may have made the decision to lower prices and increase volume: the product's price elasticity of demand has led to an increase in total revenue. Other variances are not under the control of managers: for example, a national pay agreement outside the firm's control could have an adverse effect on its wages budget.

Budgets and variances are also adjusted for changes in volume. Comparing production budget figures based on an expected output of, say, 3,000 units with the actual production costs of making 3,500 units is not comparing like with like: the budgeted costs have to be scaled accordingly and these new budgeted figures are then compared with the actual costs.

Standard costing

A 'standard cost' is a cost estimated by managers from information on expected prices and efficiency levels of production. Like budgets, standard costs provide **targets** for managers against which their individual performances can be judged.

Standard costing is therefore another control technique comparing actual against a predetermined target (the standard cost) to produce variances. It is linked with budgetary control: for example, it is easy to establish sales and production budgets once standard costs have been set.

Variance analysis in standard costing explains the difference between actual and expected results. There are three main variance groups.

Sales variances The **sales price** variance measures the difference between the standard and actual selling prices. The **sales volume** variance measures the effect on profit of the difference between the actual and expected numbers sold.

Production cost variances Total cost variances are calculated for direct labour, direct materials, and production overheads. Each of these variances is subdivided to show variances in both 'price' and 'quantity'.

Direct labour	Calculations:
A rate variance based on the difference between actual and standard pay.	**(standard – actual rate) x actual hours worked**
An efficiency variance based on whether output is above or below standard.	**(standard – actual hours) x standard hourly rate**
Direct Materials	Calculations:
A price variance based on the difference between actual and standard unit prices.	**(standard – actual price) x actual quantity**
A usage variance based on the difference between actual and standard quantities.	**(standard – actual quantity) x standard price**
Production overheads	
Variances based on differences between expected and actual volumes of use, efficiency, and expenditure.	

Other cost variances These include marketing cost variances and administrative cost variances.

Chapter roundup

Chapter 6 has concentrated on the importance of the accounting function. It has explained and illustrated how accounting creates and summarises financial records from various source documents. Once this information is obtained, it is analysed using appropriate ratios. The chapter has shown how these ratios and other accounting techniques, such as budgetary control and standard costing, concentrate not only on present but also on future events, to allow accurate forecasts to be made.

Illustrative questions

1 A business purchases a fixed asset for £400,000. This has a useful life of five years and a residual value of £80,000. By what amount will this asset be depreciated annually if the company uses the straight line method of depreciation?　(3)

AEB

Tutorial note

You have to recall the formula for straight line: there should be no confusion with reducing balance (there is no % figure for writing down in the question). Do show your workings: if you make an error in calculation you can still receive some marks for using the right approach.

Suggested answer

Cost to be written off = £400,000 − £80,000 = £320.000

Useful life of 5 years

$$\text{Annual depreciation} = \frac{£320,000}{5} = £64,000$$

2 (a) What factors cause cash flow problems?　(5)

(b) Outline **two** ways in which a business might overcome these problems. State **one** drawback associated with each.　(8)

Tutorial note

A 'textbook' answer is required here. Part (a) does not tell us the number of reasons required: three, with basic explanations, should be sufficient. Each answer to part (b) should consist of a named method, a brief description of the method, and a stated drawback.

Suggested answer

(a) Reasons include: increased delay by debtors in repayment, thereby slowing down receipt of cash and leading to a lack of working capital; creditors are being paid earlier than before or earlier than necessary, reducing cash levels; more cash than necessary is tied up in stocks.

(b) A firm might decide to sell its debts to a factor (finance house): this provides quick cash, but the full debt is not received by the firm (the factor charges for the service). Secondly, the firm might try to use suppliers' (trade) credit to a greater extent, extending the credit period taken from creditors: the drawback is that this might affect trading conditions (e.g. eventual withdrawal of credit by supplier) and the firm's reputation. (Other areas include borrowing, improved budgeting/budgetary control, sale and leaseback or disposal of surplus assets.)

3 (a) Outline the various parties who are likely to be interested in the published accounts of a PLC. (8)

(b) Explain the ways in which accounting may be of use to the managers of a company producing soft drinks. (12)

WJEC

Tutorial note

In answering (a), your answer should include 'shareholders' since we are referring to a limited company. Part (b) can be approached not only from accounting, but also by including key management terms such as planning, control and communication.

Suggested answer

(a) The parties include the following, together with their main reason(s) for interest: shareholders (levels of profit, share prices), employees (job security, possible profit-sharing schemes), creditors (recovery of money), long-term lenders such as banks (ability to pay interest, likelihood of recovering money loaned), tax authorities (tax due), competitors (indication of financial stability), potential buyers (realistic share value?).

(b) Any organisation needs to keep control of its finances. The accounting function records the movement of cash and value (through bookkeeping); by doing so, the firm can implement its own security systems. Also, through the use of standard costing and budgetary control, costs of manufacturing the drinks are identified and prices can be set using a 'cost-plus' approach. The firm can calculate whether it is better to 'buy in' items such as bottles, or whether it makes financial sense to make them on the premises. Credit control systems – used by the firm to monitor its debtors when selling soft drinks on credit – can also be established. Any variations (variances) are brought to the attention of managers, which is known as management by exception. As well as future planning, ratio analysis of past accounts enables management to identify key areas for action.

An efficient accounting function will enable management to plan ahead, for example through budgeting; to co-ordinate its various functions through meetings to discuss budget levels; to communicate financial performance and achievement; and, by doing so, to motivate staff through involvement in these processes.

4 This question is specifically about the appraisal of the performance of supermarkets using their published accounts. You will be expected to include knowledge relevant to business accounts and the changing retail market in your answers.

Figure 1 is an extract from a spreadsheet file called 'plc ACCTS' that was used by a firm of financial advisers to assess the viability of investing clients' money on the Stock Exchange. This part of the file contains a summary of the published company accounts of Iceland plc, Sainsbury plc and Tesco plc for 1992.

Action required

(i) Use the information in Figure 1 to produce a detailed ratio analysis of the companies' accounts. (8)

(ii) Incorporate the most important of these into a report which **evaluates**, *with qualifications*, which of the three businesses would have been the 'better' company in which to invest. (24)

(iii) Explain how the use of information technology could have helped you with this exercise. (8)

Figure 1 *Summary of the published company accounts of Iceland, Sainsbury and Tesco*

	Iceland	Sainsbury	Tesco
PROFIT AND LOSS ACCOUNT (£'000s)			
Sales Turnover	1,037,277	8,695,500	7,097,400
Gross Profit	96,745	870,500	661,500
Net Profit after Taxation	39,874	438,200	395,600
Earnings per share	41.31p	25.43p	19.95p
Dividend per share	10.00p	8.75p	6.30p
BALANCE SHEET (£'000s)			
Fixed Assets	306,752	3,861,100	3,552,000
Current Assets*	114,573	843,800	600,300
Current Liabilities	193,734	1,468,200	1,003,500
Net Assets (Capital) Employed	161,972	2,640,900	2,447,000
*Stocks	66,806	362,200	221,700
Debtors	29,341	80,800	39,600
Cash at Bank	18,426	173,900	38,300

London Examinations

Tutorial note

The ratios are not identified for you: the examiner will expect you to concentrate on liquidity and profitability ratios. In such questions it is usually important to mention that ratios are not the complete answer when analysing the strengths and weaknesses of a firm.

Suggested answer

(i)

Ratios	Iceland	Sainsbury	Tesco
Gross Profit %	9.3	10.0	9.3
Net Profit %	3.8	5.0	5.6
Return on Net Assets (Capital Employed)	24.6	16.6	16.2
Working Capital ratio	0.59:1	0.57:1	0.60:1
Quick Assets ratio	0.25:1	0.17:1	0.08:1

(ii) Profitability ratios based on turnover indicate that Tesco is particularly efficient at controlling its administrative and distribution costs (9.3 − 5.6 = 3.7% expenses as a percentage of sales; Sainsbury is 5% and Iceland 5.5%). Tesco also has the highest NP margin of 5.6p in the £ sales, which suggests that in any price war (reduced prices cut into profit margins) it will be extremely price-competitive.

Profitability ratios based on investment suggest that Iceland is the most efficient at generating profit from its resources: it has virtually a 25p in the £ return on its net assets. Tesco has the lowest return of 16p in the £, which might suggest to potential investors that greater returns may be made elsewhere. This is supported by the calculations given in Figure 1; earnings per share and dividends per share, at 41.3p and 10p respectively, are highest for Iceland and lowest for Tesco.

In liquidity terms, all companies have seemingly low ratios: for example, the working capital ratios are all about 0.6 to 1. The retail industry normally has low ratios due to the relative lack of debtors and the extremely quick turnover of stock (which generates the cash needed to remain in business). Tesco has the lowest Quick Assets ratio, at 0.08 to 1: in one sense, the lower the Quick Assets ratio the better, because the company is 'working' with other people's (i.e. creditors') cash, although for a smaller firm this would be extremely dangerous.

In summary, an investor will apparently receive the highest return from Iceland, although the earnings and dividend per share information is incomplete (for example, we need to know share prices, to calculate the P/E ratios). Furthermore, the accounts for a number of years should be available to make more meaningful judgements, and we should acknowledge that ratios of past performance are no guarantee of future success. Finally, ratio analysis is only one area of analysis that an interested investor should consider: there are many other financial and non-financial factors such as the age of the company assets and the state of its technological development, that need to be taken into account. For the investor more interested in the longer term, perhaps Tesco, with its greatest efficiency on expenses and its highest NP%, might be the best buy.

(iii) Using information technology could have helped calculate the relevant ratios, for instance by using a spreadsheet. The basic rules of arithmetic are applied: for example, to calculate NP percentage, if the Iceland column in Figure 1 is column D, and Iceland sales are in row 7 and its net profit in row 9, we would enter (in cell D10) the formula 'D9*100/D7'. This formula calculates the percentage net profit, and it could be replicated (copied) into cells E10 and F10 for Sainsbury and Tesco respectively. The spreadsheet can also produce visual displays (e.g. comparative graphs) of the information. For comparative figures, a database package can be used to store previous years' information; and a word-processing package can be used to generate reports.

Practice questions

1   A company's annual sales are £16.5m and cost of goods is £11m. Average stock is £550,000. Calculate the stock turnover ratio.   (2)

Pitfalls

One common error is to divide average stock into the sales figure and not cost of sales. You must remember to express the answer as 'times' and not as a percentage figure.

Key points

£11,000,000/£550,000 = 20 times per annum.

2   Limited companies are obliged to produce a:
Profit and Loss Account;
Balance Sheet;
Cash Flow Statement.

Describe the purpose of each, and state why all three are required for a full assessment of company performance.

Pitfalls

Examiners' reports often point out that candidates simply include a list of ratios and possible data users, and fail to explain why each document, on its own, gives an incomplete picture of the company's performance.

Key points

Profit and loss: historical statement of revenues and expenses which calculates net profit (gross profit calculated in trading account).

Balance sheet: historical statement of what a firm owns (assets) and what it owes (liabilities): i.e. a financial summary as at a point in time.

Cash flow: statement of cash receipts and payments during the period.

On its own, each gives an incomplete picture of a firm's position. Various parties wish to assess a firm's liquidity, profitability and the use of assets; each document only tells part of the story. As an example, the profit and loss account states net profit: profitability is assessed when this is compared against capital employed (found in the balance sheet).

3 Fowles Ltd are a boat building firm. The top part of their balance sheet as at 31 December 1994 is shown.

FOWLES LTD BALANCE SHEET (PART) AS AT 31.12.1994

	£	£
FIXED ASSETS	1,500,000	
Depreciation	300,000	1,200,000
CURRENT ASSETS		
Stock	300,000	
Debtors	150,000	
Cash	100,000	550,000
CURRENT LIABILITIES		
Creditors	150,000	
Tax payable	300,000	450,000
NET CURRENT ASSETS		100,000

(a) The company accountant forecasts the following during the coming half year.

	Jan	Feb	Mar	Apr	May	June
SALES £	120,000	600,000	600,000	120,000	120,000	120,000
MATERIALS £	90,000	90,000	90,000	90,000	90,000	90,000

Sales on one month's credit, materials on two months' credit.

Debtors from 1994 will have paid by 31 January; creditors on two months' credit.

Operating overheads at £30,000 paid each month.

Wages are paid in cash at £90,000 per month.

Tax is payable in March.

(i) Prepare a monthly cash flow forecast for Fowles Ltd from January to June 1995. Include a cash balance for each month. (9)

(ii) Give one recommendation regarding cash flow you would make to the Board of Fowles Ltd. State your reasons. (2)

(b) Explain the purpose of depreciation and how it affects company accounts. (4)

(c) Fowles are considering spending £400,000 on some specialist equipment. Discuss financial methods of appraisal the company could use when evaluating this investment problem. (5)

Cambridge

Pitfalls

We have the normal problem of identifying when the cash movement takes place. The awkward items are sales (one month's delay) and purchases (two months).

Key points

(a) (i)

	Jan	Feb	Mar	Apr	May	June
Receipts (£000):						
from debtors	150	120	600	600	120	120
Payments (£000):						
to creditors	75	75	90	90	90	90
overheads	30	30	30	30	30	30
wages	90	90	90	90	90	90
tax			300			
Net cash inflow (outflow)	(45)	(75)	90	390	(90)	(90)
Opening cash balance	100	55	(20)	70	460	370
Closing cash balance	55	(20)	70	460	370	280

(ii) One recommendation: a very uneven cash flow, so plan for short-term investment of large surpluses from April.

(b) Its purpose is to adjust fixed asset values to a more accurate one than original cost, and to spread the cost of the asset over its useful life. It reduces profit and reduces the stated fixed asset value.

(c) Popular methods (see Chapter 10) include Discounted Cash Flow, Return on Investment, and Payback.

4 A company's balance sheet reads as follows:

	£	£	£
Fixed assets (net of depreciation)			40,000
Current assets			
stock	8,000		
debtors	10,000	18,000	
Current liabilities			
creditors	20,000		
overdraft	20,000	(40,000)	(22,000)
			18,000
Financed by			
Share capital (£1 ordinary shares)			50,000
Reserves			(32,000)
			18,000

(a) What is meant by
   (i) 'fixed assets (net of depreciation)'?
   (ii) reserves (32,000)?

(b) Using appropriate ratios, analyse the financial situation of the company.

(c) Some companies now include their brand names in their accounts. Explain why this is the case.

(d) How can shareholders influence the actions of their company? (20)

NEAB

Pitfalls

Part (a) (ii) is difficult, since reserves are shown in brackets (i.e. a negative figure). Always check each figure carefully to see whether the question shows it as negative. Also note that, for (b), profitability ratios (e.g. NP%, return on capital) cannot be calculated.

Key points

(a) (i) The net book value of the long-term assets owned by the company (e.g. furniture, equipment).

  (ii) Reserves are undistributed profits: in this case, however, the company has distributed more profit than it has made.

(b) Working capital = 18,000:40,000 = 0.45:1
Quick Assets = (18,000 – 8,000) 10,000:40,000 = 0.25:1

  From a liquidity viewpoint, the company seems to be in difficulties. Also, negative reserves suggest financial problems.

(c) Inclusion of brand names reinforces identity of the company and the brand. There may also be analysis and comment regarding the financial performance of individual brands.

(d) By voting (assuming they have a vote) and speaking at general meetings; by calling an extraordinary general meeting (if sufficiently high percentage); by letters/contacting the media; by selling their shares.

5 (a) What is a business budget?   (4)

  (b) How are budgets used to assist the control (that is to say, monitoring and review) function of management?   (6)

  (c) Discuss the advantages and disadvantages of using ratio analysis as a means of assessing company performance. Give examples.   (15)

SEB

Pitfalls

The question suddenly switches from budgeting to ratio analysis. When answering (c), we need to explain clearly that ratio analysis is on past information.

Key points

(a) A plan, expressed in monetary terms, relating to a future time period.

(b) Since a budget is a forecast, the actual performance of the firm can be compared to this forecast; a variance can be calculated and analysed (management by exception).

(c) Ratios can be used to give objective measures of company performance, and to summarise detailed and specialist information for non-specialist managers; e.g. return on capital employed, stockturn. They are limited in that they only measure the firm's financial performance (e.g. NP margin) and ignore other aspects such as product age, competitor performance in the market place (though competitors' ratios can be used for comparison). They also look at past events and are of limited value only for future projections (though future problems with cash flow, for example, can be seen from ratio analysis).

MARKETING

Units in this chapter

Chapter objectives

Chapter 7 is devoted to the role of the marketing function in modern business. It explains why more and more firms are becoming market-oriented in outlook, and how they examine potential markets before undertaking production. The 'marketing mix' ingredients of product, price, place and promotion are also explained.

There are close links between Chapter 7 and other chapters in the Guide. Market supply and demand (Chapter 1) provides the background to market price and the firm's pricing policy. External factors such as government and European Union policies, social and demographic trends, technological influences, and consumer law (all in Chapter 4) influence the work of a typical Marketing Department.

The key topics and concepts covered in this chapter are:

- the marketing concept;
- markets;
- segmentation;
- market research;
- product;
- price;
- place;
- promotion.

7.1 MARKETING AND MARKETS

THE MARKETING CONCEPT

If firms are to survive and be successful, research and development of new products cannot be limited solely to the influence of production: the activity needs to take on the role of studying the market and the consumer. Marketing looks at the firm and its activities through the eyes of its customers. The basis of the 'marketing concept' is that the customer is seen as the start of a business cycle, not as its end. Fig. 7.1 shows how the marketing concept influences this business cycle.

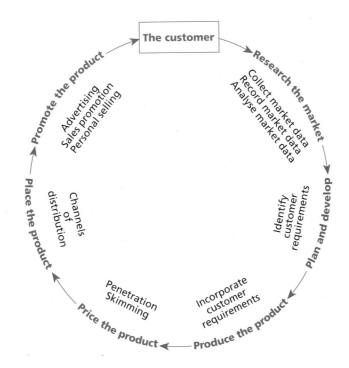

The customer

Research the market
Collect market data
Record market data
Analyse market data

Promote the product
Advertising
Sales promotion
Personal selling

Identify customer requirements

Plan and develop

Place the product

Channels of distribution

Penetration
Skimming

Incorporate customer requirements

Produce the product

Price the product

Fig. 7.1 Marketing influence on the business cycle

The traditional production-led approach to manufacturing focused on the product. It would be made using processes which were heavily cost-influenced, and the end product tended to be standardised. The firm would then place the product on the market and expect it to sell.

A criticism made of IBM during its difficulties in the 1990s (see page 86) was that it had remained technology-oriented, rather than market-oriented: key business decisions were dictated by technology, with sales staff selling to DP users – the technologists – compared with other computer firms selling smaller PC machines and software to end-users who were not technologists. As computers reduced in size, they had become commodities, less important than their software, and the market-oriented approaches of IBM's competitors acknowledged this by concentrating more on the software.

A marketing-led approach involves analysing the market and then making what the market appears to want: it seeks to differentiate products on the basis of market requirements. Production methods and processes are still important, and costs influence what is made and how it is made, but the emphasis remains on the **consumer** and the **market**.

The role of marketing

The marketing function plays three key roles within any organisation.

1 It supports and encourages the process of exchange through **techniques aimed at the consumer**.

2 It **collects and analyses data** on both the consumer and the market.

3 It acts as a **co-ordinating function** for the organisation through the action of the marketing concept.

The marketing function is often seen as the most important co-ordinating or integrating force in an organisation. It is the one function which looks outwards from the firm: the information it collects on external markets and consumers is then disseminated throughout the other functions.

MARKETS

Chapter 1 explained that economists regard a market as the place where buyers and sellers determine price. Markets can be local (a street market), national (the UK labour market) or international (the capital market).

The term 'market' in a marketing context refers to people and/or businesses having a need or a desire for the firm's product. Marketing classifies markets as 'consumer' or 'industrial'.

Consumer and industrial markets

Consumer markets exist for consumer goods and services, products which are bought for their own satisfaction. There are three main types of consumer goods.

❶ **Single-use consumer goods** such as food and fuel have a short life and are normally income-inelastic: often referred to as FMCGs ('fast-moving consumer goods'), they are bought to satisfy physical needs (food and medicines), psychological needs (cosmetics and 'fashion' clothes), or on impulse (magazines and sweets).

❷ **Consumer durables** such as video recorders, televisions and some clothing are longer-lasting and more expensive goods: they are carefully planned purchases which are bought infrequently and which have an income-elastic demand.

❸ **Consumer services** such as hairdressers and plumbers are used more frequently as income grows, and are associated with satisfying physical (eg personal appearance) and safety (e.g. house repair) needs.

Industrial markets consist of products used by industries in making their own products. There are:

- capital goods, e.g. new premises and equipment
- industrial consumables, e.g. fuel and stationery
- industrial services, e.g. cleaning, printing, distribution.

	Consumer markets	Industrial markets
Customers	Many: allowing price to be set by firm	Few: firm negotiates price and terms with customer
Channel	Through wholesalers and retailers	Usually direct to customer
Product	More standardised: differentiation does take place	More personalised: may be made to end user's specific requirements
Methods	Resources concentrated on advertising: mass media widely used	Less generalised: more personal selling and use of specialist journals

MARKET SEGMENTATION

Segmenting a market involves dividing it into distinct subgroups. This can be achieved using either the product or the consumer as the basis for segmentation: the product or consumer characteristics in one segment must differ from the characteristics in other segments. The tasks of the marketing function are to:

❶ identify segments which are economically viable;

❷ position the firm's products in the identified segments; and

❸ target the relevant consumers in the segments.

SEGMENTING THE MARKET

A major part of Lloyds Bank's business is providing services to other businesses. The financial needs of these corporate customers change as they themselves expand and develop, and so the Bank has organised itself to deliver services tailored to meet the requirements of businesses grouped by size as follows:

Small Businesses

For smaller businesses (annual turnover up to £1m.) the Bank has a network of some 350 Business Centres based in key branches in the UK, whose staff are specially trained to cater for their needs. A Business Starter Pack is provided for those setting up in business for the first time, and a Small Business Guide is available covering the many aspects of day to day business management.

Medium Sized Companies

For medium sized companies, Lloyds Bank Commercial Service has the expertise and experience to provide rapid solutions to the problems of business customers.

Dedicated relationship managers are ready to work alongside customers to the same end: the success of the business. This means that they visit companies to ensure a full understanding of the operation and banking needs – as well as saving customers' valuable time.

The national team of Commercial Service bankers have access to the full range of services available from Lloyds Bank. By understanding the business they are able to provide a service tailored to the customers' individual needs. Their expertise has been earned where it counts – serving business customers.

Larger Companies

For larger companies, which include major multi-national corporations whose activities typically have an international dimension, there are account teams who specialise in different sectors of industry. They work closely with other areas of the Bank and co-ordinate delivery and marketing of all types of domestic, international and electronic banking services, which meet the needs of the customer.

Source: Lloyds Bank plc

Firms which concentrate on small market segments – the Tie Rack and Sock Shop chains in clothing are good illustrations – are carrying out **niche marketing**. This involves creating a known name and image, and establishing a specific position in the market. Problems associated with niche marketing are based on arguments of scale and specialisation.

- The firm may have to remain small because overheads need to be kept low – if competitors can benefit from economies of scale, they will be strongly price-competitive.

- The firm is at risk due to the lack of diversification – the single-product or 'niche' approach depends for its success on consumer demand levels and tastes remaining at least constant.

Consumer characteristics

Consumers are often segmented according to the following characteristics:

Age (demographic factors) People's propensity to save or spend, and their buying habits, change as they grow older – e.g. banks segment their consumers by targeting both young (school leavers for new current accounts) and old (pension and savings schemes).

STUDENT BARCLAYCARD

If you're aged 18 or over you can apply for a Student Barclaycard. If your application is accepted, Barclaycard is issued free of charge for you as long as you're in full-time higher education.

Barclaycard can help you manage your money by offering you a £250 credit limit with up to eight weeks' interest-free credit. This credit facility can help you bridge gaps between terms and cope with unexpected expenses. Barclaycard is useful for travelling too. You can use it wherever you see the VISA sign, at over ten million outlets worldwide and at over 425,000 places in the UK.

Barclaycard also offers Purchase Cover, Barclaycard International Rescue and Barclaycard Holiday Club.

If your application for a Barclaycard is successful you get a free gift.

STUDENT INSURANCE

Barclay offers a tailor-made policy for students underwritten by Norwich Union, one of the leading UK insurers.

Special low rates apply for students in halls of residence.

YOUNG SAVERS

The Junior BarclayPlus account is a fun way to start saving for the under elevens who have £1 or more to save.

BarclayPlus is a savings account for young people aged 11–16.

RETIREMENT: THE FACTS

Service.	A package of services specially selected to meet the needs of people of retirement age.
Who is it for?	People about to retire, or those who have retired.
Advantages.	Free banking, investment and pensions advice and a wide range of other services to help you make the most of your money.

Fig. 7.2 Age-based segmentation by Barclays

Source: Barclays Bank plc

Sex   There are gender-influenced products such as cosmetics. Some products might be targeted at one sex: this can be linked to age, socio-economic or other factors, e.g. mothers with young children being targeted by manufacturers and advertisers of small 'supermini' hatchback cars.

Socio-economic status   Advertisers use a lettered scale to summarise occupational and social class groupings.

Social group code	Social category	Illustrative occupation	Percentage of population
A	Upper middle class	Professional, senior managerial	4
B	Middle class	Managerial	10
C1	Lower middle class	Supervisory, clerical	22
C2	Skilled working class	Skilled manual	32
D	Working class	Unskilled manual	22
E	Other	Students, unemployed, pensioners	10

This system identifies consumer groups by income and other characteristics such as education and leisure interests. It provides basic market segmentation information, e.g. for newspaper proprietors when targeting their readership: picture-based tabloid papers such as the *Daily Mirror*, more 'middle-class' tabloids like the *Daily Mail*, and broadsheet 'qualities' such as the *Guardian* are believed to represent different socio-economic groups. It also influences advertisers in these newspapers, who must ensure that the paper's target readership correlates with the advertiser's targeted segment.

Geographical factors Income, tastes and leisure interests vary between the UK's regions. For example, on average in 1992:

- households in Northern Ireland spent £5 per week on hotels and holidays, less than half the UK average of £11;
- families in East Anglia spent £4.20 a week on their pets compared with £1.61 in the North of England;
- Scots spent £7.40 per week on tobacco, compared with £4.50 in the South East of England.

REGIONS	Car	Central heating	Washing machine	Fridge/ fridge-freezer	Freezer or fridge-freezer	TV	Cable TV	Phone	Video	Computer	Second home
1. North	60	92	91	99	81	98	6	80	69	15	3
2. Yorks and Humber	61	71	88	99	81	98	8	87	70	19	3
3. North West	62	75	88	99	83	99	12	87	70	18	3
4. East Midlands	77	84	93	100	87	98	10	90	74	21	3
5. West Midlands	69	79	88	99	83	99	9	88	74	19	3
6. East Anglia	76	86	91	100	87	99	13	92	68	17	4
7. South East	71	86	85	99	86	98	10	92	70	22	5
8. South West	78	80	87	99	83	98	6	90	68	19	5
9. Scotland	57	82	91	99	77	99	9	85	65	15	1
10. Northern Ireland	63	84	92	99	70	98	4	83	55	9	2
All regions	68	82	88	99	83	98	9	88	69	19	3

Fig. 7.3 Ownership of consumer durable goods

Source: Family Spending Survey, 1992, ONS

Fig. 7.3 illustrates the differences in the regional ownership of certain durable goods. Such differences allow advertisers and producers to target by region as well as by country.

Neighbourhood analysis The ACORN – A Classification Of Residential Neighbourhoods – system analyses residential areas into a number of groups. These groups reflect expected buying habits for the given neighbourhood type. This information is recorded using postcodes, and can be used for techniques such as direct marketing.

Psychographic profiling 'Lifestyle' profiles are based on segmenting consumers and products (which may be designed specifically for certain types of lifestyle). Examples include varying clothing and car styles: for example a hatchback can be differentiated according to factors such as engine size, power and styling, and then aimed at two different market segments – young male drivers, and families with young children.

Fig 7.4 summarises what we look for when we buy a car. It illustrates how cars can be differentiated by factors such as body styling and safety features, and then aimed by the manufacturer at different market segments, for example, safety features may be promoted in order to appeal to families with young children; the styling and accessories of a different model may be selected to have more appeal to young single drivers. Such analysis also allows the manufacturer to direct advertising and promotion to other forms of segmentation, e.g. on the basis of consumer geographical location (whether the cars are to be sold in the UK or the rest of Europe, with their different influences on car purchase).

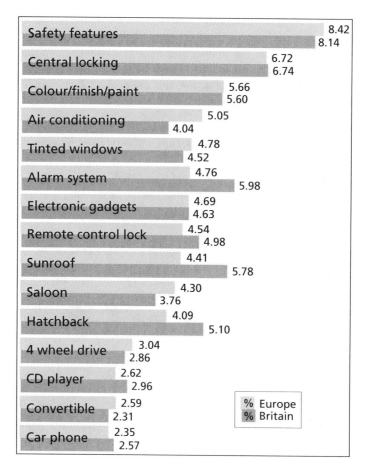

Fig. 7.4 Influences on buying a car

Source: Press Association

7.2 SOURCES OF INFORMATION

Consumers are one of the categories about which firms need information. Consumer habits and spending patterns are analysed. Products, markets and the firm itself are other categories about which information is required.

RESEARCHING THE FIRM AND ITS PRODUCTS

All firms need to reflect upon and analyse their position, and that of their products, in the market-place. They are interested in their

- **past performance**: sales and market share for each product;
- **present position**: the different market segments where they operate, and levels of customer satisfaction;
- **likely future situation**: future sales and market share, and product development.

Two well-known techniques are used to analyse past, present and future market performance.

SWOT analysis

This is used to identify the firm's

- strengths (S);

- weaknesses (W);
- opportunities (O);
- threats (T).

Strengths and weaknesses are mainly **internal** to the firm; opportunities and threats are essentially **external**. As an example, a company producing garden sheds which is planning to diversify into the manufacture of greenhouses might find its SWOT analysis identifies the following factors:

- (S): existing contacts/outlets; a known trade name; a reputation for a quality product; existing suppliers for glass (shed windows); a competent and contented workforce.
- (W): lack of labour with suitable skills; no experience in producing glass-based products; no specific knowledge of the market for greenhouses; limited capital for purchase of equipment required.
- (O): expand the capital base through new share issue; diversify to spread risk; reduce the seasonal effect of shed sales and production by making a product with a different seasonal peak; there is no local or regional competitor supplying greenhouses.
- (T): most competitors operate nationally – difficult for the firm to compete on cost (fewer economies of scale); uncertainty of the climate (seasonal and long-term) affecting levels of demand.

The firm's marketing strategy is influenced by this analysis, assuming the decision is taken to manufacture the new product.

The Boston growth and market share matrix

'Boston Box' analysis is suitable for larger companies with a wide product range. It groups the products under four headings.

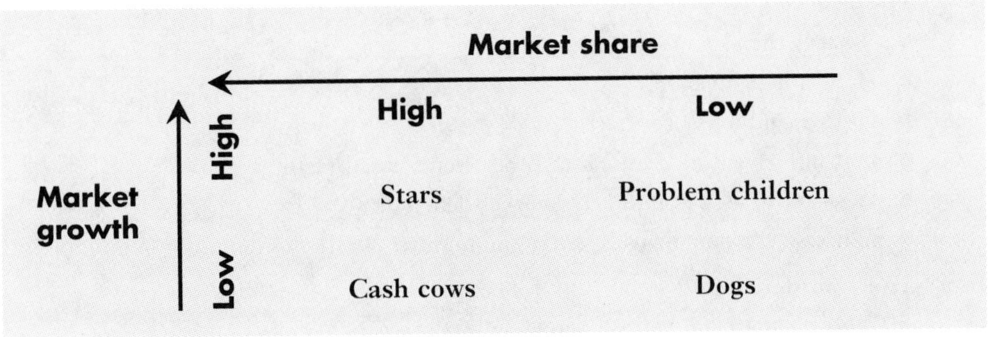

Fig. 7.5 Boston Box analysis

Products are grouped on the basis of their market share, probable market growth, and the stage they are at in their product life-cycle (see page 178).

- 'Stars' are potentially highly profitable, requiring large investment for development and promotion: this should result in a large market share and development of the product into a 'cash cow'.
- 'Problem children' also require large investment, but are in a market segment which might suffer low growth: they may plug a hole in the firm's product range (to prevent competitors from entering the segment) but if not disposed of, they can turn into either 'stars' or 'dogs'.
- 'Cash cows' form the basis of the firm's profits and sales: the firm continues to invest enough in them to retain market share, and they help finance development of 'stars', but if not managed properly they risk becoming 'dogs'.
- 'Dogs' are heavy users of resources, but remain unprofitable: the firm will divest itself of these unless there is a chance of making them profitable, or they are being held for strategic reasons (e.g. to maintain market share against competitor penetration).

The Boston Box technique should not be seen as a one-off approach to product analysis. Product status will change over time as (for example) market demand falls and additional promotion is needed. It illustrates the importance to larger companies of having a balanced product portfolio.

MARKET RESEARCH

The purpose of market research is to obtain information on market conditions for the firm's products, both new and existing. It concentrates on three areas.

1 The Product
- Who buys it?
- How often do they buy?
- What point is it at in the life-cycle?
- How can its life be extended?
- How does it fit into the portfolio?
- Can it be improved?
- Is its price competitive?
- How effective is its – promotion?
  - distribution?

(For a new product):
- How should it be – tested?
  - packaged?
  - launched?

2 The Market
- What is the size of the total market?
- How is it segmented?
- Is it expanding or contracting?
- Is it influenced by seasonal or other trend-based factors?
- What other factors influence market demand?
- Is it easy for new firms to enter the market?

3 The Competition
- Who are the main competitors?
- What are their – pricing policies?
  - promotion policies?
- How do they compete in the different segments?
- What are their strengths and weaknesses?

Market research varies according to the purpose and type of research undertaken, and the results generated by the research. The 'seven Os' of market research are as follows.

● **Occupants**	Who are in the market (customers)?
● **Opposition**	Who are in the market (competitors)?
● **Objects**	What do the consumers buy?
● **Occasions**	How frequently do the consumers buy?
● **Organisation**	Who is involved in the buying decision?
● **Objectives**	Why do they buy?
● **Operations**	How do they buy (which distribution channels)?

The purpose of the research The purpose of carrying out research may be to obtain either quantitative or qualitative data.

Quantitative research	**Qualitative research**
concentrates on factual information (e.g. units sold, % of total market share)	concentrates on attitudes and opinions (consumer tastes, likes and dislikes)

The type of research

This varies according to whether the techniques used in the research are 'field' or 'desk'-based.

Field research This is also known as **primary** research, because original data are obtained. Various techniques are used to obtain primary data.

- **Questionnaires:** designed specifically for the task and completed face-to-face, by telephone or by postal surveys.

- **Test marketing:** a potential new product is marketed regionally to gauge reaction to it, before committing the firm to mass production and national launch.

- **Consumer panel:** an identified group of consumers receives the product and makes individual comments on it.

- **Observation:** people's reactions (e.g. to a new display or form of packaging) are observed whilst they shop, to provide information from the market-place.

If field research is to provide relevant information, it must be based on a representative sample: the consumers selected as the sample must represent the population as a whole in the market. (The nature of sampling is explained on pages 219–20.)

The main advantage of field research over desk research is that it is tailored specifically to the product: most desk research has been undertaken for different purposes and so the data are not always fully relevant to the product.

Desk research Desk or **secondary** research is based on existing information sources such as:

- the firm's own national and regional sales statistics;

- government publications, such as *Regional Trends* and *Social Trends* (from the Office for National Statistics);

- trade association publications;

- information from local chambers of commerce;

- market research agency reports;

- articles from the quality papers.

As an information source, desk research is less expensive than field research, and the information – being already available – is quicker to obtain.

The results of the research Another way of classifying market research is to examine the information it generates. This information may be classed as:

1. **controllable:** it is within the organisation's power to alter a variable identified through research, such as poor packaging or an inappropriate method of promotion.

2. **uncontrollable:** the research identifies factors which are beyond the control of the organisation, such as an economic downturn affecting sales/market size, or a new technological development which is influencing sales of its current model.

7.3   THE MARKETING MIX

The 'mix' consists of the four Ps – product, price, place and promotion. It identifies the different elements, and the weighting given to each element, when an organisation markets its products. This mix varies according to the stage of the product's life, the organisation's financial situation and its own stage of development, and according to external factors such as the degree of competition.

THE PRODUCT

'Products' consist of both goods and services. These can be grouped into consumer market and industrial market goods and services (see page 33). Products are also defined in terms of the benefits they bring to a consumer, who might buy the product for its image or for a service associated with it, rather than for its physical presence. A product may possess **core**, **secondary** and **tertiary** attributes.

As an example, people buy cars because they offer a transport service.

- The core attribute of this product is that it allows a certain freedom of movement from A to B.

- The secondary attributes possessed by the product are based on its additional features – it may be 'comfortable', 'economical', 'reliable' or 'spacious', may offer a choice of colours and paint finishes, and include extras such as a stereo or sunroof: these secondary attributes are summarised in Fig. 7.4.

- The tertiary attributes of a product are external to it: with cars, these include the warranty and delivery date, as well as status or self-expression factors.

The manufacturer must therefore ask the question, 'What market are we in?' and not simply 'What product are we making?'.

The product mix

Most firms produce and market several products. Their marketing strategy for one product can influence the sales and marketing of their other products.

The 'product mix' is the term for the complete range of products in all markets and segments. The mix consists of different product lines – the group of products aimed at one particular market or segment – and the **mix width** identifies the number of product lines in the product mix. The wider the mix width a firm has, the more diversified it is and the better chance it has of survival if one market segment collapses.

Each product line also has a **mix depth**: this is a reference to the number of different products in a single product line. The deeper the mix depth, the more segments the firm has to operate in to avoid its products competing with each other. Promoting one product could lead to a fall in sales of the others when they are in the same segment. Firms therefore seek to rationalise their products, keeping them compatible if they cannot be placed in different market segments.

The effectiveness of the firm's product mix is assessed by analysing individual products. The use of product life-cycle analysis establishes product age, and techniques such as the 'Boston Box' are also used to categorise products in the mix.

The product life-cycle

The concept of a product's life-cycle is based on the assumption that it has only a limited life once it is introduced into the market-place. It is therefore important that a firm has a balanced 'product portfolio' (product mix), replacing those in the 'maturity' and 'decline' stages of their lives with newer products.

The product life-cycle has four stages. These are shown in Fig. 7.6.

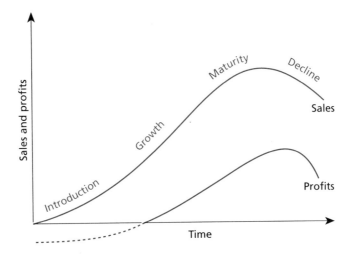

Fig. 7.6 Stages of the product life-cycle

Introduction Following the product planning and development stages, the product is introduced onto the market. Characteristics of this stage are:

- low initial sales, due to limited knowledge and no consumer loyalty;
- heavy promotion to build brand image and consumer confidence;
- low profits at best, due to high development and promotion costs being set against low sales volume;
- product modifications taking place;
- limited distribution levels (but high stockholding for the manufacturer), and distribution channels not fully established;
- a strong likelihood of product failure.

Attempts will be made to gain a market share, for example by using penetration pricing policies. If, however, the product looks as though it will fail, the firm will probably abandon it.

Growth As consumer knowledge and loyalty develop, sales increase and profits start to be made (helped by greater economies of scale for the firm). If the product appears successful, or if it is exploiting a gap in the market, competitors will introduce similar products: if the new product is competing with existing brands, competitors may adopt different pricing policies to counter the challenge to their existing market share. The product is gradually changing from a 'star' into a 'cash cow'.

Maturity This stage is characterised by a slowing of growth as the product reaches its saturation (maximum) sales level. Profits are maximised during this stage, but the firm has to fight to defend its market share against stronger competition. Sales are maintained through additional promotion, customer loyalty (repeat purchases) and attempts at product differentiation, by alterations such as new packaging or through reduced price. The product is one of the firm's 'cash cows'.

Decline Total sales will fall, both for the firm and the industry. To counter this, the firm may reduce price again, cutting into its profit margin. The firm may decide to maintain production as other firms abandon their products, in an attempt to gain a larger share of the (smaller) market. It may also undertake niche marketing in a particular market segment.

Extending product life

By extending the product life, the firm hopes to extend the maturity (high-profits) stage. To do this, it alters:

- the product. Approaches include:
  - changing image (the 'new, improved' model);
  - introducing additional models, such as a diesel engine version for a car;
  - extending the product into other formats, for example chocolate bars extending into the ice cream market (e.g. ice-cream 'Mars', 'Galaxy' and 'Bounty') and washing powders becoming washing liquids.

- the marketing strategy, by changing the product image and/or its appeal – an example is where personal computers are promoted not only for work purposes, but also for games and educational use.

It is important for the marketing function to undertake this analysis so that the firm's product portfolio can be evaluated. Product life-cycle analysis also determines other aspects of marketing policy. The stage of a product's life influences the firm's policies on advertising, distribution, pricing, branding and product development: sales and profit forecasts and cash-flow forecasts are also affected.

Product life-cycle analysis illustrates how the marketing function integrates other business functions. Co-ordination of activity includes research and development (new product planning and development), production (phasing products in or out), sales (planning the new product promotion), personnel (if new skills are required to make new products) and accounts (for any new capital expenditure).

Product life-cycle analysis can be criticised:

1 It can overstate the importance of developing new products, rather than seeking to extend the lives of existing ones through diversification or by exploiting new markets and market segments. New product development is also expensive and risky, compared to the more secure and less expensive option of extending the life of a known and successful product.

2 Some products have proved to have a substantial or almost endless life, given occasional updating or modifications.

3 The four stages are not discrete – it is rarely possible to identify precisely where a product lies on the cycle.

4 The life-cycle can become a self-fulfilling prophecy – some niche market companies ignore the life-cycle concept, yet still succeed.

New product development

Firms develop new products to maintain a balanced product mix. A product can be classed as 'new' if it is:

- **Innovative**: it is the original model or type, such as the portable Sony Walkman, the Mini (with its compact, 'transverse' engine), and Nintendo's Game Boy.
- **Imitative**: products which copy the innovative original once it proves successful (the different makes of training shoe are a good example).
- **Replacement**: where a new model of an existing product is brought out.

Innovative products result from a **proactive** approach to product development: the firm attempts to create or manipulate the market. This strategy carries the highest risk, but also the highest potential rewards. The alternative approach, where imitative and replacement products are marketed, occurs when a firm is **reactive** and a market follower.

New product development has a number of stages.

1 Assess the demand	• What does market research tell us?
	• Is the product feasible?
	• Is there a gap in the market?
2 Obtain ideas	• What can research and development suggest?
	• Who else can contribute ideas?
3 Evaluate the ideas	• What does market research tell us?
	• Do the ideas fit the corporate plan?
	• What are the potential 'limiting factors' (suppliers, demand, market size, productive capacity, capital expenditure, break-even point, etc.)?

④ Develop the idea	● What do we need to develop the product?
	● What does the prototype look like?
	● What test marketing can we do?
	● Do we have a timetable for equipment purchase, staff training, and financial planning?
⑤ Launch the product	● What forms of promotion do we need?
	● What does the test marketing tell us?
	● What is our pricing policy?
⑥ Evaluate success	● What is the consumer reaction?

Two important areas of product development are screening and test marketing. **Screening** takes place at the ideas evaluation stage. The first process of 'wide-mesh' screening eliminates many ideas on the grounds of funding or lack of expertise. Additional screening analyses:

● labour availability and cost;

● possible market reaction from competitors;

● compatibility with:
  – corporate objectives
  – the existing product mix;

● likely future market growth;

● profit potential;

● anticipated length of the life-cycle.

Test marketing relies on the production of prototypes or pilot products. The purpose is to simulate as closely as possible the market, the product, and the marketing support which will be given.

Even if the new product is successful, difficulties remain with its progress. These are:

● high capital costs;

● increased revenue expenditure through retraining labour, additional stockholding, and new advertising, which put pressure on the firm's liquidity;

● establishing and dealing with new channels of distribution;

● difficulty in creating consumer confidence and loyalty.

Product differentiation and branding

The process of giving a 'name' to a product has developed this century. Brand marketing grew alongside the consumer society, supported by the surge in consumer durables and the expansion of commercial television. Branding gives consumers the assurance that their next purchase of a product will give them one which is virtually identical. **Brand loyalty** is created (and exploited by the manufacturer) through the guarantee of quality and consistency.

The benefits to the manufacturer from branding products include:

● assistance in selling new products, because an existing respected brand name or image has a 'goodwill' value and can confer attributes of quality, value for money, ease of use, reliability, etc. on a new product – for example, in a 1993 survey on car sales in the UK, Volvo was seen as the safest and most environmentally friendly car, attributes which it can use to promote any of its new models;

● the promise of repeat purchases as a result of brand loyalty;

● a greater chance of gaining display space;

● extending the brand into another market (e.g. chocolate into the ice-cream market);

● market segmentation is made easier;

● less personal selling is required (which saves costs).

Branding depends largely on packaging. Originally there solely to protect the product, the packaging now has additional functions. It carries the brand name or logo, it displays product information that is legally required, and offers space which the manufacturer uses to persuade the consumer to buy the product: 'what innovation there has been in consumer goods has come largely from packaging suppliers and grocery retailers' (McKinsey Marketing Consultants, 1993).

Modern packaging offers:

- a communication base;
- ease of display;
- impact;
- environmental acceptability.

Own-label brands These are goods branded with the retailer's name, and not the manufacturer's name. Manufacturers gain through using excess capacity to produce own-brand items: there is also the hope that their existing brand names can survive through consumer loyalty. The retailer can offer own-brand products at lower prices to compete with manufacturers' brands.

In 1988, a number of 'brand-driven' takeovers took place: for example, Philip Morris bought Kraft for $12.9 billion, and Rowntree was sold to Nestlé for $4.5 billion, both purchase prices being well in excess of the net worth of the company book values. Brand performance was a major influence in the acquisitions. There is now increasing evidence that the brand manufacturers are losing power to the retailers, and that **price sensitivity** is becoming more important than brand loyalty. The growing power of retailers, increased consumer sophistication and the tendency to 'channel-hop' and avoid advertising have been accompanied by increased customer scepticism about the claims made by manufacturers for their branded goods. One specific factor producing pressure on leading brands is 'PPP' – perceived product parity – with increased consumer belief that there is little difference between many rival brands. The age of many of the leading branded goods is a further factor. A survey in 1993 identified only nine of the top fifty UK brands as having been introduced after 1975, while twenty of them had been in the shops before 1950.

Table 7.1 *Private label share of the market*

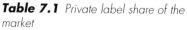

Category	% Share
Wine	75
Cheese	65
Fruit juice	60
Desserts	56
Frozen foods	56
Canned vegetables	50
Bakery items	46

Source: *The Guardian*

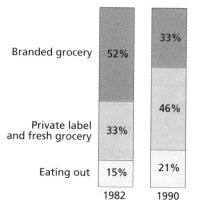

Fig. 7.7 *The decline of grocery brands*
Source: ONS

Branding allows manufacturers to create or highlight apparent differences between products. These differences are supported by advertising. Different pricing policies allow differentiation on the basis of price, and there are other bases for differentiation. These non-price bases include service, quality, packaging, reliability, and extended guarantees.

PRICING DECISIONS

Price is another element in the marketing mix. It represents a profit objective to the seller and a measure of value to the buyer. The firm's pricing decisions are influenced by external and internal factors, and prices which result may be fixed or negotiable.

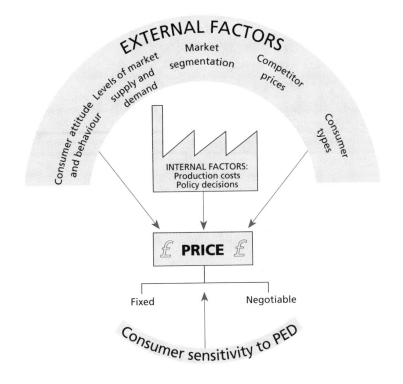

Fig. 7.8 Price influences

Supply, demand and price

Chapter 1 explains how economists stress the interaction of supply and demand in price determination. A situation exists where producers supplying the product and consumers demanding it reach a point of equilibrium through market price: at this price the same quantity of product is demanded and supplied. Changes in supply and demand are analysed to establish the level of elasticity, which affects the firm's total revenue.

Most marketeers regard this analysis as useful but limited, arguing that the role of other factors such as promotion are understated in economic analysis (probably because their effects are uncertain).

Price and costs

Chapters 6 and 8 explain the nature of costs. Accountants play an important role in pricing policy through establishing and analysing costs. The most popular method of fixing the price of a product is to use this cost information. Costs are calculated using either absorption costing or marginal costing techniques, and a profit element is added: this is known as the mark-up if it is expressed as a percentage of cost, and as the margin if expressed as a percentage of selling price.

Cost-plus pricing Cost-based pricing methods are based on classifying the firm's costs as either fixed or variable.

- Fixed costs such as rent of premises and office salaries remain constant and must be paid regardless of the level of output.

- Variable costs such as raw materials and direct labour alter as the firm's output alters: an increase in output leads to an increase in these costs.

Cost-plus pricing is an absorption cost method and is also known as **full-cost** pricing. The firm calculates its expected output. Total fixed costs are divided by the expected output, to calculate the fixed cost per unit. The unit variable cost is added, then the percentage profit mark-up, to give the selling price.

Example:	Expected output:		100,000
	Total fixed costs:		£600,000
	Variable costs (£) per unit:		
	(Direct) raw materials	1.40	
	(Direct) wages	1.85	
	(Direct) other expenses	0.75	
			£4.00
	Profit mark-up:		40%

The expected output yields a unit fixed cost of £6.00: the total unit cost is therefore £10.00 and the selling price will be £14.00. If the firm's calculations are correct, the profit will be £400,000.

The major drawback of this approach is that it might produce a price (and profit margin) acceptable to the firm but not to the market. Some products can be sold temporarily at a price below cost – for example 'loss leaders', offered to attract custom or to establish market share – but this cannot be maintained in the long term.

The cost-plus approach therefore assumes that all output will be sold. In the above example, if actual sales are only 80,000:

- total revenue is: £1,120,000: 80,000 × £14;
- total costs are: £920,000: £600,000 fixed and £320,000 variable (80,000 × £4);
- profit is halved to £200,000.

Other difficulties include forecasting fixed and variable costs accurately, and classifying costs as fixed or variable – in practice, many are semi-variable because they contain both fixed and variable elements.

Contribution pricing This marginal cost method of pricing is closely linked to break-even analysis. It is based on calculating the contribution to total fixed costs made by each product sold.

Selling price – variable cost = contribution

In the above illustration, if the unit selling price is £14 and unit variable cost is £4, contribution is £10. The firm's break-even point is calculated by dividing total fixed costs by the unit contribution.

$$\frac{£600,000}{£10} = 60,000 \text{ produced and sold to break even}$$

Each product made and sold over 60,000 makes £10 profit: each product below 60,000 generates a £10 loss.

Contribution pricing takes greater account of market conditions. The firm can analyse the effects of changing price. By lowering the selling price it also lowers the contribution and creates a higher break-even sales point: but this might reflect more accurately the external pricing factors, such as the level of competitors' prices.

Contribution pricing, with its emphasis on marginal costs, can be used to implement differential pricing. Rail and airline transport illustrate this. Low-fare, stand-by or off-peak, and customer category (e.g. as 'students' or 'senior citizens') pricing is used to fill seats: the marginal cost of these passengers is very low and any contribution which the transport company can get helps to cover its fixed costs. Differential pricing can be based on different:

- customer types;
- customer location;
- amounts purchased.

Market-led pricing policies

The market structure influences the pricing policy of individual firms. The firm is either a price-taker – in a market structure where it cannot (or chooses not to) exert control over the market price – or a price-maker, if it is in a monopoly position. The firm may decide not to try to influence the present market price: if it is an oligopolist (one of a small number of firms dominating the market) it may settle for the prevailing price, to avoid costly price wars. In such cases it relies on non-price competition through advertising and other forms of promotion, to maintain or improve its market share.

There is still flexibility in pricing even where firms are price-takers. The firm can adopt one of the following pricing strategies.

Skimming   A skimming or 'creaming' strategy is a high-price one used when a new product is introduced. The firm might have a temporary monopoly before competitors enter the market: the creaming strategy helps it recoup heavy initial expenditure as well as to exploit its monopoly position. Consumers are prepared to pay high prices for status or prestige reasons, but the resulting high profit margins encourage early and strong competition.

One form of skimming is where **prestige pricing** is used by a firm. This strategy can be used when a product is regarded by consumers as being of high quality. Prestige pricing is a permanent strategy which gives a high profit margin, although sales volume can be small due to the existence of lower-priced alternatives.

Penetration   This strategy is one of lower prices and profit margins and is used with both new and established products. The purpose is to improve market share. Penetration pricing is often used:

- with products which are:
  - high-volume
  - long-life
  - price sensitive;
- if the firm:
  - wishes to become market leader
  - has a cost advantage over its competitors
  - can benefit from substantial economies of scale;
- where the market is expanding.

A conglomerate may decide to cross-subsidise the penetration or predatory pricing of one product with profits made from others. Cutting the weekday cover price of *The Times* newspaper in September 1993 from 45p to 30p by News Corporation (and later to 10p) followed a trial in the Kent area (which had reportedly increased sales by 14 per cent). This was seen by some commentators as predatory pricing and an attempt to capture the share of the 'quality' segment of the newspaper market held by a competitor, *The Independent*: the lower price of *The Times* could be supported, if necessary, by profits from other News Corporation operations such as BSkyB.

The benefits of a penetration strategy can be quick growth for the firm, coupled with a positive effect on competition: existing inefficient competitors are eliminated and potential new ones are discouraged from entering the market.

It is also a high-risk strategy. Price cutting reduces profit margins and affects the firm's profitability and liquidity (if the product's demand is more inelastic than anticipated). Competitors are encouraged to react to preserve their own market share, and price wars result. Any errors in cost estimation might result in losses being made because profit margins are small.

PLACE

Firms making products for a particular market have to decide how their products are to reach that market. Distribution forms the basis of 'place' in the four Ps. Physical distribution has the task of delivering the correct quantity of goods whilst at the same time maintaining the product's physical quality and security.

Channels of distribution

The channels shown in Fig. 7.9 represent the main ways that manufactured goods are distributed from producer to consumer.

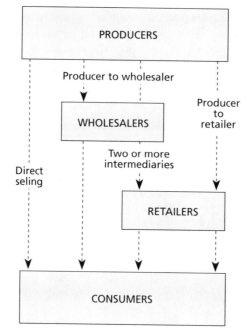

Fig. 7.9 *Channels of distribution*

All distribution channels offer a level of effectiveness which must be offset against their relative cost. The choice of channel also depends on the level of control over the outlets required by the manufacturer. Mass-marketed items such as newspapers are not affected by the image of the outlet, whereas products with an 'exclusive' label or a high degree of technical complexity are distributed with the manufacturer exerting much greater control over the number and quality of outlets.

Direct selling   Many products are sold directly from producer to consumer. Some manufacturers operate 'factory shops' for their consumer products; consumer goods are also sold through mail order or 'door-to-door'; and many industrial goods use the direct channel. Direct selling of some consumer products has been criticised for its high-pressure approach, though there is now increased legal protection for consumers. General benefits to the seller from using this method include:

● controlling the product's promotion – it is sold by the seller's own sales force;

● closer customer contact – the seller receives consumer feedback quickly and directly.

Producer to wholesaler   This is a popular channel for small producer firms making a limited or incomplete product range. Wholesalers provide several important services for these producers:

❶ **Risk bearing**: the producer has a guaranteed market, with the wholesaler bearing the risk of not selling the goods,

❷ **Storage**: stockholding costs are reduced,

❸ **Advice**: market feedback is given by the wholesaler,

❹ **Promotion**: the wholesaler helps promote the product.

The producer loses control over the final product outlets and receives lower profit margins (compared with direct selling, for example).

Producer to retailer   The traditional wholesaler channel is inappropriate for major high-street and retail park stores such as Asda and Tesco. They have their own warehouses where bulk delivery of stock is made by the producer: the store breaks the bulk at this point for dispatch to its outlets. Other forms of producer–retailer link include the tied outlet approach operated by breweries and petrol producers.

Suppliers again have the benefit of a concentrated market for their products, but are subject to greater control – of price, quality, credit terms and delivery date. They have no direct contact with the final consumer, and little say over the product's final promotion.

Two or more intermediaries This traditional chain is still widely found. It is used where products are sold through smaller retailers: using wholesalers allows wide product distribution without the producer having major transport and administrative costs. The producer again lacks contact with the final consumer and control over product promotion.

PROMOTION

Firms promote their products to:

- increase sales of existing products, for example by selling in a different market segment;
- introduce a new product onto the market, informing potential consumers of its availability;
- compete with others, to maintain or increase market share directly or indirectly (e.g. by attacking a competitor's product);
- improve corporate image: 'Our advertising splits reasonably neatly into two compartments: one, creating a positive image for the Bank, for which we tend to use television…' (Lloyds Bank plc marketing strategy report, 1993).

The amount of promotion varies according to the organisation: as an example, McDonald's spent £33 million on marketing in 1993.

The promotion mix Promotion consists of two different cost categories: 'above-the-line' costs of promotion (advertising), and 'below-the-line' costs – personal selling, sales promotion, and other influences such as packaging and public relations. The mix of promotional activities is influenced by their relative cost and effectiveness. They must also be compatible with each other, and appropriate to the company image.

Advertising

Advertising attempts to **inform** and/or **persuade** potential customers. The emphasis of informative advertising is to give factual information about the product.

Most advertising contains an element of persuasion. The objective of persuasive advertising is to convince customers that they need the product: it includes persuading them to buy the firm's version rather than a competing one. Persuasive advertising is assisted by the use of branding and other forms of product differentiation, and seeks to establish brand image and customer loyalty through repeating its persuasive statement.

Advertising is criticised for:

- **making outlandish claims**, although strictly false claims are illegal under the Trade Descriptions Act and the EU's Misleading Advertising Directive, and are also monitored by watchdog bodies such as the Advertising Standards Authority;
- **manipulating consumers**, by using approaches involving sex or status to make the product more appealing.

Choice of media The firm can choose from a variety of advertising media. The main limiting factor is the size of the advertising budget. Other influences include the market – its nature and size will influence media selection – and the product, for example, specialist products are often advertised in specialist (industrial or hobby) magazines.

The following are the main media available to an advertiser.

❶ Television and radio Commercial stations provide mass coverage and are therefore suitable for mass-appeal goods. Drawbacks include the expense (of TV advertising), the increasing tendency of viewers to channel-hop and avoid adverts as the number of available stations increases, the temporary nature of the advertisement, and the lack of selectivity of this approach.

2 **Print-based media**   This advertising is more permanent: the advert can be cut out for future reference, and may include a reply slip. It also provides more information than broadcast advertisements: it allows the advertiser to act more selectively, because consumers can be targeted by socio-economic or interest group (e.g. through advertising in special-interest magazines). It is also less expensive than TV advertising. It does, however, lack the impact of sound, vision and movement.

3 **Other media,** including
  - cinema advertising – often targeted at a youth audience
  - posters – used to sell mass-appeal products
  - leaflets and mailshots – these reach a mass, but not a captive, audience.

Below-the-line promotion

Sales promotion   The main techniques of sales promotion are
- **free samples:** these allow the customer to try the product, and can establish brand loyalty;
- **price reductions:** the use of discount or money-off coupons to get the consumer to repeat the purchase;
- **premium offers:** free gifts, following the collection of product labels encourage repeat purchases;
- **competitions:** acting as an inducement to buy the product;
- **after-sales service:** used to persuade customers to buy a particular brand of a consumer durable.

Point-of-sale (**POS**) advertising is carried out in conjunction with sales promotion. POS includes any advertising or merchandising which takes place at the point of sale: it often concentrates on packaging and display to provide product recognition, and is associated with impulse-purchase products such as sweets.

Personal selling   Advertising is impersonal, because it is directed at a mass audience. The benefit from personal selling is that the firm can **target its message** to suit the recipient.

The use of personal selling allows the firm's message and promotion to be individually tailored to the customer. It can have close control of this promotional technique through employing the sales staff or agents. The firm also receives directly any consumer comments, and its sales staff can handle non-sales matters such as customer queries and complaints.

The main disadvantage of personal selling is its high cost. Other drawbacks include the relatively high turnover and lack of continuity of sales staff and agents.

A decision must be made whether to train and use a sales force or to hire outside agents. The nature of the product is normally the deciding factor: a sales force is used for high-cost or technically complex consumer and industrial products, and agents where the account or product value is small (such as cosmetics).

Chapter roundup

Chapter 7 has outlined the role of marketing in linking the outside world to the organisation's internal functions, and its co-ordinating role for the organisation. The chapter has explained why many firms adopt and apply the 'marketing concept', describing how market research is undertaken and examining the elements of the marketing mix (the 'four Ps').

Illustrative questions

1 What is meant by the term 'SWOT analysis'? (2)

AEB

2 Identify **three** ways in which a firm seeks to extend the life of its products. (3)

Tutorial note

Both questions require brief answers only. Your answer to 2 should distinguish carefully between the three identified ways.

Suggested answers

1 This term refers to the analysing of a firm's current and likely future situation in terms of its strengths and weaknesses, and the possible opportunities and threats it faces from the outside world.

2 Three ways include: launching the product in a new market (e.g. abroad) or new segment of an existing market; changing the product specification and supporting with the 'new, improved' promotional approach; reducing the price of the product.

3 Read the following passage and then answer the questions that follow.

> Smarties were originally launched in 1937 by Rowntree Mackintosh as a sugar-coated chocolate aimed at the adult market. However, the following year tactics were altered and Smarties were targeted at children and this led to the sweets subsequently being packed in tubes.
>
> Over the years, demand has increased and Smarties have become a strong brand in an established part of the confectionery market.
>
> Smarties are brightly-coloured sugar-coated sweets with a milk chocolate centre. The mix comprises of eight colours: red, yellow, orange, green, mauve, pink, brown and blue. They are available in four distinctive standard packs: a tube with coloured tops and embossed letters; cartons; a 3 tube multipack and since 1980, a mini carton for the 'smaller size' market.
>
> Mars is another of the major chocolate and sweet manufacturing groups in the UK. Mars produces a range of well-known products including Mars Bars, Twix and Maltesers.
>
> In July 1985, Mars prepared to launch M&M's in the UK market. The product was already a major seller in the United States and other countries. M&M's are brightly coloured, chocolate-centred buttons and the closest thing to Smarties currently available.

(a) The importance of packaging is dependent on many variables, most of which are attributable to the product itself. List **four** factors that Rowntree Mackintosh would have taken into account when designing the packaging for Smarties. (4)

(b) Rowntree Mackintosh is a 'market-led' company. What do you consider to be the main objectives of this type of company? (6)

(c) How might the marketing mix adopted by Rowntree Mackintosh for Smarties alter in view of the introduction of M&M's on to the market? (8)

WJEC

Tutorial note

The question is structured into distinct sections. To gain full marks you need to refer to the situation described in the case study. Don't forget that a basic list only is required in part (a).

Suggested answer

(a) Rowntree Mackintosh would have considered the following:
- aesthetics (the attractiveness of the packaging design);
- cost of the raw materials;
- packaging used by competitors (to allow a Unique Selling Disposition/Proposition);
- storage and protection (to protect the product).

(b) The main objectives of a market-led company focus on the consumer (often referred to as 'client'). The objectives will probably refer to the size of the market, the clients' wants in this market, how to meet these wants, and setting targets to achieve this. This approach contrasts with the traditional 'production-led' approach, where the product is made and then put on the market; with a market-led company, the end user is the primary concern.

(c) 'Marketing mix' refers to the 'four Ps': product, price, place and promotion. It identifies these elements, and the relative importance given to each of these by a firm's marketing function. Rowntree Mackintosh would have considered the effect of M&M's on its product, and whether Smarties needed re-styling (e.g. through new packaging). It would also consider the comparative price of the two products, and may have adjusted the price of Smarties to compete with M&M's. Thirdly, it would examine its channels of distribution ('place'), comparing the nature and efficiency of these channels with those being used by its rival. Finally, Rowntree Mackintosh would review its promotion strategies, to see how best to respond to the new product on the market.

4 This question is specifically about Market Research. You will be expected to include knowledge relevant to this aspect of business studies in your answers.

Read the following extract from a newspaper article then answer the questions which follow it. You may draw on evidence from the article to support your answers.

> 'The European Union Tax Commissioner has pledged to abolish tax free shopping for European citizens travelling between member states. In response, the Managing Director of United Distillers pointed out that "duty free sales are to a great extent impulse driven" and "lost duty free sales are unlikely to be recovered in domestic markets". A similar message was delivered by the Managing Director of Pringle (the Scottish knitwear firm): "This will mean our firm will have to face new problems and adopt new strategies to remain competitive".'
>
> From *The European* (November 4 1994)

Before Pringle can begin to adopt new strategies, the firm must commission some market research.

(a) (i) Identify and explain a major marketing aim for Pringle.
   (ii) Explain how this might determine the kind of market research commissioned by the firm. (4)

(b) The market research agency employed by Pringle is considering primary research. Explain with reasons which methods would be most suitable. (8)

(c) Explain what you would expect this market research to find and how such information could influence Pringle's marketing of its products. (8)

(d) Identify which secondary data would help Pringle's market research and explain how this would help with a marketing strategy. (4)

(e) Pringle requires a questionnaire suited to its market research aim. The questionnaire must be designed to collect information which can be collated using a database.

Explain, with examples:
- how the use of such software will influence the questionnaire
- how the database should be structured
- how the database would be used to search and sort the information gathered.
(16)

London Examinations

Tutorial note

This is a reasonably straightforward question, though note that (a) (i) requires you to identify a **major** marketing aim. Choose this aim carefully, with your answer to part (ii) in mind. A good answer should identify the various market research points and then relate them to Pringle's situation.

Suggested answer

(a) (i) A major marketing aim for Pringle could be to expand into new markets in Europe (the EU) for the company's existing products. This aim would be realistic if the company's products are not represented in all EU countries.

   (ii) Pringle's market research would therefore have to be tailored to specific countries, where the company did not export. This would influence how consumer attitudes to the company's goods are assessed.

(b) Suitable methods include postal questionnaires, face-to-face interviews, surveys at the point of sale, and telephone interviews. Face-to-face interviews, whilst an expensive method, would at least involve the use of questionnaires designed specifically for the task, and give respondents the opportunity to query questions asked (compared with postal questionnaires). Better responses are also usually obtained from these street surveys.

(c) This research might obtain information regarding the price elasticity of demand for the products, the opinions and attitudes of potential customers abroad, and their possible reactions to various marketing strategies (e.g. mailshots) that the company might use. This information would influence Pringle's marketing strategies: for example, the company will have information regarding how its market(s) might be segmented, how its pricing policy might have to be varied, what channels of distribution it might pursue, and how its product range might need to be diversified.

(d) Secondary data will be obtained from UK and EU governmental agencies, trade associations, the CBI, and other sources of statistics. Statistics from the DTI on exporting, and statistical analyses in periodical publications such as *Social Trends* are useful sources of information. Whilst this information is more general, it can help Pringle establish where sales of its goods are likely to be high (e.g. by examining personal/regional/national wealth statistics).

(e) The database will have the power to collate, search, cross-reference, sort and report on the various records kept. Handling data is easier if questions are closed rather than open, perhaps supported by the use of multiple-choice questions. The overall structure could be by respondent category, with fields such as age, gender and socio-economic status. Sample questions might be along the lines of:

Who purchases knitwear items in your household?	I do My partner Both of us Neither of us
About how often do you shop for knitwear items?	More than once a month Once a month Once every three months Once a year I don't purchase these items
Where do you/your household normally buy knitwear from?	Shop name A Shop name B (etc)

5 This question is specifically about marketing planning. You will be expected to include knowledge relevant to this aspect of business in your answers.

First examine the information provided about 'Super Soft Ltd' and then answer the questions.

Super Soft Ltd

Super Soft is a comparatively new firm. It was set up by two entrepreneurs 5 years ago to develop and sell software packages to business customers. Each year, the owners of the firm have invested 60% of the annual profits in product development work. This investment has helped Super Soft to gain a reputation for its innovative approach to software design. It has also enabled the firm to establish a dominant position in the UK business software market (78% share in 1993).

However, since the advent of 'The Single European Market', Super Soft has begun to face increased competition from European software firms which are beginning to market their products aggressively in the UK. 'Stuttgart Informatiks' from Germany are specialists in computer-aided design software and 'Real Soft' of Spain have been awarded a substantial Spanish Government subsidy to assist them in their research and development work on integrated software packages. Both firms have lower overheads than Super Soft which helps them to price their products competitively.

Currently, Super Soft has three main products in its range: 'Smart Sums' (a financial control and accounting package), 'Smart Design' (a small computer-aided design package) and 'Smart Pack' (a fully integrated word-processor spreadsheet and database package). Each of these products sells to different size markets and yields different products (see Figure 1).

Figure 1 *Super Soft Product Range*

SALES PROFITS (£000s)	1989	1990	1991	1992	1993
Smart Pack	50	60	75	90	100
Smart Design	8	12	14	13	10
Smart Sums	50	65	85	105	115
UK MARKET SIZE (£ MILLION)	1989	1990	1991	1992	1993
Smart Pack	7.2	8.1	10.1	12.6	13.7
Smart Design	1.5	1.6	1.7	1.7	1.6
Smart Sums	2.4	3.2	4.5	6.5	9.1

(a) Using your knowledge and understanding of marketing, provide an **analysis** of Super Soft's current product range. (16)

(b) How could the use of computer software applications have assisted you in your analysis of Super Soft's product range? (8)

(c) **Evaluate** which aspects of Super Soft's marketing mix are the most important in the firm's Marketing Plan and why. How should the Super Soft marketing manager plan to develop these and what would be the implications of this for the firm. (16)

London Examinations

Tutorial note

The words in bold indicate the level of response expected from you. In part (a) you should offer an analysis of the product range strengths and weaknesses. Part (c) is particularly tricky, because it consists of three questions: remember you should give reasons for your choice of marketing mix items.

Suggested answer

(a) Whilst Super Soft is dominant in the UK market, it is facing increased competition. Its price competitiveness is weak due to its higher overheads, and the product range is therefore likely to be over-priced. Super Soft's export potential would therefore seem rather limited on a price argument. Examining the range's figures, whilst Smart Pack has doubled profits – and Smart Sums more than doubled – Smart Design's profits have declined, whilst its market size is static. Although Smart Sums yields the highest total profits, its relative profitability seems low (its market size has had to increase four-fold to generate this profit). If, however, the company dropped Smart Design from its product range, this might allow its competitors to penetrate the software market to a greater extent. Perhaps the company might alter its pricing strategy to increase its competitiveness.

(b) The company's numerical information could have been entered into a spreadsheet. This has the capacity to produce a range of relevant figures, such as the contribution made by individual product lines to overall profits, sales trends, and individual costs. Graphical display of information such as market share and net profit percentage is also possible using a spreadsheet/graphics package. An analysis of customer purchasing patterns, habits and locations becomes possible when relevant information is entered into a database.

(c) The firm must consider all aspects of the marketing mix. Super Soft must review its **pricing** policy to ensure it is price-competitive with its competitors. This might necessitate reduced expenditure on R&D (a long-term risky strategy) in order to conserve expenditure so that prices can be cut and profit margins retained. This might also 'free up' expenditure for additional **promotion**, to ensure the company and its products stay in the public eye. Super Soft might consider the benefits from competing with the other software suppliers in their own countries: it will need to review its **products** (e.g. to evaluate new product development needs) and use market research to assess the viability of exporting. If a decision to export is taken, the firm needs to consider the **place** part of the 'mix', by assessing the most appropriate channels of distribution to use.

Practice questions

1 (a) Why do large companies use advertising agencies? (2)

(b) State **two** functions of packaging. (2)

(c) A company is researching the market for chocolate snacks. What market research techniques might it use? (4)

Pitfalls

You have to make sure that the points in your answer to part (c) relate to the given market, i.e. a mass consumer market with many competitors, national advertising, etc.

Key points

(a) Gain from specialist knowledge and expertise which is not present in the firm.

(b) Protect the product; advertise/promote the product (also inform the consumer).

(c) (General points, to be related to chocolate snacks market): field research – questionnaire/interview; desk research – existing sales data, external statistics e.g. Social Trends/other government sources, information from sales reps, analysis of competitors' activities.

2 One of the world's leading consumer electronics firms develops a new product which incorporates a major technological breakthrough.

Examine the principles which should guide the company in setting the price of the product. (25)

AEB

Pitfalls

Although this is a question on pricing, you should not limit your answer to a description of the various forms of pricing: they need to be put into the context of the question.

Key points

Principles include: competitor pricing; price elasticity; nature of market (price it will take); firm's rate of return required on investment; firm's existing pricing policy; image of firm; likely break-even point(s); whether short-term profit-maximisation or longer-term market share objective.

3 (a) In what circumstances should a firm use direct channels of distribution? (5)

(b) Outline briefly the various methods a firm might adopt to distribute its products abroad. (5)

NEAB

Pitfalls

Both parts receive the same marks, so obey the instruction 'briefly' in part (b). Your answer to part (a) could include specific examples.

Key points

(a) Direct channel involves distribution from manufacturer straight to user (e.g. many industrial products). Common situations are: when the product is large/bulky and/or 'one-off'; where orders are not placed by the customer on a regular basis; when a customer orders large amounts.

(b) These include: market research into company and culture; using government/chamber of commerce support; deciding whether to establish a franchising system, grant licences; find and use distributors or agents.

4 (a) Explain what is meant by **market segmentation**. (5)

(b) How may a knowledge of market segmentation enable a firm to improve the effectiveness of its marketing? Give examples. (12)

(c) Discuss whether the strategy adopted for selling into a **declining market** should differ from that for selling into an **expanding market**. (8)

SEB

Pitfalls

There is a temptation to include points in your answer to part (a) which should be included in part (b). Limit your answer to (a) to a definition and basic description of segmentation, perhaps supported by an example (which could then be referred to in your answer to (b)).

Key points

(a) Division of the market into distinct subgroups or 'segments'. Examples include a shoe manufacturer analysing the market on bases of age, gender, fashion and use (e.g. casual/formal).

b) Segmentation brings clarity and focus to the marketing function. Market research into different segments allows the firm to adapt its marketing strategy and to focus on particular segments to improve its competitiveness and/or market share. Advertising can be directed to specific media and given a specific message; sales promotion can focus on particular audiences and segments; personal selling can be tailored to individual segments. Also, employees can specialise in particular segments, thereby gaining greater expertise. Segmentation also allows product differentiation, and niche markets to be exploited.

(c) Strategies for a declining market are more likely to be defensive in nature, also short-term 'one-off'; those for an expanding market involve greater aggression and activity (e.g. heavier involvement of sales force to establish market share).

OPERATIONS MANAGEMENT

Units in this chapter

Chapter objectives

The role of the production function is to turn input into output by changing factors of production into finished goods or services as efficiently as possible. Chapter 8 explains how this function plans and controls the different elements in the production process, and how major long-term production decisions are arrived at. It links with Chapter 4 – where government regional policy on the location of firms is described – and with Chapter 6, which explains how the accountant is concerned with measuring costs and values.

The key topics and concepts covered in the chapter are:

● production engineering, planning and control;
● work study;
● quality control;
● stock control;
● costs;
● break-even;
● production methods;
● location of production;
● stock valuation.

8.1 PLANNING, CONTROL AND COSTS

A typical Production Department contains several related sections or functions. Their combined role is to create a viable manufacturing programme for the products identified by the Marketing Department as being in demand.

Production engineering

Once the decision on what to make has been taken, the production engineering section decides how best to apply technology and other resources in manufacture, by determining the work processes required. Decisions are taken on the:

- quality of raw materials needed;
- manufacturing processes to be used;
- capital equipment needed;
- length of the production run for each product.

The production engineer uses **work study** to analyse labour and production efficiency. Work study consists of work measurement and method study.

Method study   This seeks to determine how a job should be carried out. The need for method study is highlighted where there are production bottlenecks, idle machinery or high levels of scrap and waste. It is based on the assumptions that there is a 'best' method of doing a job, and that this method can be determined by studying the job. The recognised steps in method study are:

Identify the job

Record the job details

Examine the details

Develop the new method

Install it

Monitor it

Work measurement   This is used to reveal the work content of a task and to establish how long the task should take to complete.

It uses the concepts of **standard time** – the time taken in normal conditions by a competent worker to complete the task – and **standard performance** – an average output rate achieved by competent workers using agreed production methods. Standard times are used for production planning (e.g. machine loading calculations) and are also used as a basis for pay incentive schemes and in establishing standard costs.

The main methods used to measure work are by direct observation (through time study or activity sampling) of the work, and by synthetic methods (using standard data, or PMTS) which do not involve observation.

- **Time study**   uses a stop-watch to measure job times and is the basic measure used where work is repetitive in nature. The elements of the job are timed and adjusted according to an assessment of the operative's speed and efficiency: a rating for the job is therefore established.

- **Activity sampling**   consists of several observations made during the work cycle at random intervals. Working and idle times can be calculated from the sample.

- **Standard data**   uses information gained from previous measurements and observations which were undertaken for similar activities. A synthetic time for the new job can be constructed from these secondary data.

- **PMTS** – predetermined motion time systems – uses established tables for times taken to carry out basic movements such as 'reach', 'turn' and 'grasp'. The times from these tables are summated to estimate standard times for job operations.

Production planning

The role of production planning is to establish short-term and long-term **production schedules**. To be successful, the production planning policy must be realistic and achievable: it therefore includes elements of stock control (to ensure stocks are obtainable at the right time and in the right numbers), sales forecasting (linking with the demand for the products being made), and labour (quality and availability). As an example, a sudden surge in demand for a product being made requires the production planners to consider:

- introducing overtime;
- subcontracting some work to other manufacturers;
- re-equipping with more productive machinery;
- reducing stock levels to boost production in the short term.

Production control

Production control ensures that the plans made at the production engineering stage are being followed, and that the production deadlines set by production planning are being met. There are a number of areas of control under this heading, including quality control, and stock control, which are explained in depth later in this chapter.

- **Cost control** The Production Department budget includes labour, material and overhead costs which require controlling to ensure budgeted total production costs are not exceeded.
- **Machine control** Machine loading is reviewed to account for individual machine capacity.
- **Progress control** Production schedules are controlled and factory production is 'chased' to ensure deadlines are met.
- **Quality control** The product standard or quality is inspected and monitored.
- **Stock control** This is undertaken to ensure production can be carried out as and when required.

Purchasing

The main role of the purchasing function is that of materials management. Production can be a highly complex operation, requiring many different items at different points in the production process. In such cases, purchasing is normally a centralised function, employing specialist buyers. Benefits of centralising the purchasing function include discounts for bulk buying, and greater expertise and efficiency. The organisation's buyers must obtain items:

- at the correct **price**;
- in the correct **quantities**;
- to the correct level of **quality**;
- at the correct **time**.

Fig. 8.1 Work of the purchasing function

ASSURING QUALITY

The term 'quality assurance' refers to the various activities concerned with quality, including quality control. The speed of manufacture on mass production lines and incentive payments for quick work can result in a fall in quality of the finished output. **Quality control** is an important element in production control, through its identification and scrapping of unsuitable output. The purpose of quality control is to ensure that standards are being maintained, especially where mass and flow production methods are being used. Specific costs associated with quality control include the costs of:

- materials scrapped;
- labour time wasted;
- rectifying poor workmanship;
- inspection and measurement;
- training employees to monitor the quality of their output;
- loss of customer goodwill when poor quality products escape the inspection net.

Quality control charts are used in mass production systems. The percentage of defective items is plotted against the vertical axis, and time against the horizontal axis: increases in the percentage of defective products can be seen and action taken. Samples of the product are taken at random for inspection: the larger the sample, the more accurate the results.

Some UK firms have used the Japanese idea of establishing **quality circles**, small groups of employees who have a common interest and who meet to discuss work matters. The quality circle attempts to improve product quality, employee morale and employee productivity through increased involvement. It is associated with the 'just-in-time' (**JIT**) approach to stock control and production described below. To be successful, a system of quality circles requires management and union support, and basic training (e.g. in JIT) for those involved.

Quality standards

Most firms seek to adopt a 'quality culture' which attempts to give customers high quality and good value. The quality culture is based on the premise that it is cheaper to get the job done correctly in the first place than to incur the costs and delays associated with failure. Reproduced below is the type of statement made by major organisations to indicate their awareness of the importance of quality.

Lloyds Bank plc
Mission statement:

The Bank will provide 'The best retail banking service – quality products, delivered well, at the right price'.

Source: Lloyds Bank plc

To be able to assure customers that quality standards are being maintained, the organisation must first set specifications. Many firms have adopted **ISO 9000**, which lays down sets of specifications for a quality system and gives a framework allowing organisations to be certified as having quality management systems. It provides detailed specifications in the areas of design, manufacture, installation and final inspection.

An alternative approach centres on the philosophy of 'Total quality management' (**TQM**). The TQM approach was adopted by the Japanese and is becoming increasingly popular in the UK. It stresses the role of all employees – not just those in the inspection department – in establishing a framework within the organisation which allows quality to be achieved. It implies that quality is assured at all stages of production, not simply checked at the inspection stage. An example of the TQM approach is the idea of 'zero defects', which encourages employees to develop a commitment to accurate work: there may be rewards associated with achieving zero defects. A TQM approach is also associated with the 'just-in-time' (JIT) or Kan Ban method of stock control and production. This is based on getting stock

> ## J Sainsbury plc
> ### Group Objectives
>
> *To discharge the responsibility as leaders in our trade by acting with complete integrity, by carrying out our work to the highest standards, and by contributing to the public good and to the quality of life in the community.*
>
> *To provide unrivalled value to our customers in the quality of the goods we sell, in the competitiveness of our prices and in the range of choice we offer.*
>
> *To achieve the highest standards in efficiency of operation, convenience and customer service in our stores, thereby creating as attractive and friendly a shopping environment as possible.*
>
> *To offer our staff outstanding opportunities in terms of personal career development and in remuneration relative to other companies in the same market, practising always a concern for the welfare of every individual.*
>
> *To generate sufficent profit to finance continual improvement and growth of the business whilst providing our shareholders with an excellent return on their investment.*

Source: J Sainsbury plc

and other inputs onto the production line in **just the right quantities at just the right time**. Items must be available when needed, be of the right quality and fit first time, and supported by adequately trained (and motivated) employees and efficient equipment.

CONTROLLING STOCK

Firms must hold sufficient stocks of different items, for a number of reasons.

Stock item	Reason	Costs of zero stock
Raw materials and work in progress	To meet production requirements.	Idle time (worker and machine); knock-on effect of delayed production.
Finished goods	To meet customer demand.	Loss of goodwill/orders; financial penalties for missing deadlines.
Consumables, equipment and spares	To support sales and production.	Idle time (worker and machine); delayed production.

The Purchasing Department carries out a balancing act shown in Fig. 8.2.

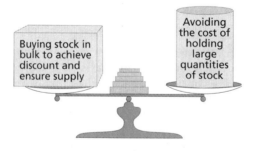

Fig. 8.2 The purchasing balancing act

If stocks are too high, unnecessary **holding costs** will be incurred. Holding costs not only include the costs of storage and stores operations, but also interest charges on the capital tied up in the stock, insurance costs, and costs of deterioration, obsolescence and theft.

Efficient stock control is based on establishing the most appropriate, i.e. the optimum, stock levels. There are four critical control levels used in keeping optimum stock levels.

1 Reorder level   Stock is ordered at this level, which is established by:

> **reorder level = rate of usage × maximum lead time:**
>
> (maximum lead time = ordering time + delivery time
> + inspection and storage time)

2 Reorder quantity   The economic order quantity (**EOQ**) is calculated in order to minimise the total costs of holding and ordering the stock. The EOQ takes into account the full range of stock costs and makes a number of assumptions:
- that there is a constant demand for the item of stock;
- that there is a constant lead time (i.e. the time between placing an order and receiving the goods);
- that stock-outs (an item out of stock when required) are not acceptable;
- that costs of making an order are constant, regardless of the order size;
- that costs of holding stock vary proportionately with the amount of stock being held.

Where these conditions exist:

$$\text{EOQ} = \sqrt{\frac{2od}{h}}$$

where o = ordering cost for the item
d = demand (annual) for the item
h = holding cost of one unit per annum

As an example: the annual demand for an item is 5,000 units; the cost of ordering the items is £80; and the cost of holding an item in store for a year is £5.

$$\text{EOQ} = \sqrt{\frac{2\,(80)\,(5,000)}{5}} = 400 \text{ units}$$

3 Minimum stock   This is a buffer stock level, which is calculated by:

> **minimum stock level =**
> **reorder level − average usage × average lead time**

4 Maximum stock   This is a warning that the stock level is at a maximum and is calculated by

> **maximum stock level =**
> **reorder level + reorder quantity**
> **− (minimum usage × minimum lead time)**

As an example, the following information relates to item D45:

maximum stock   10,000

weekly usage: 2,200 maximum
1,800 minimum

delivery time: 8 weeks maximum
4 weeks minimum

Reorder level is 2,200 x 8 = 17,600 units.
Minimum stock is 17,600 − (2,000 × 6) = 5,600 units.

Computers are widely used in stock control and ordering: for example, in materials requirements planning (MRP) they can calculate lead times for stock delivery, and in manufacturing resource planning (also known as MRP) they calculate the times taken at the various stages of production.

PRODUCTION AND COSTS

Chapters 1, 6 and 7 explain different approaches to establishing and classifying costs.

- **Opportunity cost** (see page 30) is the cost of forgoing the available alternatives.
- **Standard costs** (see page 160) are used to establish cost targets for the organisation.
- **Direct costs** (see page 157) are linked with particular product lines, whereas indirect costs are shared between the product lines because they do not relate to one product in particular.
- **Fixed costs** (see page 183) do not change as output changes, whereas variable costs alter as the level of production alters.

BREAK-EVEN ANALYSIS

The classification of costs into their fixed and variable elements allows break-even analysis to be undertaken. This is particularly useful for contribution pricing (see page 184) and also provides important information for production purposes. The break-even point can be calculated mathematically and/or displayed graphically.

Calculation of break-even

The calculation is based on the idea of 'contribution' already explained in marginal costing and pricing decisions (see page 184). The contribution that each item made and sold makes towards the firm's fixed costs is calculated by:

$$\text{Contribution} = \text{selling price} - \text{variable cost}$$

If the firm has fixed costs totalling £6,000, variable costs of £1.00 per unit and a unit selling price of £2.50, the unit contribution is £1.50.

$$\text{Break-even} = \frac{\text{fixed costs}}{\text{unit contribution}}$$

The firm must make (and sell) 4,000 units to break even: every unit sold above this figure increases net profit by £1.50, and every item which the firm fails to make and sell below 4,000 produces a loss of £1.50. At an output of 4,000 units, total revenue (TR) is £10,000 and total costs (TC) are also £10,000: £4,000 variable plus £6,000 fixed.

If the firm currently makes and sells 6,000 units, its margin of safety is 2,000 units: production and sales can fall by 2,000 before it starts to make a loss. The contribution from the 2,000 units made and sold above the break-even point is all net profit: 2,000 × £1.50 = £3,000 net profit. This is proved by

		£
TR	= 6,000 x £2.50	= 15,000
TC	= fixed cost	(6,000)
	+ variable cost 6,000 × £1.00	= (6,000)
Net profit		3,000

Graphical display

This is shown by Fig. 8.3. The sales revenue line is plotted and the total cost line is represented by the fixed cost line (parallel to the horizontal axis) plus the variable cost line. The information used above in calculating the break-even point is also used here.

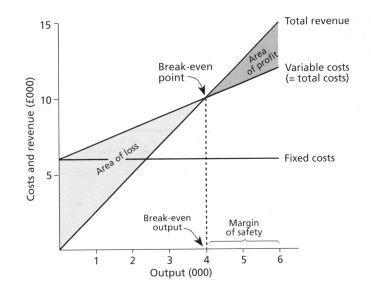

Fig. 8.3 Break-even chart

Break-even analysis is helpful to management in planning production and selling levels, but it has the following limitations.

- the chart only applies to a single product, or to a fixed mix of products;

- not all costs can be easily classified as fixed or variable (e.g. those with a standing charge element are semi-variable);

- sales prices are assumed to be constant at all activity levels;

- production and sales are assumed to be the same;

- fixed costs change over time and can change with volume (e.g. extra premises may be required if output is increased above a certain level);

- unit variable costs change with output, due to economies of scale (e.g. raw material unit prices falling through bulk-buying discounts).

Other production costs

Average and marginal costs   Break-even analysis uses the concept of the 'marginal item' in calculating contribution. The marginal cost of a product represents the cost of making that particular product: it therefore represents the product's variable cost. Average cost of production is calculated by dividing the total cost by the number of units produced. In the break-even illustration the average cost at a production level of 4,000 units is £2.50 (£10,000 for 4,000 units). At a production level of 6,000 the average cost has fallen to £2, because the additional 2,000 produced have only a variable (marginal) cost associated with them.

Social costs   The above costs are internal to the organisation. They appear in the organisation's accounts in some form. Social costs are an **external** cost of production: they are production costs met by the local community and society in general. Examples include smoke, noise and other forms of pollution generated by a firm's activities. In practice these costs are controlled through legislation (e.g. clean air laws) and by the organisation itself wishing to maintain good local relations and a positive image with the general public. The organisation balances the extra cost of controlling or reducing these social costs with the benefits and prestige it gains: for example, National Power has incurred additional costs by running cables underground rather than overhead, in some areas of natural beauty.

8.2 PRODUCTION DECISIONS

The production manager is involved in decisions concerning the method of production to use, the costing of the stock which is issued for production, and the location of the firm itself.

TYPES OF PRODUCTION SYSTEM

Production of goods and services is either intermittent or continuous in nature. Four types of production system can be distinguished, which normally depend on the scale of production being used and which themselves influence the physical layout of the production area.

Job production

This type of production involves the output of a **single product**, to individual specifications. Examples include the manufacture of a single machine tool or a ship, and the construction of an individually designed building, a bypass or a bridge (the Humber and Severn Bridges and the Channel Tunnel are typical examples). Each product is therefore a 'one-off' which requires its own costing system, the costs initially being calculated to provide a quotation based on the buyer's specification. One difficulty with job production is the accurate calculation of these costs: other problems include the high level of machine idle time and the non-existence of repeat orders.

The construction of the Channel Tunnel has illustrated the problem in job production of estimating accurately the 'three Cs': costs, cashflows and completion date. In 1993, Eurotunnel, the UK constructors, had to meet an increase in the project cost of £0.8 billion, with a corresponding rise in funding required. Postponements of the tunnel's opening date also caused pressure on the company's cashflow.

The characteristics of job production are:

- focusing on the customer and not the market;
- a high-priced product;
- highly skilled and versatile labour;
- centralised management;
- plant and equipment which is sufficiently flexible to meet the demands of the individual jobs;
- the use of techniques such as critical path analysis to plan and monitor the production process.

Batch production

This involves the output of a batch or quantity of a product without a continuous production process. Examples include producing bread and cakes in batches, constructing similar houses on a new estate and making a number of furniture items to the same design. The characteristics of batch production are similar to those of job production, although unit costs are often lower through fixed costs being spread over the number of items in the batch. The production area is often organised by grouping together similar machines and processes (such as welding and assembly).

An economic batch quantity (EBQ) can be calculated by using the same basic formula as EOQ (see page 201).

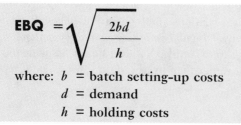

$$\text{EBQ} = \sqrt{\frac{2bd}{h}}$$

where: b = batch setting-up costs
d = demand
h = holding costs

Mass production

This involves the output of **identical and standardised products**. Examples include cars, televisions, audio equipment, washing machines and other 'black' and 'white' consumer durable goods. Production is continuous and the production inputs tend to be highly specialised, with each being employed continually on the same productive operation. Mass production relies on the support of an advanced marketing function and is associated with products which have high and long-term levels of demand. It is also associated with low morale problems arising from worker boredom, and production stoppages through equipment failure.

Its characteristics are:

- a lower-priced product;
- a greater proportion of unskilled or semi-skilled labour;
- high capital investment costs;
- economies of scale (e.g. through bulk buying and the division of labour);
- specialised plant and equipment, therefore little flexibility;
- a production layout organised to minimise the movement of parts and sub-assemblies;
- highly automated production and assembly lines;
- greater emphasis on specialised support services;
- costs being subject to standard costing and budgetary control procedures.

Process production

This method of production involves the output of a product type determined by the technological process used. Examples include oil refining and much of the production in the chemicals industry. Like mass production, the production process is continuous and tends to use even more capital equipment and more automation.

MATERIALS VALUATION

Details of the quantity of materials issued to production are recorded on a stores record card. It is also necessary to put a value on the stock issued, to charge the cost of materials to the relevant cost centre and to value the materials remaining in store.

The main methods used to price materials are FIFO (first-in, first-out), LIFO (last-in, first-out), average cost, standard cost and replacement cost. The following transactions are used to illustrate these methods.

Transactions during July				
		Units	Unit cost £	Total cost £
1st	Opening balance	50	1.00	50
3rd	Receipts	200	1.05	210
8th	Issues	100		
15th	Receipts	150	1.06	159
23rd	Issues	200		
26th	Receipts	50	1.20	60
29th	Issues	50		
31st	Closing balance	100		

FIFO

FIFO makes the assumption that materials are issued from stock in the order in which they have been received. Stock issues are therefore priced at the cost of the **earliest delivery** remaining in stock.

In the example, the costs of issues would be:

- 8th   50 at £1.00 and 50 at £1.05 (total cost £102.50)
- 23rd   150 at £1.05 and 50 at £1.06 (total cost £210.50)
- 29th   50 at £1.06 (£53)

The total cost of issues is £366 and the value of stock remaining is 50 at £1.06 and 50 at £1.20 (ie £113.00), these two totals equalling the value of opening stock plus the total value of stock received.

FIFO has the advantage of being a logical pricing method which reflects the practice of issuing the oldest stock first. It also values closing stock at or near its current market value and is acceptable to accountants and the Inland Revenue.

LIFO

The oldest physical stock is likely to be issued in practice, but the LIFO method assumes that materials are issued out of stock in the reverse order, i.e. prices used for the issue are based on the **last stock received**. In the above example the costing under the LIFO method would be:

- 8th   100 at £1.05 (£105)
- 23rd   150 at £1.06 and 50 at £1.05 (total cost £211.50)
- 29th   50 at £1.20 (£60)

The total cost of issues is £376.50 and the value of stock remaining is 50 at £1.05 and 50 at £1.00: total £102.50.

LIFO has the advantage of issuing stocks at prices close to current market values (FIFO does not do this, especially in a period of high inflation). The LIFO method, however, does not reflect the typical physical movement of oldest stock first and is not acceptable under accounting rules, nor to the Inland Revenue.

AVCO

The average cost method issues stock at its **average price**. In the above example:

- The stock on the 8th is issued at £1.04 per unit, based on a total stock at this date of 250 at a total cost of £260.
- The stock left (150 units) is valued at this average price of £1.04, and a new average is calculated when additional stock is received.
- The 150 units of stock received on the 15th at £1.06 each create a new average of £1.05.
- This new average is used to price the stock issued on the 23rd.
- The 100 units now remaining at £1.05 each are increased on the 26th by 50 (at £1.20 each), producing a closing average of £1.10.

AVCO is easier to administer than FIFO or LIFO, because there is no need to identify each stock batch separately, and it is acceptable to accountants and to the Inland Revenue. Its disadvantage is that the averaging causes its price to lag behind inflation.

Standard cost pricing

A standard cost pricing method uses **predetermined standard costs** to set the price for stock issues. All issues are made at constant price and so it is a system which is easy to administer. One drawback is the problem of determining accurate standard prices, and the issues may not be priced at current market values. If in the example the standard cost was set at £1.03 per unit, issues would be based on this price and a materials price variance could be calculated.

Replacement cost pricing

Replacement cost pricing is based on the argument that whenever stock is issued, it has to be replaced: the cost of the issue should therefore be based on the cost of the replacement stock. It is a method of pricing issues and closing stocks at **current replacement cost**. In the example, the stock issued on the 8th would be based on the replacement price (of £1.05 or £1.06) at that date. Replacement cost pricing has the advantage that materials are issued at current prices, which informs managers of any recent trends in price: although like LIFO, it is not a method acceptable either to accountants or to the Inland Revenue. Companies normally make a statement in their annual accounts that (if correct) the replacement costs of the stock are not materially different from their balance sheet values.

LOCATION OF PRODUCTION

An organisation combines the various factors of production as efficiently as possible to produce the goods or services it must sell to make a profit. The lower it can keep its unit costs, the greater its potential profit. The eventual choice of location of the firm's production is often based on compromises between different factors (Fig. 8.4).

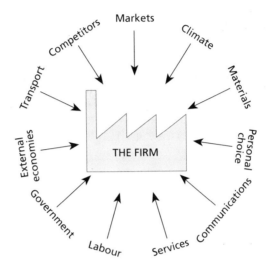

Fig. 8.4 Influences on location

Historical and natural influences

A significant historical influence on the location of production was the availability of power: for example water power, coupled with a suitable climate, encouraged the location of the old staple industries of cotton and wool weaving in the North of England.

The agricultural industry has always been influenced by the suitability of local climatic and soil conditions. Other physical advantages such as good natural harbours near to areas of high population influenced industries such as shipbuilding to locate in cities like Belfast and Sunderland. The topography and location of the land can also influence location: for example, a chemical factory complex often needs a large flat area of land by the coast.

Transport and communications

Location near to an efficient transport network has become an increasingly important influence. Many firms now examine the possible road and air links for their final products, whereas railways and canals were once the more important influences. Good transport systems are also required for the firm's labour and raw materials.

Although the whole country has national postal and telecommunication services, some 'high-tech' firms will plan to locate in areas offering more advanced technological support (e.g. advanced cable technology for telecommunications).

Labour

The availability of a both sufficiently large and well-trained labour force is an influence, although the move by many firms towards more capital-intensive production and a greater willingness by employees to commute to work have reduced the importance of this influence. When relocating, a firm has to offer a range of financial inducements to encourage its workforce to move with it, due to the geographical immobility of labour: the alternative is to meet increased training costs.

The cost of labour, as well as its availability, varies from area to area. If the firm is labour-intensive it might be tempted to move to an area of the country with relatively low wage costs.

Materials and markets

Firms involved in 'weight-gaining' production, where the end product is heavier or bulkier than the inputs (for instance, the brewery industry), have traditionally located close to their markets. Those firms using 'weight-reducing' production processes (e.g. sugar refining, and sawmills), with bulky raw materials incurring large transport costs, have tended to locate near the supplies of these materials.

Many firms and industries thus originally located close to their supply of raw materials: examples include the china industry locating in and near the Potteries and the steel industry being based near Sheffield. Now that these industries import their raw materials from abroad, newer firms are found elsewhere (often by the coast, to reduce transport costs), although the existence of external economies and 'industrial inertia' might still encourage them to locate in the traditional areas.

Some firms are heavily influenced by the population distribution of the final consumers: for example, many firms providing consumer goods locate production close to dense population areas, such as southern England (though other influences such as property and land costs can discourage this). Many extractive industries have no choice and must be based by their materials (e.g. coal mines). Firms whose market comes to them (e.g. shops and other organisations providing consumer services) also have little choice but to be geographically dispersed.

Government

The UK government and the European Union, through their development of regional policy, have become increasingly important influences. The availability of grants and other financial support have encouraged entrepreneurs to base their businesses in Development and Assisted Areas and Enterprise Zones.

Central government has played its own part in locating some of its activities outside the South East, for example in locating the National Girobank in Bootle and the DVLC in Swansea.

Personal and social influences

The personal preferences of the entrepreneur are an important influence. Some entrepreneurs have ties to particular areas of the country and may not be prepared to move elsewhere: there is geographical immobility of entrepreneurship as well as of labour.

Pressure groups and others can influence a firm's location. Concern over factors such as waste disposal and the protection of wildlife and natural habitats is an increasingly important influence, as well as the 'Nimby' (not in my back yard) attitude to the location of firms involved in the less attractive industries such as toxic waste disposal.

External economies

The existence of external economies of scale and concentration encourages firms to base their production in certain areas. For example, the UK car industry developed in the Midlands, which led to a supply of skilled labour and component manufacturers in the area.

Chapter roundup

Chapter 8 has concentrated on production methods and influences. After studying this chapter you can explain the various controls associated with production, the methods of production and the influences on the location of production.

Illustrative questions

1   Why does a retailer such as Tesco require an efficient stock control system?   (2)

2   What are 'social costs'? State **one** example.   (3)
AEB

Tutorial note

Both questions are short-answer. Question 1 is in the context of retailing, so avoid manufacturer-specific points in your answer.

Suggested answers

1   To reduce stockholding costs such as overstocking to a minimum; to ensure stock is available for shoppers as and when required.

2   Costs met by the community through a firm's activities, e.g. noise (also traffic, pollution, unemployment).

3   Total quality management (TQM) has been said to be the responsibility of every member of the organisation. What do you understand by TQM? To what extent does the achievement of TQM depend on teamwork throughout the organisation?   (20)
NEAB

Tutorial note

The second part of this question is likely to carry more marks than the first part. Make sure you distinguish between the 'get it right first time' approach of TQM and the more systems and procedure-based approach of ISO 9000.

Suggested answer

The Total Quality Management (TQM) philosophy seeks to involve all employees of an organisation in a continuing attempt to understand, meet and then exceed the expectations of the organisation's clients. It requires all members of the organisation to ensure that – at all stages of the production (or service) process – quality is achieved. It therefore sets out to establish a quality 'framework' within which the organisation operates.

   To achieve total quality, employees must identify and analyse several factors, such as client needs. In addition, each member of the organisation must realise and accept that the work he or she carries out relates to another user in the organisation. These other users can also be thought of as 'clients'. For example, an assembly worker will be producing a product which is then operated on by the assembly worker's colleague, or 'client'; in turn, this employee may liaise with his/her supervisor who is also a client. Members of the organisation's management are therefore also clients, and they in turn have their own clients within the organisation (for example, when delegating tasks).

   This acceptance of one's colleagues as clients therefore requires effective teamwork to take place. All employees must work together with shared aims and goals in mind. This team effort is reinforced in TQM through, for example, the operation of 'quality circles' of people who have a shared interest in some aspect of the organisation's activities.

4   NEW INDUSTRY IN THE NORTH EAST

   A new industry has grown up in the North East of England, automotives. It is centred on the purpose-built European production plant of Nissan, in Sunderland. Since the Japanese firm selected the North East in 1984 following a locational search throughout Europe, Nissan has invested £700 million in Sunderland.
5   Employment at the plant has grown continuously to reach 4,750 workers

including the 200 staff at its European Technology Centre. 90% of its targeted production of 222,000 cars is destined for export to 29 countries in Europe, Japan and the Far East.

10 Nissan's investment decision has introduced a new focus for the region's economy, that of automotive components. Over 40% of the Japanese component suppliers locating in the UK have chosen to do so in the North East. Joint ventures have taken place such as Ikeda – Hoover and Marley – Kanto producing car seats and plastic mouldings. 30,000 tyres and over a million sealing parts are delivered each week through the productive activity of Sumitome Rubber

15 Industries and Freudenberg Angus/LP.

From Tyne and Wear Development Corporation, *New Horizons.*

(a) Analyse the advantages and disadvantages of Nissan's policy of having a single plant to serve a number of countries rather than separate plants in each country. (8)

(b) Explain what factors you would expect Nissan to have considered in making its decision to locate its plant in Sunderland. (8)

(c) Evaluate the case for and against Nissan buying components rather than manufacturing them itself. (9)

London Examinations

Tutorial note

This question links aspects of production to locational factors. At each stage, link your answer to information in the case study where possible. The answer to (a) is quite easy once you have established that the question is referring to mass production and economies of scale.

Suggested answer

(a) The advantages of Nissan having a single plant are that it will gain from economies of scale. A single plant will be capable of mass production, which in turn generates economies such as technical ones. For example, Nissan can afford to employ at this plant expensive vehicle-manufacturing machinery such as specialist presses, which become economical in use due to the large output that is possible. Other examples of relevant economies of scale include financial economies (e.g. Nissan being able to make arrangements to borrow at low cost) marketing economies (e.g. a centralised marketing function at a single plant is less expensive, and specialists can be employed) and purchasing economies (the company can buy in bulk, for its single plant, not only raw production materials but also items such as stationery).

There are disadvantages associated with single-plant production (i.e. diseconomies of scale). As an example, the company's plant may grow too large in terms of management being able to control efficiently: there will be over-long spans of control. Another example could be if Nissan faces labour relations problems at the plant, the whole of its production will be affected.

(b) Nissan will have considered the factors we generally associate with locating a plant. The major ones in this case will include: financial incentives offered by the UK government to locate in the North East; the relative costs (such as wages) compared with other areas of the UK and the EU; the ease and cost of access to UK and EU markets for the company's vehicles; the nearness to major suppliers (e.g. of vehicle components) and ease of delivery to the plant; the availability of a suitably skilled/trained workforce in the area.

(c) The advantages Nissan will gain from buying in components include: the relative expertise of suppliers such as Lucas, and therefore the avoidance by Nissan of major expenditure on research and development; the fact that the suppliers effectively hold many of Nissan's stocks on behalf of the company, thereby reducing its storage costs and allowing it to operate a 'just-in-time' production policy; the fact that there are many (possibly hundreds) of components involved in making vehicles, and therefore it would be a complicated operation for Nissan to schedule production for, then store, all these components. There are also substantial disadvantages to this policy. Nissan is relying on outside suppliers, and the failure of one supplier could halt total production. Furthermore, there is only an indirect control over quality which might be reflected in vehicle performance at a later date, in turn affecting the company's reputation.

5 (a) The break-even chart below relates to Arrow soap, a brand of soap made by Smellies plc and distributed by Cosgrave Wholesalers to a variety of retail outlets from department stores to mini-supermarkets. Sales to retailers are currently 13,000 cases per month.

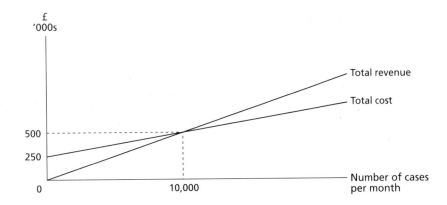

(i)   Calculate the price per case, the average variable cost per case and the current level of profit. (4)
(ii) What would be the change in the margin of safety if Smellies cut its price to £45? (2)
(iii) Comment on the limitations of break-even charts in decision making. (2)

(b) Smellies' direct production cost of a bar of Arrow is £0.14. A case of 100 bars is sold by Smellies to Cosgrave at £22.50. A bar in a department store retails at £0.59p. Define 'direct production cost' and account for the differences in prices at each stage. (4)

(c) Explain the advantages and disadvantages to Smellies of using a wholesaler. (5)

(d) Discuss why branding is important to firms like Smellies and suggest how they might create and maintain brand loyalty. (8)

Cambridge

Tutorial note

You have to read the chart quite carefully: for example, don't forget that values in the revenue/costs line are in thousands.

Suggested answer

(a) (i) Price per case: $\dfrac{£500,000}{10,000} = £50$

Average variable cost: $\dfrac{(£500,000 - £250,000)}{10,000} = £25$

Current profit level:
Total revenue: $13,000 \times £50 = £650,000$
Total variable cost: $13,000 \times £25 = £325,000$
Total fixed cost: $= £250,000$
Profit $= £75,000$

      (ii) Current margin of safety (13,000 – 10,000) = 3,000 items

           If the new sales price is £45, new contribution (£45 – £25) = £20

           New break-even point will be: $\dfrac{£250,000}{£20}$ = 12,500

           New margin of safety (13,000 – 12,500) is 500 units.

           Reduced margin of safety (3,000 – 500) is 2,500 units.

      (iii) Break-even charts assume linear relationships: in other words, fixed costs are assumed to be unchanging, also unit selling price and unit variable cost. This is unrealistic in practice. Also, the analysis assumes a single product, or an unchanging product sales mix.

(b) 'Direct production cost' is a cost directly associated with the manufacture of a product, and is therefore traceable to a cost centre. In this case, the differences in stated prices are due to mark-ups being made at each stage of the production/sale process.

(c) The advantages to Smellies from using Cosgrave Wholesalers include the support of a specialist, receipt of information about the demand for Arrow, and the ability of Cosgrave to break bulk for the company. The disadvantages to Smellies include the loss of control of distribution, and the requirement Cosgrave has to make a profit for providing this service.

Practice questions

1 (i) What factors should an entrepreneur consider when deciding where to locate a business? (5)

    (ii) Which of these factors are important for a multinational vehicle producer? (5)

Pitfalls

This question requires a specific answer to support general statements in part (i). You need to apply the relevant points to the given situation.

Key points

(a) Availability/cost of: land, labour, capital, support services, power, infrastructure; quality of access to ports, market, etc.; stability of the area/country; labour relations; government incentives.

(b) We can argue that all the above could apply: in particular, those associated with movement of production and goods between countries (e.g. stability, government incentives).

2 (a) What is meant by 'just-in-time' production? (5)

    (b) What benefits are gained by organisations from using this approach to production? (5)

Pitfalls

This is a straightforward question, though it is important to put JIT into the context of mass production.

Key points

(a) 'Just-in-time' suggests stockholding is reduced to amounts required to just meet production demand. Tight delivery schedules are set, possibly involving delivery of stock only hours before it is needed for production.

(b) A company should find that its cash flows are improved (less stock held) and wastage, obsolescence and other stockholding costs are reduced. The customer gains from lower prices, with the company therefore becoming more price-competitive.

3 Andy produces a toy selling for £7.50 each. The material costs are £2 per toy, labour costs £3 per toy and fixed costs £2,500 per month. Andy can make and sell 1,500 toys each month.

(a) Calculate Andy's:
  - unit variable cost;
  - break-even point;
  - monthly profit

  Show your workings. (5)

(b) What must Andy consider if he wishes to increase the price of his toys? (5)

(c) What are the benefits of Andy forming a limited company to operate and expand his firm? (5)

(d) (i) What benefit will Andy gain from expanding his product line to make other toys?

  (ii) If he did expand his product line, Andy would use 'batch production'. Explain this term. (5)

Pitfalls

With any numerical problem it is important to show workings so that the examiner can see how you have arrived at the relevant figures (you are advised in (a) to show workings).

Key points

(a) Unit variable cost (£2 + £3) is £5.

  Break-even point is fixed costs £2,500 divided by contributions (£7.50 – £5) £2.50 = 1,000 units.

  Monthly profit is margin of safety (1,500 – 1,000) 500 units × £2.50 contribution = £1,250.

(b) Elasticity of demand for his product; reaction of customers and competitors.

(c) Limited liability; easier to obtain finance; greater expertise/specialisation.

(d) (i) Entering new/different markets; safer (not dependent on one product).
  (ii) Production of a quantity without using a continuous production process.

COMMUNICATION IN ORGANISATIONS

Units in this chapter

Chapter objectives

Effective communication is one of the main elements contributing to the efficient management of an organisation. This chapter explains the purpose and methods of business communication, the barriers which can make it ineffective, and the various pictorial and statistical methods commonly used to summarise and communicate information. Links exist with other chapters, notably Chapter 6 – which looks at published final accounts and ratio analysis, as important methods of communicating financial information – and Chapter 8, which shows how break-even charts can be used to communicate cost and profit information.

The key topics and concepts covered in this chapter are:
- oral, written and electronic communication;
- barriers to communication;
- data and information;
- pictorial representation;
- index numbers;
- measures of central tendency;
- measures of dispersion.

9.1 THE NATURE OF COMMUNICATION

The purpose of communication is to **transmit information**. Managers need to be aware of the nature of communication and of the special skills required when communicating information.

The following are the elements which comprise the communication process, together with examples of the training in them which can be offered by organisations.

Element	Examples of training
the transmitter	training in report writing and speech making
the message being transmitted	training in systems analysis, computer programming, precis skills, memo and report writing, telephone technique
the medium chosen for transmission	training in how to use technological and telecommunications equipment
the recipient	training in company-specific and technical terms, and in listening techniques

METHODS OF COMMUNICATION

An organisation deals with various groups of people, who are either based internally (employees and managers) or externally (customers, shareholders, suppliers, central and local government). Internal and external communication takes place using oral, written and electronic means.

Oral communication

This method is most appropriate for transmitting basic, low-volume information quickly. Face-to-face oral communication is the most common form and it can be either formal or informal in nature. The use of the telephone is the principal alternative to face-to-face contact.

Oral communication has the advantage over written forms of being a two-way process which is quick and flexible – comments and phrases used can be queried by the parties – and it also has immediate impact, but it does not provide a written record of what was said or decided.

Three popular formal oral communication methods are meetings, interviews and presentations.

- **Meetings** follow formal procedures, the order of business being determined by an agenda. Since the main drawback of oral communication is its lack of permanence, written minutes are kept of decisions made. Examples of formal meetings include a company's annual general meeting (AGM) and board meetings. Meetings can also be informal: for example, some quality circle meetings (see page 199) do not have formal agendas, and minutes are not taken.

- **Interviews** are another formal method of oral communication. They are widely used in selection procedures and in grievance or disciplinary procedures.

- **Presentations** are sometimes used in formal situations, for example for a press conference or a training session. They provide structured information, but often need supporting written or diagrammatic material to assist retention of the message.

Non-verbal communication is also important in both formal and informal social situations. It includes the use of facial expression, tone of voice, gestures, body contact, physical appearance and physical proximity. The communicator must ensure that any non-verbal signals support the oral message, rather than contradict it.

Written communication

Written communication is widely used when high-volume and/or technical information must be transmitted. It has traditionally been used when the speed of delivery is not important, but the development and popularity of facsimile transmission (fax) machines now allows instantaneous transmission of written information to take place. Written communication is appropriate where a formal long-term record of the detail is required, or where such a record is to be used in a future transaction or communication.

- **Memoranda** (memos) are the main internal written forms for an organisation, for example being used by departmental heads to communicate with their staff: they are informal and summary in nature.

- **Business letters** are the main external and formal method of communication: they are also used internally, for example to make a formal statement to an employee.

- **Manuals** are used to make written summaries of technical specifications and procedures: an example is the budget manual.

- **Reports** are used to provide written details of activities such as research, or the financial performance of a company (e.g. the Annual Report).

DIRECTORS' REPORT
Sixty-fourth annual report of the directors of
Ford Motor Company Limited

The directors submit the annual report and accounts for the year ended 31 December 1992 for Ford Motor Company Limited and the group, which comprises Ford Motor Company Limited and its subsidiary undertakings.

Principal activities

The principal activities in which the group is engaged are the manufacture and sale of motor vehicles, together with associated and other finance operations.

Disposal of activities

On 21 May 1992, the Company sold its shares in A. C. Cars Limited.

Share capital

During 1992, 330 million ordinary stock units were issued for cash at par to broaden the capital base of the Company.

Directors

During the year under review, Mr. I. G. McAllister was appointed Chairman and Chief Executive on 1 January and Mr. B. J. Coughlan resigned as a director of the Company on 1 December. Since the year end, Mr. L. L. Halstead and Mr. L. R. Ross resigned as directors of the company on 1 January 1993 and Mr. B. L. Blythe and Mr. J. W. Hougham resigned as directors of the Company on 31 January 1993 and 1 March 1993 respectively. The directors express their appreciation of the valuable contribution each has made to the Company and the Ford organisation during his period of service.

Dividend

The directors recommend that no dividend be paid in respect of 1992 (1991 nil).

Donations

Money given by the group for charitable purposes in the UK during the year amounted to £140,559 (1991 £224,000).

Auditors

In accordance with Section 384 of the Companies Act 1985, a resolution proposing the reappointment of Coopers & Lybrand as auditors to the Company will be put to the annual general meeting.

By order of the Board.
C. C. Page Secretary
8 April 1993

AUDITORS' REPORT
Report of the auditors to the members of
Ford Motor Company Limited

We have audited the accounts in accordance with Auditing Standards. In our opinion the accounts give a true and fair view of the state of affairs of the company and the group at 31 December 1992 and of the losses of the company and the group and cash flows of the group for the year then ended and have been properly prepared in accordance with the Companies Act 1985.

Coopers & Lybrand
Chartered Accountants and Registered Auditors
London, 8 April 1993

Fig. 9.1 Extracts from Directors' Report and Auditor's Report

Source: The Ford Motor Co Ltd

Electronic support for communication

- **Fax machines** are used to transmit exact duplicates of an original document (text and/or diagram) from the sender to the recipient: the document image is scanned electronically and transmitted down the telephone line which connects the two fax machines. This system overcomes one of the principal drawbacks of written communication, that of slowness of delivery.

- **Electronic mail** (e-mail) also uses telephone lines, to link computers in different locations. The mail (letter, memo, etc.) is transmitted by one computer and received by the other, which informs its user that a message is waiting.

- **Teletext services,** such as those seen on most domestic televisions, allow a one-way or two-way link with an electronic database. They are widely used to obtain current business information, for example in the international financial and currency markets: the tourism industry is an example of where an electronic database is used to link supplier information (e.g. an airline company and the number of seats available on a flight) with consumer requirements.

Computers form the backbone of many communication systems. The advantages to be gained from the use of this modern technology in communication include: improved quality (e.g. through desk-top publishing and laser printing); reduced costs of storing, manipulating and retrieving mass data and information; and greater security of information stored.

The Ford Motor Co Ltd illustrates how a company can benefit from the use of information technology in communication.

- Satellite communications provide a video-conferencing link between the UK Research and Engineering Centre in Essex and its counterpart in Cologne, Germany.

- Satellite links are also used for conferences between company locations in the US, Australia, Japan and Europe.

- A Picture Tel facility is used to transmit images in parallel with video-conferencing.

- FCN, the Ford Communications Network, uses television screens installed in Ford premises throughout the UK which are linked by telephone lines and satellite to transmit continuous teletext news items, video news programmes and special information bulletins to employees.

- Ford Dealer Television Network (FDTN) broadcasts news to Ford's main and retail dealers and offers an interactive communications facility between dealers and Ford management.

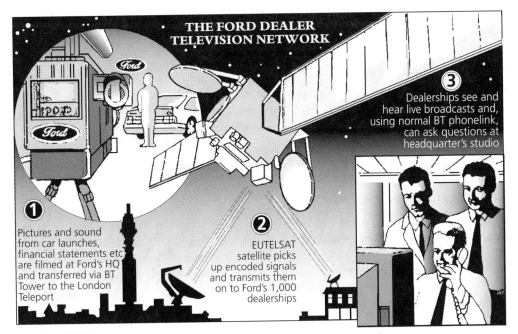

Fig. 9.2 FDTN

Source: The Ford Motor Co Ltd

BARRIERS TO EFFECTIVE COMMUNICATION

The efficiency of communication is affected by its four elements: the transmitter, the message, the medium and the recipient. Problems arise in the following situations.

The transmitter uses:

- an inappropriate level of language, e.g. jargon or over-complex terms;
- inaccurate technical terms or specialist vocabulary;
- over-long sentences or poor sentence structures;
- summaries which omit important information;
- unsuitable or inappropriate non-verbal communication to support the message.

The message is sent:

- over a long distance, which might encourage the use of less appropriate non-direct methods;
- through a long chain of command (see page 74), resulting in it being transmitted through too many people and levels;
- containing a high level of redundancy (i.e. the amount of information being transmitted is far more than is required);
- between a transmitter and recipient of unequal status, such as communication between the managing director and a group of shopfloor workers: one party might refuse to listen to the other party's message.

The medium is:

- unsuitable for the information being transmitted;
- too slow in getting the message to the recipient in time for it to be acted upon.

The recipient:

- has a poor listening technique;
- interprets the message in an incorrect way, due to personal bias or the wish to hear something else;
- is in an unsuitable physical or emotional state to receive the message accurately.

There is the additional general problem of 'noise', a term which describes any impediment to the transmission of a clear message. Examples of noise include actual background noise, or faulty transmission equipment, which distract the transmitter and/or the recipient.

Improving communication

Communication can be improved by: training the transmitter in the use of appropriate language (including body language) and the selection of appropriate media; obtaining efficient support technology, such as fax machines; and training the recipient in listening techniques and methods of feedback. Specific listening techniques include:

- **repeating or restating,** to ensure the meaning is understood;
- **clarifying,** to obtain additional information;
- **summarising,** to focus on the perceived key issues.

Communication networks

All communication takes place within formal or informal networks. Formal networks are closely associated with the organisation's structure, as shown by its organisation chart. The chart shows the lines of authority and the relationship between departments or functions: it also illustrates the formal communication networks that exist within the organisation.

A formal, 'chain' network is based on the existing chains of command within the organisation. Communications are transmitted from superior to subordinate along the chain, and this network is therefore associated with 'tall' structures and authoritarian organisations such as the police and armed forces. Horizontal communication networks and channels also exist: as an example, members of a team communicate with each other at team meetings or through issuing memos.

Informal networks coexist with formal ones. The human need for contact, friendship and recognition helps to create these informal channels. They assume greater importance where the formal networks are not working efficiently. The main characteristics of an informal network are:

- it transmits information quickly (and often accurately);
- the quality of its communication is heavily influenced by the subjective judgements of those transmitting the information.

9.2 PICTORIAL AND STATISTICAL METHODS OF COMMUNICATION

COLLECTING THE DATA

Data consist of unorganised facts and figures which require organising into information. Data can be:

- quantitative (number-based) or qualitative (descriptive);
- primary (original) or secondary (collected elsewhere with another purpose in mind);
- internal or external to the organisation.

Sampling

Where primary data are needed – for example, in surveying prospective customers, following the test launch of a new product – a decision has to be made on the extent and nature of the sample of the population required. For the sample to be valid, it must reflect accurately the whole population. The target population (sample) is drawn by using one of several different sampling methods.

❶ **Simple random sampling** This is a method where every member of the population stands an equal chance of being selected for the sample and there is therefore no bias in the sample selection. Computers are used to generate random numbers for this task.

❷ **Stratified random sampling** This is a suitable method where the population consists of subgroups with their own unique qualities or attributes. For example, a population could be stratified on the basis of age, sex or income. Each sub-group can then be sampled on a random basis.

❸ **Multi-stage sampling** This involves selecting a number of (geographical) areas which are regarded as representative of the whole, and a random sample is taken in these areas. It is a way of reducing the costs associated with full random sampling, although the results of the sampling process may be more biased and thus less reliable.

❹ **Cluster sampling** This develops the idea of multi-stage sampling by selecting everyone – not just a random sample – in an area thought to be representative of the whole. It can cut time and costs even further than multistage sampling, but the reliability of its data is more suspect.

❺ **Quota sampling** A quota of the number of people or items to be sampled is set, and the data are then collected from anyone or anything fitting the relevant category, until the quota has been filled. This is a popular market research method used by street interviewers and can work effectively in conjunction with stratified sampling techniques, although it is often the least accurate of all the sampling methods.

Systematic sampling This method sets an interval and then samples every nth (10th, 50th, 600th, etc.) person or item on the basis of this interval. It is a popular method, used in quality control systems, although it can be an inaccurate approach because it does not use truly random numbers.

PRESENTING THE INFORMATION

The way that information is presented diagrammatically or numerically can be almost as important as the content represented by the information. Information which is presented satisfactorily uses an appropriate

- **display**, using correct columns or a correct scale;
- **level of detail**;
- **method of presentation** for:
  - the information;
  - the user(s);
- **series of labels** which describe the:
  - sources
  - heading
  - axes
  - units being used.

Tables

The purpose of tabulation is to group and organise data so that they become manageable and capable of being understood. **Tally charts** are used to count the frequency of items occurring within each group. The number of items per group can then be recorded in a table consisting of labelled rows and columns.

Tables are effective in displaying summarised information accurately and concisely, although they are not as visually stimulating as pictorial forms of presentation and they do not always display trends clearly.

Examples of tabulated information can be seen throughout this Guide, for example on pages 53, 80 and 81.

Graphs

These are diagrams plotting values as points, which are then joined together to form a continuous line. They are easy to construct and can show clearly any trends. Fig. 9.3 shows how a graph can be used effectively in displaying seasonal trends.

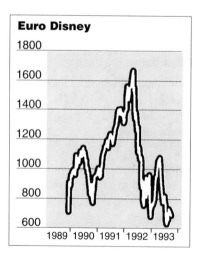

Fig. 9.3 Euro Disney attendance

Source: *The Guardian*

Fig. 9.4 plots three graphs to highlight the gap between them.

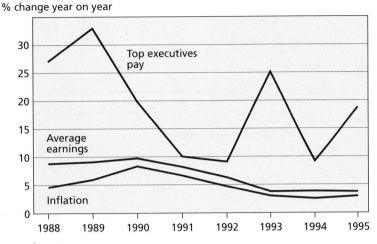

% change year on year

Fig. 9.4 Top executive pay

Source: *The Guardian*

Other examples of graphs can be seen on page 52.
Special types of graph include:

- **Semi-logarithmic graphs:** whereas ordinary graphs summarise the absolute changes which have taken place, these semi-logarithmic graphs show the percentage or proportional rates of change which have occurred.
- **Lorenz curve graphs:** these show the equality or otherwise of two distributions. They illustrate the level of inequality in the way that a figure is shared between two competing ends: for example, the Lorenz curve graph is often used to display inequalities in wealth or income.
- **Z charts:** these are really three graphs in one, containing lines which show monthly data, cumulative data, and a moving annual total. The name derives from the shape of the graph, which looks like the letter Z.
- **Break-even charts:** see page 203.

Pie charts

These consist of circles divided into segments. The circle represents the whole population, the segments representing the parts which make up this whole. The 360 degrees of the circle is therefore divided in proportion to the figures making the total. Pie (and bar) charts are popularly used in company reports to summarise trading and other financial information. A Pie chart is effective in showing how a total is made up, but is an unsuitable display method if there are too many segments. It has been traditionally difficult to construct, but most computer spreadsheet packages can now generate pie charts quickly and easily. Fig. 9.5 shows a pie chart being used to break down a total. Another pie chart can be seen on page 96.

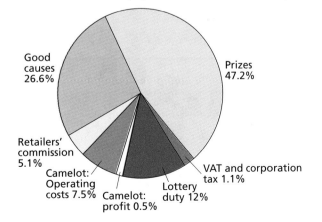

Fig. 9.5 Breakdown of sales to 31 March 1995

Source: Camelot Group plc

Bar charts

In a simple bar chart the figures being compared are represented by bars. The height of each bar reflects the relative size of the figure it represents. This is shown clearly by Fig. 9.6 on satellite dish ownership, and can also be seen on pages 34 and 127.

A component or 'stacked' bar chart is constructed by first drawing a bar to represent the total population, and then dividing it into its component elements. It enables totals to be compared and also shows clearly how these totals are made up from their components, as shown in Figs. 9.7, 9.8 and 9.9.

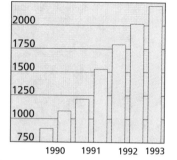

Fig. 9.6 Number of satellite dishes (thousands), June and December figures

Source: The Guardian

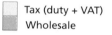
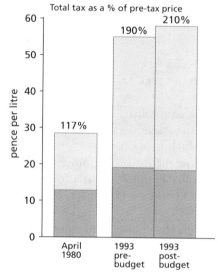

Fig. 9.7 Tax in UK 4-star leaded petrol price

Source: Esso UK plc

A percentage component bar chart – an alternative form of display to the pie chart – shows the relative percentage or proportion of each component, and therefore its relative importance. All the bars are the same height, because each one represents 100 per cent. Fig. 9.8 shows percentage component bars.

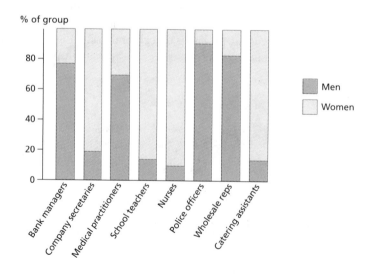

Fig. 9.8 Male and female employment by type of occupation

Source: The Guardian

A compound (or multiple) bar chart is used where the component figures need to be compared. Each component has its own bar, the bars for each time period being drawn side by side. The relative size of each component is shown and can be compared, although the overall total cannot always easily be seen. Fig. 9.9 shows population changes using this method.

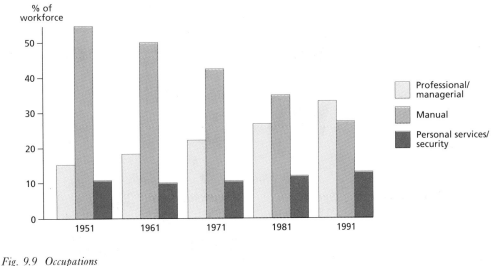

Fig. 9.9 Occupations

Source: OPCS

Pictograms

These are simple diagrams using pictures or symbols to represent numbers. Their purpose is to give a quick and basic idea of relative size, for purposes of comparison. An alternative approach is to have one symbol or picture for each organisation, time period, etc. The size of each symbol represents the size of the amount being illustrated, as in Fig. 9.10.

Although pictograms provide a quick and basic summary of the situation, they fail to show fractions accurately, and they can often give a false impression of size (especially when the width of a symbol is increased as its height increases).

Index numbers

These are used when it becomes necessary to compare information from different time periods. A common base – the base year – is established and figures from this base year are given the value 100. Other years' figures are then expressed against this base value. Index numbers therefore make comparison of different years' figures more meaningful. Index numbers are used to measure changes in price, quantity and value.

FREQUENCY DISTRIBUTIONS

Large amounts of data are more easily understood if they are organised into frequency distributions. Tally charts can be used to arrive at the frequency for each set of data. The data are then grouped into various classes or values which state the number of items in each class. The following illustrates a grouped frequency distribution of firms employing different numbers of people.

Number of people employed	Frequency
under 50	2
50 but under 100	6
100 but under 150	24
150 but under 200	44
200 but under 250	16
250 but under 300	4

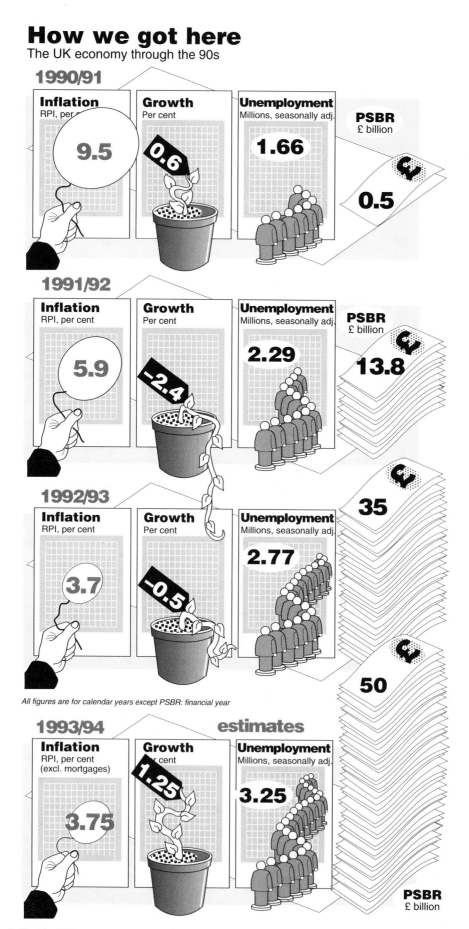

Fig. 9.10 *The UK economy through the early 1990s*

Source: Paddy Allen, *The Guardian*

Histograms

These are diagrams which are used to illustrate frequency distributions. The horizontal scale is used for the variable of interest and the vertical scale indicates its relative frequency. Using the information above, the horizontal scale shows the employee size of the firms and the vertical scale shows the number of firms per class. Fig. 9.11 illustrates the histogram.

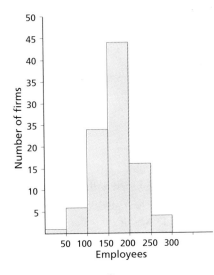

Fig. 9.11 Histogram of the number of employees per firm

Each bar of the histogram represents one class, its width reflecting the class width. The histogram can be converted to a **frequency polygon**, a graph which plots the mid-point height of each bar. The advantage of the frequency polygon is that it highlights the shape of the distribution, as shown in Fig. 9.12.

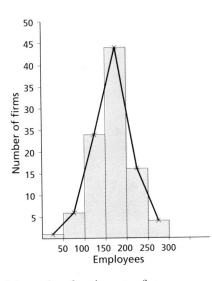

Fig. 9.12 Frequency polygon of the number of employees per firm

INTERPRETING THE DISTRIBUTION

We are interested in three features of a distribution of data:

- Its central tendency – a measure of its 'average'.

- Its dispersion – a measure of its spread (i.e. are the numbers widely dispersed or closely grouped?).

- Its skewness – how symmetrical the raw data are ('skewness' is the term used to describe a lack of symmetry in the raw data).

Measuring central tendency

The three most popular methods used to calculate an average value are the arithmetic mean, the median and the mode.

The arithmetic mean This is a simple average of the total values of the data. It is calculated by totalling the values and dividing by their number. If the following are the values:

$$42, \quad 34, \quad 58, \quad 35, \quad 51$$

the mean is

$$\frac{220}{5} = 44$$

The mean has the following characteristics:

● it is easy to understand and calculate;
● it uses every value in the distribution;
● it can be used for further statistical manipulation;
● it can be distorted by extreme values in the distribution;
● it can give, as the answer, a value which does not exist in the original data (such as in the example above).

The median This is the middle value of an ordered set of items. To establish the median value, the data must be organised into an ordered set – an array.

If the raw data are:

$$5, \quad 3, \quad 3, \quad 8, \quad 2, \quad 7, \quad 5, \quad 4, \quad 3$$

the array is

$$2, \quad 3, \quad 3, \quad 3, \quad 4, \quad 5, \quad 5, \quad 7, \quad 8$$

The median value is 4 because it is in the middle of this array. A problem arises where there is no middle value, i.e. the array consists of an even number of values. If the above array had the first value missing it would be:

$$3, \quad 3, \quad 3, \quad 4, \quad 5, \quad 5, \quad 7, \quad 8$$

and the median value is taken as the mid-point of the middle two items. In this illustration the median is 4.5.

The median has the following characteristics:

● it is easy to understand;
● it is not influenced by extreme values in the data;
● half the values are greater, and half are less than, the median value;
● it requires the data to be organised;
● it may be unrepresentative where there are only a few values.

The mode This is the value which occurs most frequently in a list of data. In the data used to construct the histogram, the modal group is '150 but under 200', because the greatest number (44) of firms employed this range of workers. In the data used to illustrate the median, the mode is 3 since this is the value occurring most frequently.

The mode has the following characteristics:

● it is easy to understand;
● it is an actual single value with discrete (whole-number) data;
● its value is not affected by extreme items in the population;
● it requires the data to be organised.

Choosing the average

If a firm's managers wish to assess the order or rank of something – for example, where the firm stands compared with others in the industry – the median is normally used. If they need to establish the most commonly occurring value – in the clothing and footwear industries, for example – the mode is used. If they wish to establish an equal distribution, for example in calculating the average number of times their products are bought by a consumer per annum, the mean is an appropriate measure to use. Table 9.1 illustrates the use of the median when the best 'typical' average value for pay was required.

Table 9.1 *Percentage of workforce in EU countries earning low pay (defined as less than two-thirds of male median earnings)*

UK	20.0
Spain	19.0
Ireland	18.0
Denmark	15.8
Italy	14.5
France	14.0
Germany (W)	13.0
Portugal	12.0
Netherlands	11.0
Belgium	5.0

Source: EU 1992

MEASURING DISPERSION

Measures of location – the mean, median and mode – tell a manager what is an 'average' or 'typical' value. The manager may also wish to know how the population is spread, or dispersed, around the central value. As an example, a quality control manager could use the arithmetic mean to calculate whether metal tubes being made average 3 cm in diameter. It is also necessary to measure whether enough tubes fall within the acceptable tolerance limits of 2.9 cm and 3.1 cm. A machine producing tubes with an average size of 3.01 cm is apparently efficient, yet may be unacceptable if most of the tubes have widely dispersed measurements ranging from 2.7 cm to 3.3 cm.

The range, quartile deviation and standard deviation are popular methods used to measure dispersion.

The range

This is the difference between the smallest and the largest value in the population. If these items comprise the total population:

$$24, \quad 25, \quad 72, \quad 44, \quad 28, \quad 65$$

then the range is 48 (72 – 24).

The range is easy to understand and to calculate, but it ignores all but two values and it is directly affected by extreme values. It is useful in providing a quick measure of dispersion and can be used effectively when there are only a few values in the population.

The quartile deviation

The quartile deviation is often used as the measure of spread when the median is used as the measure of location. Quartiles divide the data into four equal parts. The interquartile range is the difference between the first and third quarters – Q3 and Q1 – which represent the central half of the data. The quartile deviation (QD) is half this amount and is calculated by:

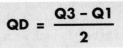

$$QD = \frac{Q3 - Q1}{2}$$

The quartile deviation has the following characteristics:

- it is easy to understand;
- it concentrates on the more representative central 50 per cent of the values and is therefore not affected by extreme values;
- it can involve lengthy calculations.

The standard deviation

This measure of dispersion is used where the mean is used as the measure of location. It represents the average deviation from the mean and is calculated by using the formula:

$$\sigma = \sqrt{\frac{\Sigma (x - \bar{x})^2}{n}}$$

where σ = **the standard deviation** $\bar{x}$ = **the mean**
         Σ = **the sum of** n = **number of values**
         x = **a value**

(In practice, the standard deviation is easily calculated on modern calculators.)
The standard deviation has the following characteristics:

- it is easy to calculate;
- it uses all values in its calculation, but can be distorted by extreme values;
- it can be developed mathematically.

Chapter roundup

Chapter 9 has concentrated on the process of communication: after studying this chapter you can explain the nature of oral and written communication, together with the main barriers to communicating successfully. The chapter has also illustrated the main pictorial and statistical methods of communicating information.

Illustrative questions

1 Distinguish, with the aid of examples, between formal and informal communication.

(4)

AEB

Tutorial note

The mark scheme is likely to give 1 mark for a general comment about each form, and 1 mark for each of two examples.

Suggested answer

Formal communication is communication that takes place along formal channels, such as oral presentations to managers, or is otherwise formalised (e.g. minutes of a meeting). Informal communication is communication that takes place in less formal social situations (e.g. when employees talk during a lunch break about a business matter), or when the event taking place is deliberately designed to be informal, such as many Quality Circle meetings.

2 A travel agency is reviewing its information storage system.

   (a) Design a simple database record card to record details of actual or potential business customers.

   (b) Describe how this database might be used in a direct mail promotion.

Tutorial note

The question involves the work of a travel agent: your thoughts might be based on personal use for holidays, but remember that 'business customers' are referred to. This will influence the fields you choose for the record card, which could be drawn simply (this allows you to indicate likely field lengths).

Suggested answer

(a) Possible database record card fields:

Organisation name _____	Telephone _____
Organisation address _____	Extension _____
_____	
_____	Fax _____
_____	
County _____	
Post-code _____	
Client name _____	
Position_____	
Request _____	
_____	
_____	
_____	
Date _____	Operator initials_____

Fields might also include the client's main foreign country interests, and the services used by the client (air travel, hire car, hotel, conference facilities, etc.).

(b) The database could be used in conjunction with a word processing package (which might be part of an integrated software package with the database). The software would allow labels for envelopes to be generated (via a printer) from the name and address fields of the database. Each letter could be customised, by the business customer's name being inserted into appropriate places on a standard letter using the name field from the database and the word processing package's mailmerge facility. Having different (or additional) fields would enable the organisation to target certain customers when undertaking promotions.

3 'Research suggests that managers read on average one million words a week, and forget 80% of what they have learned inside a month.'

   (a) What features of a business report determine how easy it is to read? (8)

   (b) What are the main advantages of good presentation in a report? (7)

   (c) Discuss whether, if their long term memory is poor, managers should read less and devote more time to other tasks. (10)

SEB

Tutorial note

Parts (a) and (b) are quite straightforward, where all you need to do is identify and explain the main points. A phrase such as 'Discuss whether…' is often an indication that there is not a precise answer (and that the examiner expects you to recognise this in your answer).

Suggested answer

(a) A good report has a number of features which make it readable. It needs to be structured logically, include content which is descriptive and unbiased, and it should be written in language that is accessible to the reader. The writer needs to answer a number of questions in order to write a readable report: who are the users of the report? What do they need to know? How much information is required, how quickly, and at what cost?

(b) Good presentation in a report requires the use of an acceptable structure such as title; terms of reference; procedure; findings; conclusions; recommendations. In addition, numerical information is often presented most effectively by the use of appropriate diagrams and charts. The advantages of good presentation are that the information is communicated efficiently and effectively. This assists management or other users of the report in controlling and co-ordinating the business functions.

(c) In modern business life, there is an ever-increasing amount of information at managers' disposal. This has been particularly noticeable in the 1990s, with the development of electronic communications. Given this increase in volume, it becomes more important than ever for managers to prioritise the tasks they face. Associated with this is the need for managers to delegate routine tasks. It is not a valid argument to say that, simply because managers forget much of what they read, they should devote more time to other tasks. These 'other tasks' may not be important, and therefore should involve others who are not employed to make the high-level decisions associated with management. The information that the managers need to read should be relevant to them, for example in their strategic roles.

4 Study the following information and then answer the questions that follow.
John Roberts is a builder who currently employs 250 workers on the construction of a new supermarket. The earnings of the workforce for the week ending June 1995 are illustrated below.

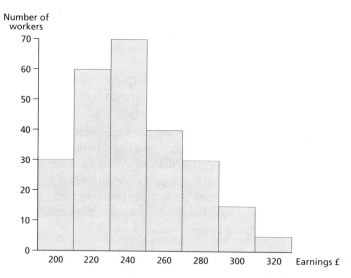

The workforce is currently in dispute with John over a pay claim. They have submitted a claim of 5% for all workers. John has offered them an increase of £11 per worker. This increase he argues is above the current rate of inflation as measured by the retail price index and will increase the standard of living of all the workforce.

The dispute seems likely to escalate.

(a) Calculate the mean wage of the workforce. (3)

(b) Explain why some workers might be prepared to accept John's offer whilst others are not. (6)

(c) How useful is the retail price index as a measure of the cost of living? (9)

WJEC

Tutorial note

Graphs and charts can be difficult to read accurately under examination pressure. You therefore need to be careful in identifying the relevant figures in (a).

Suggested answer

(a) ($200 x 30) + ($220 x 60) + ($240 x 70) + ($260 x 40) + ($280 x 30) + ($300 x 15) + ($320 x 5) = $6,000 + $13,200 + $16,800 + $10,400 + $8,400 + $4,500 + $1,600 = $60,900.

Total employees = 30 + 60 + 70 + 40 + 30 + 15 + 5 = 250.

Mean wage $= \dfrac{£60,900}{250} = £243.60$

(b) Some workers will want to accept John's offer because the return of £11 is greater than a 5% increase. Examples include workers earning £200: a 5% increase on this would only be £10. Those employees earning £240 and above will be worse off if they receive a £11 increase.

An associated argument is that a percentage increase maintains differentials, which is what higher-paid workers often look for. A flat-rate increase will narrow differentials, which is often supported by lower-paid workers in the system.

(c) The retail price index (RPI) is a measure of how the prices of a 'basket' of goods have moved over time, set against a base year. The index is not perfect, because it consists of various popular household goods weighted to reflect their relative importance for a typical household. The problems are in establishing what is a 'typical' household, and also that the relative importance of each good in the basket changes over time (the weights therefore need to be updated regularly). Given this updating of the weights (and the items included in the 'basket'), the RPI is a reasonable representation of what many people spend.

Practice questions

1   Give **two** disadvantages of using a pie chart to present data. (2)

AEB

Pitfalls

Questions normally ask for both advantages and disadvantages, or just advantages. Here you need to state briefly two disadvantages.

Key points

Two disadvantages are that the pie chart may not show clearly an item divided into many segments, and that it can be visually misleading in certain circumstances (e.g. when displayed at an angle).

2   (a)   Why does the growth in a firm's size often cause communications to deteriorate, and what steps should its management take to control this deterioration?

(b)   What other factors affect a firm's information system?

(c)   To what extent can communication barriers be overcome by efficient systems design?

Pitfalls

Part (a) really contains two questions in one ('...why does... ..and what'). The wording in part (c) 'To what extent...' is often an indication that there is not a precise answer (and that the examiner expects your answer to acknowledge this point).

Key points

(a) Larger size extends the channels of communication and chain networks: there are more layers of personnel through which the message must pass. Systems analysis should be undertaken to evaluate the efficiency of the present organisational structures and routines; communication media should also be assessed for suitability and clarity; staff training in communication procedures and techniques should be undertaken.

(b) Staff morale; staff numbers; the size of the organisation (e.g. whether it is a 'flat' or a 'tall' structure); the state of the technology being used; the present level of training; the degree of geographical dispersion of the organisation, its employees, suppliers and customers.

(c) Systems design seeks to improve and develop procedures and routines which are suitable for a specific organisation. Effective communication forms the foundation for efficient systems, but still depends on the level of human involvement, expertise and morale for success.

3 (a) What are the most important non-verbal methods of communication? (8)

  (b) What uses do non-verbal methods of communication have in the **internal** communications of a business? (12)

  (c) Discuss the regulation of non-verbal communication in advertising and other promotions. (5)

SEB

Pitfalls

Your answer needs to be precise, concentrating on non-verbal communication in the contexts given.

Key points

(a) Gestures (facial and body); eye contact; mannerisms; appearance; physical proximity.

(b) They reinforce and support internal communications, helping explain them, e.g. by speakers emphasising the points they are making with body movement.

(c) Control is required of subliminal messages, for the public good; use of NVC can be misleading in certain circumstances, and therefore against the recognised advertisers' code of conduct.

MAKING DECISIONS

Units in this chapter

Chapter objectives

All managers have to make business decisions. Most of the earlier chapters contain units which illustrate the different areas of decision-making: examples include decisions on recruitment, organisational structure, size, location, and price. Chapter 10 examines the nature of financial and investment decisions, and explains the major decision-making techniques available to managers. Making decisions brings about change, and the chapter ends by outlining how change affects people at work.

The key topics and concepts covered in this chapter are:

- sources of finance;
- investment appraisal;
- linear programming;
- critical path analysis;
- simulation;
- change.

10.1 FINANCIAL DECISIONS

All organisations must obtain finance to meet their various financial commitments. A firm's managers must decide:

- how much finance is needed;
- whether it is needed to cover capital or revenue expenditure;
- whether it can be obtained internally;
- whether it should be borrowed or obtained permanently;
- (if borrowed) whether a short-term, medium-term or long-term source is best.

The amount and nature of this finance varies from firm to firm and is influenced by a firm's size, its form of ownership, the type of technology currently being used in the firm, the relationship between capital and labour, the length of credit periods allowed and taken, and the age of the firm's assets.

A firm's financial commitments are classed as either capital expenditure or revenue expenditure (see page 144). The firm must acquire fixed assets (see page 144) to use in making its goods or services. Long-term (fixed) capital is needed for this capital expenditure. Short-term working capital is used to finance the revenue expenditure running costs such as wages and the purchase of stock. The firm's liquidity measures its short-term financial stability in terms of its ability to meet these debts.

The firm can obtain finance from internal and external sources. The advantage of using internal finance is that this does not carry interest or other borrowing costs, nor does it need to be repaid in future. A drawback of relying on internal sources is the lack of certainty of the amounts available, since these depend largely on sales and profit activity levels.

INTERNAL SOURCES OF FINANCE

1 **Retained profits**   Private sector firms and owners are legally obliged to pay tax on profits, but then face a choice with the balance remaining. They can either 'spend' it, in the form of personal (sole trader or partnership) drawings or owner (shareholder) dividends, or 'save' it as retained profit. Retaining profits preserves the firm's cash through not spending it in the form of distributed profit. This is the main internal source of funds: it is also known as undistributed or ploughed-back profit, and may at the end of the financial year be transferred to a reserve such as a general reserve.

2 **Sinking funds**   As a fixed asset is used and starts to wear out, the accountant may invest in a sinking fund an amount equal to or slightly above (to take account of inflation) the level of depreciation charged, to finance the replacement of the asset.

3 **Sale of assets**   A firm might have surplus assets, for example during a recession or a period of rationalisation. These assets can be sold to raise finance. A variation on the standard sale for cash is 'sale and leaseback', where the firm sells the asset to a purchaser and at the same time agrees to lease it back over a long time period. Funds are therefore generated, while the firm retains the use and control of the asset concerned.

4 **Control of working capital**   Extending its average credit period taken and/or reducing the average credit period it allows improves the firm's cashflow. Other controls include reducing stock levels and postponing the payment of expense creditors (e.g electricity and telephone bills), to increase finance for investment.

EXTERNAL SOURCES OF FINANCE

Share issues

A limited company normally obtains most of its permanent capital by issuing ordinary and/or preference shares. Its memorandum of association contains a capital clause which states the amount and types of share capital it is allowed to issue.

- The **nominal capital** is the maximum share capital that can be issued.
- The **issued capital** represents the nominal capital actually issued at a given time.
- **Called-up capital** refers to the amount the company has called on the shareholders to pay. It may issue more shares than it requires as capital, to avoid the expense of a future share issue, only calling on the shareholders to pay initially a fraction of the share value (many privatisation issues adopted this strategy).
- **Uncalled capital** represents the balance owing by the shareholders on partly paid-up shares.

Share capital

The authorised share capital of the Company is £500.0 million (1994/95 – £500.0 million).

Details of the share capital issued and fully paid are set out below:

	1996 Shares	£m	1995 Shares	£m
5.25% Cumulative Preference shares of £1 each	300,000	0.3	300,000	0.3
4.9% Cumulative 'A' Preference shares of £1 each	2,000,000	2.0	2,000,000	2.0
8.75% Cumulative Preference shares of £1 each	498,280	0.5	498,280	0.5
Ordinary shares of 25p each	1,522,628,617	380.7	1,515,790,099	378.9
		383.5		381.7

Fig. 10.1 Share capital

Source: Sears plc

Ordinary shares, or 'equity capital', carry the greater risk, from the investor's view being at the end of the line for repayment of capital. They are also not awarded a fixed rate of return but a variable dividend which relies on surplus profits after loan interest (paid out of gross profit), tax and preference dividends (from net profit) have been paid. The advantage to the ordinary shareholder lies in times of high profits, especially in high-geared companies (see page 155) which have a low proportion of ordinary shares amongst which the remaining profits are shared.

Preference shares carry less investment risk than ordinary shares. Different types of preference shares can be issued:

● **Redeemable** preference shares are repayable at some future date.

● **Cumulative** preference shares allow their owners, in times of good profits, to receive any dividends owed from previous years when the company was unable to pay the full amount of dividend because of low profits.

● **Convertible** preference shares give their owners the opportunity to convert these shares into ordinary shares.

	Ordinary	**Preference**
Voting rights	Usually one vote per share	Usually non-voting
Payment of dividend	Variable, depending on profits and the decisions of the directors	Fixed percentage rate
Repayment of capital	After loans and preference shares	After loans and other creditors, but before ordinary

Long-term sources of finance

'Long-term' normally refers to a period in excess of five years. The benefits to managers from using long-term finance are:

● the interest payments are eroded in real terms by inflation;

● these payments are made out of gross profit (untaxed income), whereas share dividends are payable out of taxed net profits;

● the lender has no direct vote or say in controlling the firm.

Unlike dividends, however, the interest payments must **always** be met by the firm: this can create liquidity problems at times of losses or low profits.

Debentures and mortgages form the main sources of long-term loan capital.

- **Debentures** are normally secured against either a specific asset, or assets in general: the lender can recover the asset if the borrower fails to make the required payments. The term 'debenture' refers to the document issued outlining the nature of the loan. This loan is usually redeemable at a given future date.

- **Mortgages** are similar to debentures, although they are obtained from one source (a financial institution), rather than from a number of subscribers.

Medium-term sources of finance

'Medium-term' involves finance of between one and five years. Bank (or other finance house) loans, hire purchase, credit sale and leasing are the main sources of medium-term finance.

- **Bank loans** are fixed sums agreed between the borrower and the bank, for a fixed term. Unlike overdrafts, a special account is opened for the loan, and interest is charged on the full balance. The bank requires security against the loan being made. Loans can also be obtained from specialist finance houses; the opening up of the EU Single Market has made the provision of business loans much more competitive.

- **Leasing** allows firms to obtain capital equipment without having to buy and own it. This avoids the need for large capital outlay, and brings the lessee (the hirer) several benefits: the payments are regular, known in advance and made out of untaxed gross profit; income generated from using the asset can contribute towards payments; no specific security is normally required from the lessee; and the asset can be exchanged, upgraded or the agreement ended as technological developments make its use less cost-effective.

- **Hire purchase and credit sale** agreements are often used when a firm wants to purchase and own an asset – which takes place at the start of a credit sale agreement, and at the end with hire purchase – without having to meet the full capital cost in a single payment. Many of the advantages of leasing also apply here.

Short-term sources of finance

'Short-term' refers to a period of less than a year. Bank overdrafts, factoring debts and extending trade credit are popular forms of short-term finance.

- **Overdrafts** are agreed between a bank and a firm, allowing the firm to overdraw its existing account up to an agreed amount: a charge is based on the level of the overdraft, which can make borrowing by overdraft relatively inexpensive. Overdrafts are also flexible, but the facility can (in theory) be withdrawn by the bank with minimal notice.

- **Factoring** occurs when a firm sells its trade debts at less than their face value to a factoring agent in return for an immediate cash payment. The selling company loses some of the value of the debt, but this is partly offset by the quick receipt of cash which can be set to work immediately, and through the factoring agent taking on the responsibility of any bad debts.

- Increasing **trade credit** occurs when the firm identifies and starts to use alternative suppliers who are offering better credit terms.

10.2 CAPITAL INVESTMENT DECISIONS

Organisations undertake investment appraisal to assess the quality of capital investments such as the purchase of fixed assets. These types of investment:

- tie up the firm's finance for a long period, normally for a number of years;
- generate profits over most or all of their useful life;
- often have a resale or scrap value at the end of their life.

Because of the major capital outlays involved, managers try to calculate expected profitability and cashflows for the proposed investment. These calculations also help decisions to be made between alternative capital projects. There are three main methods of evaluating capital investment.

Payback period method

This method of investment appraisal calculates how long it takes a project to repay its original investment. The method is therefore based on **cashflows**.

The payback method highlights projects which quickly repay their original investment. The following example illustrates how it works.

A company is considering two different capital investment projects. Both are expected to operate for four years. Only one of the projects can be financed.

	Project A £	Project B £
Initial cost	22,000	2,000
Profit/(loss):		
year 1	2,000	2,500
year 2	4,000	1,500
year 3	7,000	3,000
year 4	(3,000)	5,000
Expected scrap value	2,000	2,000
Depreciation per annum	5,000	5,000

The payback periods for the projects are calculated by adding annual depreciation back to the cashflows from profit: depreciation is a non-cash expense which reduces profit, therefore the profit figures given understate cash inflows by the amount of the depreciation. Cashflows in year 4 are also increased by the scrap values for each project.

Year	Project A		Project B	
	Annual cashflow £	Cumulative cashflow £	Annual cashflow £	Cumulative cashflow £
0	(22,000)	(22,000)	(22,000)	(22,000)
1	7,000	(15,000)	7,500	(14,500)
2	9,000	(6,000)	6,500	(8,000)
3	12,000	6,000	8,000	-
4	4,000	10,000	12,000	12,000

The payback period for project A is two and a half years. At the start of year 3, outflows exceed inflows by £6,000. Net inflows for year 3 are £1 000 per month: it therefore recoups its original investment after six months of year 3. Project B's payback period is three years. The manager would select project A on the basis of this method, even though project B generates a greater total cash inflow by the end of its life.

The payback period method is widely used in practice, although often as a supplement to the more sophisticated approaches to investment appraisal.

● It is easy to calculate and understand.

● Its use emphasises liquidity, because the calculations are based exclusively on cashflows.

● It also helps managers to reduce risk by selecting the project which recovers its outlay most quickly.

● Earlier cashflows can be predicted more accurately than later ones, and are less affected by inflation.

The main disadvantage of using the payback period method is that it completely ignores profit and profitability. It also takes no account of interest rates and the effect of time on the value of money.

Accounting rate of return (ARR) method

This method of investment appraisal calculates the profits expected from the investment, expressing them as a percentage of the capital invested: the higher the rate of return, the 'better' (i.e. the more profitable) is the project. The ARR – also known as the return on investment method – is therefore based on **anticipated profits**, rather than cashflows.

$$\text{ARR} = \frac{\textbf{Expected average profits}}{\textbf{Original investment}} \times \textbf{100}$$

Using the above figures, project A generates total profits of £10,000 and project B total profits of £12,000.

	Project A £	Project B £
	2,500	3,000
	22,000	22,000
ARR =	11.4%	13.6%

Project B would be chosen, using the ARR method.

- The accounting rate of return method is easy to use and simple to understand.
- It measures and highlights the profitability of each project.

Its disadvantages are that it ignores the timing of the project's contributions. High profits in the early years – which are estimated more accurately, and which help to minimise the project's risk – are treated in the same way as profits occurring later. It also concentrates on profits rather than on cashflows, and ignores the time value of money (profits in the later years being eroded by the effects of inflation).

Discounted cash flow (DCF) method

This method is sometimes divided into two elements, which complement each other:

- The **net present value** (NPV) method takes account of all relevant cash flows from the project throughout its life, discounting them to their 'present value'.
- The **internal rate of return** (IRR) method compares the rate of return expected from the project with that identified by the company as being the cost of its capital. Projects whose IRR exceeds the cost of capital are worth considering.

The principle of DCF is based on using discounting arithmetic to obtain a present value for future cash inflows and outflows. It assumes that a firm prefers to receive cash in year 1 rather than in year 2, because the earlier the cash is received, the sooner it can be reinvested and made to work.

As an example, a company receiving £100 at the start of a year might be able to invest it at 10 per cent per annum: by the end of the year this investment will be worth £110. Given the choice of £100 now or a higher sum in a year's time, the managers will choose the higher sum only if it exceeds £110. This principle works in reverse: the managers know that a project generating £110 in a year's time is worth the same as one generating £100 immediately, the project with the future value being discounted to its present value (by using a set of discounting tables). The principle of discounting forms the basis of DCF.

The NPV method calculates the present value of the project's future cashflows. Each year's cashflow is discounted to a present value, which shows how much the managers would have to invest now at a given rate of interest to earn these future cash benefits. The present value of the total cash outflows is compared to that of the total cash inflows to calculate the net present value of the project. The project with the highest NPV will be chosen.

- **If the NPV is positive** – cash benefits exceed cash costs – this means that the project will earn a return in excess of its cost of capital (the rate of interest/ discounting used in the calculations).

- **If the NPV is negative**, this tells the managers that the cost of investing in the project exceeds the present value of future receipts, and that it is not worth investing in it.

If the company planning to invest in either project A or project B has a cost of capital equal to 12 per cent, the future cashflows can be discounted to their present values using information extracted from discounting tables. The present value of £1 when discounted at 12 per cent is

Year	Present value (PV) factor 12%
0	1.000
1	0.893
2	0.797
3	0.712
4	0.636

(Thus £1 in a year's time is the same as £0.893 invested now at 12 per cent for one year; £1 in two years' time is the same as £0.797 at 12 per cent over two years; and so on.)

Year	Project A			Project B		
	Cashflow £	PV factor	NPV £	Cashflow £	PV factor	NPV £
0	(22,000)	1.000	(22,000)	(22,000)	1.000	(22,000)
1	7,000	0.893	6,251	7,500	0.893	6,698
2	9,000	0.797	7,173	6,500	0.797	5,180
3	12,000	0.712	8,544	8,000	0.712	5,696
4	4,000	0.636	2,544	12,000	0.636	7,632
			NPV = 2,512			NPV = 3,206

Both projects produce a positive NPV, but project B has the higher expected NPV and would therefore be accepted.

The IRR method involves comparing the actual rates of return – in this illustration both rates exceed 12 per cent since both have positive NPVs when a 12 per cent figure is used – with the company's cost of capital. If the cost of capital is 12 per cent, both projects are worth pursuing, if possible because the average annual returns on capital are greater that 12 per cent.

The use of the DCF method takes account of all cashflows and it acknowledges the time value of money. The main problem is in establishing a suitable discount rate to use, because this rate (and the firm's cost of capital) is likely to vary over the life of the project.

10.3 DECISION-MAKING TECHNIQUES

OPERATIONS RESEARCH

The main techniques used to improve business decision-making are based on operations research (**OR**) techniques. OR involves applying scientific techniques to problems of business operation. Its purpose is to produce factual information which managers can use in making decisions.

A systematic OR approach to decision-making involves:

- **identifying the problem** to be researched by stating all its significant factors and constraints;

- **constructing an appropriate model**, normally a mathematical representation of the problem;

- **using the model** to find a solution by supplying it with relevant data, manipulating the variables to represent different courses of action and to see their effects;

- **setting up control procedures** once the 'best' solution has been identified and implemented.

OR assesses two main types of problem. The first type focuses on problems whose main characteristic is an unpredictability in performance or behaviour: an example is:

- **Queueing problems** These evaluate how best to reduce queues and bottlenecks in business areas including production control and stock control. The basic problem is the limit on capacity, and its characteristics are 'customers' (products as well as people), a waiting period, and a service period. Simulations are undertaken to calculate how waiting and service times can be minimised in order to maximise the use of resources (money, time, labour and equipment).

The second type of problem considers how to allocate resources to a particular problem in the most effective (optimum) way. These problems are characterised by situations where several jobs are to be carried out, with limited resources which can be used in different combinations in each job. The challenge is to allocate the resources in an optimum way. Examples of such problems include

- **Transportation problems** These are often based on distribution, occurring when a firm with several warehouses has to deliver to a number of different shops. Difficulties include which vehicles (in terms of their location and carrying capacity) and delivery routes to use for individual customers.

- **Product-mix problems** These are similar to transportation problems, but apply where there is a strict limit to the number of resources. The chemical, oil and paint industries often calculate how best to minimise costs where different resource mixes are possible.

OR techniques used to solve these problems include linear programming, critical path analysis and simulation. The first technique is commonly used to solve allocation (transportation and product-mix) problems, and critical path analysis in solving queueing and allied problems. Simulation as a technique is used widely in OR.

Linear programming (LP)

This is a mathematical tool used in OR to establish how best to use alternative limited resources (labour, equipment, production time, materials, etc.). It is used where the variables have a **linear relationship** – i.e. a change in one variable causes a proportional change in the other(s).

This technique gives managers the opportunity of evaluating how different resource mixes affect costs and profits. LP traditionally used a two-variable plotting approach on a graph, but computers now allow more variables to be analysed in the mix. The relationships in the model are classified as:

- **constraints**: limits to the resources available;

- **the objective function**: the desired result, expressed as an equation.

An example of how LP can be used is as follows.

A firm makes two types of building brick: type A and type B. Both have two manufacturing processes: moulding, and firing.

	Moulding (hours)	Firing (hours)
Type A	3	2
Type B	4	6

Each process has 4,800 hours available. Maximum demand for brick type A is 1,200 in the time period. Contribution to profit and fixed costs is £40 for type A and £60 for type B.

A = brick type A
B = brick type B
M = moulding
F = finishing
C = contribution

The mathematical model of the problem can now be constructed.

For process M, 3 hours A plus 4 hours B cannot exceed 4,800:

$$3A + 4B \leq 4,800$$

For process F, 2 hours A plus 6 hours B cannot exceed 4,800:

$$2A + 6B \leq 4,800$$

The limit to A is 1,200:

$$A \leq 1,200$$

and since A and B cannot be produced in negative quantities:

$$A \geq 0 \text{ and } B \geq 0$$

The intention of the objective function must be to maximise contribution for the firm:

$$\text{Maximised } C = 40A + 60B$$

The model can now be summarised as:

$$\text{Maximised } C = 40A + 60B$$

when	$3A + 4B \leq 4,800$
and	$2A + 6B \leq 4,800$
subject to limits	$0 \leq A \leq 1,200$
and	$B \geq 0$

The problem can be solved by graph (there are only two products). Each constraint is plotted:

❶ $3A + 4B \leq 4,800$ is plotted as $3A + 4B = 4,800$. The values are 1,600 on the A axis ($3A = 4,800$) and 1,200 on the B axis ($4B = 4,800$). The area under this line contains all feasible solutions for A and B.

❷ $2A + 6B \leq 4,800$ is plotted as $2A + 6B = 4,800$: the A axis value is 2,400 and the B axis value is 800.

❸ $A \leq 1,200$ is plotted as $A = 1,200$.

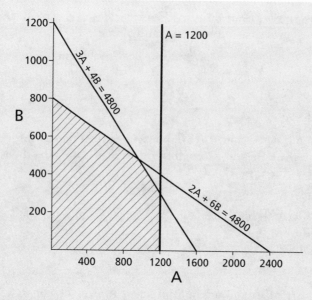

Fig. 10.2 *Plotting the constraints*

Any solution which fits these three constraints must fall in the shaded area contained by all three graph lines: this area is called the feasibility polygon. Mathematical theory tells us that contribution is at its maximum at the edge, normally at one corner, of the polygon. The objective function is now taken and increasing values are given to C: it is plotted as a series of parallel lines which move away from the graph's origin until one of the lines touches only a corner of the polygon. This occurs where C is given the value 67,200:

$$\text{if } A = 0,\ 60B = 67{,}200 \text{ and } B = 1{,}120$$

$$\text{if } B = 0,\ 40A = 67{,}200 \text{ and } A = 1{,}680$$

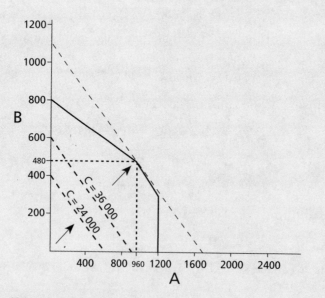

Fig. 10.3 *Maximising contribution*

Fig. 10.3 shows the C line touching the polygon at the values A = 960 and B = 480.

The optimum mix is therefore to make 960 of brick type A (a contribution of £40 × 960 = £38,400) and 480 of type B (contribution of £60 × 480 = £28,800: total £67,200).

Critical path analysis (CPA)

CPA, also known as **network analysis**, is used to identify the best way of scheduling a complex series of related tasks, to minimise the time taken in their completion. It is widely used in industries such as construction, to schedule the different phases of planning and building. Most new and complex projects which take some time to complete can apply CPA techniques. CPA consists of a network of the tasks, drawn either manually or by computer. The effect of changing either the order in which the tasks are carried out, or some other variable, can be evaluated.

CPA allows planners to:

● forecast the completion time for the project;

● identify:
  – EST (earliest start time)
  – EFT (earliest finish time)
  – LST (latest start time)
  – LFT (latest finish time)
  for the different activities which make up the project;

● highlight all stages where timing is critical – the 'critical path';

● monitor progress and delays throughout the project's life;

● establish in advance the precise resources required;

● assess ways of overcoming resourcing and/or timing problems.

The stages in the construction of the network are as follows:

❶ **Subdivide the project** into its constituent activities. Each activity uses some resources and takes a certain time to complete.

❷ **Decide on the order of completion.** Some activities obviously precede others – e.g. building materials must be bought before they can be used – although judgements often have to be made (for example, whether to plumb and fit a kitchen in a building before plumbing and fitting the bathroom). An activity might depend on several preceding ones: for example 'install heating units' depends on activities such as 'wire room', 'install floor', 'plaster room", and so on.

❸ **The network model is constructed** and the activity times are recorded.

❹ **The network is analysed.** This establishes the total time for the project and the critical path through it (i.e. the path where any delay to the activities also delays the whole project: there is no slack time). The total slack time, or 'float', represents the time the non-critical activities can over-run before they delay the project.

❺ **A timetable** is drawn up to schedule resources.

❻ **The network is used** to monitor progress of the project.

An example of the use of CPA is as follows.

The directors of a company wish to buy and assemble temporary additional office space. The activities are:

	Length (days)	Preceding activities
A. Obtain permission	3	-
B. Buy materials for base	4	A
C. Obtain assembly	6	A
D. Lay base	3	B
E. Assemble office frame	5	C
F. Attach frame to base	2	D, E
G. Paint frame	2	C

Each activity is identified by a node represented by a circle (see Fig. 10.4). Nodes are numbered for identification, and represent the start and finish of an activity. They record the earliest start time (EST) and latest finish time (LFT) for each activity.

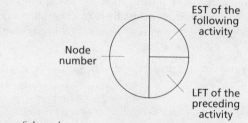

Fig. 10.4 Structure of the node

Nodes are joined by arrows representing the flow of activities (the length of each arrow is not significant). Fig. 10.5 shows the network model for the above activities. In practice, the details by each arrow of the activity's name and length are often omitted, but they are shown here for reference.

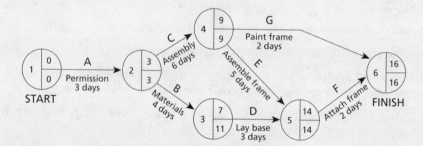

Fig. 10.5 The network diagram

The EST represents the earliest date at which an activity can commence.

- Node 1 shows the start of activity A, which is day 0.

- Node 2 represents the start time for B and C. These must follow A, which takes three days to complete, so node 2 has an EST of day 3.

- Node 3 shows the start of activity D, which must follow B: B takes four days to complete, so node 3 has an EST of day 7.

- Node 4 represents the start of E and G, which follow the end of C: C takes six days so E and G cannot start before day 9.

- Node 5 shows the start of F, which follows the end of both D and E: the earliest D can end is after ten days (EST day 7 plus three days to complete) and the earliest E can finish is day 14 (EST day 9 + five days). Activity F cannot start before both D and E are finished, therefore its EST is day 14.

- Node 6 ends with the finish of activities F (EST day 14 + two days) and G (EST day 9 + two days): the whole project must therefore take a minimum of sixteen days.

The LFT represents the latest date by which an activity must be completed to avoid delaying the whole project. Each activity's LFT is calculated by *working backwards* from the completion date.

- Node 6 represents the end of the project, so its LFT must be sixteen days.

- Node 5 shows the start of activity F, which takes two days to complete: the LFT for activities D and E shown by this node is therefore (16 − 2 =) day 14.

- Node 4 starts activity G which takes two days: the LFT is not (16 − 2) day 14 because node 4 also starts activity E. This activity takes five days and has an LFT of day 14 shown in node 5. The LFT for node 4 must be (14 − 5 =) day 9.

- Node 3 starts activity D, which has an LFT of 14 shown in node 5: D takes three days to complete therefore the LFT for activity B which precedes it must be (14 − 3=) day 11.

- Node 2 represents the LFT for activity A. Although activity B could start on day 7 (it takes four days and its LFT is day 11), activity C has an LFT of day 9 (node 4) and it takes six days to complete. The LFT for activity A is therefore day 3 (9 − 6).

- Node 1 represents the start of the project and has an LFT of day 0: the LFT at the start must be the same as the EST.

The critical path can now be seen clearly. It is shown by those nodes whose EST and LFT are the same: nodes 1, 2, 4, 5 and 6. Any delay in the activities they represent – activities A, C, E and F – will delay the project as a whole. Activities B, D and G are non-critical because they can over-run to a certain extent without the project being delayed. They have "floats' which indicate the spare time available to complete them.

- Activity B can be delayed without affecting the project: its EST is day 3 but it could start later to meet its LFT of day 11. It has a float, which is calculated by deducting its earliest start time from its latest start time (LST − EST). The LST in turn is calculated by taking an activity's duration from its LFT. For activity B:
  - the LST is day 7 (11 − 4)
  - the EST is day 3
  - its float is four days
  The other possibility is that eight days could be taken to complete B without the project being delayed.

- Activity D also has a float of four days: its LST is day 11 and its EST is day 7.

- Activity G has a float of five days: its LST is day 14 and its EST is day 9.

Critical path analysis can therefore be used as a control technique by managers, once the critical path has been established.

Simulation

Approaches to OR normally involve a model being constructed to simulate real life. The simulation could be similar physically to the area being studied (e.g. the cockpit of a flight training simulator), a computer representation of it, or even a set of mathematical formulae.

Monte Carlo simulation models are widely used. These attempt to imitate random behaviour occurring in real-life systems, so that the effects of alternative courses of action can be evaluated. Examples of their use are found in attempts to simulate arrival patterns of customers and the nature of queueing in banks, shops, airports etc. Variables to be simulated include the number of people arriving, the pattern of the arrivals, waiting time, the number of service points available, and the time taken to service the customers.

Virtual reality (**VR**) is gaining in importance. Current VR technology developed from flight-simulation. Most publicity has focused on its use in game-playing in the leisure industry. Current VR here includes arcade games and (in the USA) a VR application-telephone link allowing viewers to 'create' a TV programme.

VR also has a number of other business applications.

- Hospitals in the UK and the rest of Europe have helped create VR tools for surgeons, including the digital representation of patients and the projection onto a patient's body of internal organs (to locate surgical points).

- Interior design (e.g. for kitchens and bathrooms) using VR is possible in some furniture showrooms in Japan. This can then be linked with ordering, manufacturing and delivery processes to make and deliver the physical manifestation of the "virtual' kitchen or bathroom. In the UK, THORN EMI plc uses VR to simulate lighting layout and design for industrial applications such as new office blocks.

● VR is used for architectural applications, for example by Tyne and Wear Development Corporation to 'create' the proposed redevelopment of a dockside area of Newcastle, thus allowing interested parties to see the development in advance of its being built.

● Glaxo plc uses VR to assess the effect of new chemical processes and compounds through creating a VR model of the possible molecular structure.

Simulation has gained in importance with the increase in computing power and software packages. Firms can now buy a range of simulations to run on their computer systems.

10.4 COPING WITH CHANGE

The pace of change in the business world has become more rapid, particularly as a result of the improvements in telecommunications and other forms of technology. Organisational change results from either direct or indirect processes: individual attitudes and values may be changed directly through retraining and re-education, or indirectly through management policies which have changed the organisation's structure, technology or objectives.

The areas of business change are covered in detail elsewhere in the Guide, particularly in Chapters 1 and 4. The main areas, with some examples of the changes, are:

● **Economic**: increased levels of unemployment; medium-term balance of payments difficulties; failure of the ERM; proposals for a single European currency; decline in the revenue from North Sea oil.

● **Legislative**: introduction of European Union Directives to implement the Single Market; more domestic consumer protection legislation; additional legal curbs on the power of trade unions.

● **Demographic**: growth in the proportion of over-65s; a proportional reduction in the number of young people coming into the labour market.

● **Technological**: increased pace of implementing new technology in business; increased computer power; satellite links with overseas firms; improved telephone and transmission technology; changed production processes.

● **Social**: increased voluntary or forced leisure time; an increase in the proportion of service sector jobs paying low wages; a greater awareness of fitness and health; changing tastes and fashions.

The management of change

Employees (and managers) may resist change for a variety of reasons.

● **Personal** reasons:
  - fear of the unknown
  - a low tolerance of change
  - prejudice
  - dislike of the methods being used to implement the change.

● **Economic** reasons:
  - an increased fear of unemployment
  - lack of belief in their ability to acquire the new skills needed.

● **Communication** reasons:
  - not receiving adequate reasons for the change
  - mistrusting or misunderstanding the reasons given for the change.

- **Social** reasons:
  - existing satisfaction with present colleagues, equipment and systems
  - initial dislike of new colleagues, equipment or systems
  - dislike of outside interference.

Requirements for the effective management of change are summarised in Fig. 10.6.

Fig. 10.6 Managing change

Managers must:

- Ensure that full and clear information is given on the:
  - reason(s) for the change
  - method(s) proposed for implementing it
  - likely disruptions to current working routines
  - progress to date of the implementation.
- Give employees their own opportunity to evaluate the possible effects of the proposed changes, and the opportunity to provide feedback to management.
- Set up working parties, quality circles and training routines for all staff affected by the change.
- Provide a system to monitor the implementation, which gives employees the opportunity for feedback.
- Continue to monitor the effects of change once the new systems have been fully implemented.

The greater the level of employee participation and involvement in the process, the more effectively change will be implemented.

Chapter roundup

Chapter 10 has explained the decision-making processes and the results of these processes. It has illustrated how the decision-making process is supported by techniques such as discounted cash flow and other appraisal techniques, and linear programming, critical path analysis and simulation. These give management valuable information to use in making decisions which, when implemented, result in change. The chapter therefore concludes by examining how managers should implement this change effectively.

Illustrative questions

1   What factors should a bank manager consider in deciding whether to allow an entrepreneur to increase the business's overdraft limit?

Tutorial note

The answer needs to be phrased from the view of the potential lender: a good answer will identify, explain, analyse and evaluate each of the factors.

Suggested answer

The bank manager needs to consider: the level of business expertise of the customer (any experience of running a business, or areas of specialist knowledge); the customer's personal situation (the ability to offer collateral, how much is already owed to the bank or other lenders); the potential of the business (products, markets, the possibility of expansion); the likely survival of the business (the degree of competition, business performance measured by ratio analysis, cash flow performance); the state of the economy in general (the level of interest rates and the level of borrowing); the policy of the bank (regarding particular situations, amounts to be lent, etc.).

2 Discuss what information a bank manager might expect to be given by an entrepreneur seeking finance for a new business venture. What factors would you expect the bank manager to take into account in deciding whether or not to grant the finance? (20)

NEAB

Tutorial note

The phrase 'expect to be given' suggests that you need to identify appropriate documentation in this part of the answer. Questions asking you to 'Discuss' something in this manner require you to give reasons why. Your answer could acknowledge that you assume the entrepreneur has business experience and/or a current business involvement.

Suggested answer

The bank manager will wish to examine the entrepreneur's plans for the new venture, and the entrepreneur's past business performance. The manager will expect the entrepreneur to present a number of key documents. These are:

1. A business plan for the new venture. This plan will outline internal factors, for example how the product is to be made (or the service provided), and external factors such as proposed markets, advertising and channels of distribution.

2. A draft profit and loss account. This enables the bank manager to assess to what extent the entrepreneur has fully analysed the likely profitability of the new venture, and whether it will produce sufficient profits given the level of investment sought by the entrepreneur.

3. A draft cash flow. This forecast will enable the bank manager to see how quickly sufficient cash will be generated for the bank to get its investment repaid, and whether the venture is going to be underwritten by sufficient finance.

The manager will be interested in the entrepreneur's calculations as shown in this documentation (are they realistic? complete? accurate?). The manager will also take into account the security that the entrepreneur offers against the loan. Finally, the manager will wish to check the entrepreneur's business experience and the performance of the present business (e.g. is there sufficient finance/cash already?).

3 Wilson Ltd is a private company which manufactures engineering components for the UK market. It is financed by £100,000 of share capital, owned in equal amounts by four shareholders and by a bank loan of £300,000. The authorised share capital is £200,000.

Wilson is considering installing a new machine (Machine A) in order to produce a slightly different product which it thinks the UK market needs. Alternatively it is considering the purchase of a machine (Machine B), which will increase the output of its product line, but for the European market, of which it has no previous experience. Both machines cost £50,000 but only one project can be implemented.

Projected net cash flows from the projects are as follows:

	Machine A	Machine B
End of Year 1	£10,000	£5,000
End of Year 2	£10,000	£5,000
End of Year 3	£20,000	£30,000
End of Year 4	£20,000	£40,000
End of Year 5	£30,000	–

In addition, Machine A has an estimated scrap value of £10,000, but Machine B has no probable scrap or resale value. The cost of capital is estimated to be 10%.

(a) (i) Calculate the pay-back period, the average annual rate of return and the net present value of each project. (11)

(ii) State with reasons which project you would recommend on numerical grounds. (4)

You may find the following 10% discount table useful:

Year 1: 0.91   Year 2: 0.83   Year 3: 0.75   Year 4: 0.68   Year 5: 0.62

(b) Identify and analyse the non-numerical factors that Wilson Ltd should bear in mind before making a final decision. (10)

London Examinations

Tutorial note

Many candidates in examinations calculate the present value of a project accurately, but then fail to deduct the cost of the project to obtain the NPV. Using a table as shown below will help you overcome this. As with any numerical answer, workings should be shown.

Suggested answer

Payback: both machines cost £50,000 and both have a total payback of £40,000 by the end of year 3. The outstanding £10,000 is half of year 4's cash flow for machine A, and a quarter of the cash flow for machine B. Thus payback is 3.5 years for A and 3.25 years for B.

Average annual rate of return (ARR): A's average profits are £20,000 (£90,000 + £10,000 over 5 years). B's average profits are also £20,000 (£80,000 over 4 years). This gives both machines an ARR of 40% if average profits are expressed as a percentage of total investment.

			Net present value (NPV)		
Year	Discount (10%)	Cash Flow A	Present Value	Cash Flow B	Present Value
0	1.00	(50.000)	(50,000)	(50,000)	(50,000)
1	0.91	10.000	9,100	5,000	4,550
2	0.83	10,000	8,300	5,000	4,150
3	0.75	20,000	15,000	30,000	22,500
4	0.68	20,000	13,600	40,000	27,200
5	0.62	30,000	18,600		
5	0.62	10,000	6,200		
			NPV = 20,800		NPV = 8.400

(ii) I would recommend A: although it takes slightly longer to pay back the original investment, it receives as high a rate of return as B, and – crucially – it has a much higher NPV.

(b) An important factor in favour of installing machine A is that there appears to be demand for its products in the UK market. Its product will add to the firm's product range, which is another factor in its favour. Other factors against the choice of machine B are that it makes a product for a market (Europe) of which the firm has no experience. This means that there will be a need for other financial outlay (e.g. training, market research), and trading in the rest of Europe brings additional complications and expense (e.g. transport, fluctuations in the exchange rate, setting up channels of distribution). The main general non-numerical factor is: how reliable are the forecasts?

4 This question is about Implementing Business Decisions. You will be expected to include knowledge relevant to this aspect of business studies in your answers.

   (a) State a decision making problem that can **NOT** be solved using linear programming. Which operational research technique should be used to solve such a problem? What are the limitations of the technique you have identified?

   (8)

   Kilminster's is an engineering firm which produces flywheels and crankshafts using a shift system.
       The daily production run is made up of three eight-hour shifts. During each shift the flywheels and crankshafts have to pass through an acid bath and also spend time on a special machine. It takes one hour and twenty minutes to prepare the acid bath for each shift. The special machine is only available for five hours per shift. The storage space that is available to the firm during any shift for the finished flywheels and crankshafts is a thousand square feet.
       The firm knows that during production each flywheel needs four minutes in the acid bath while each crankshaft needs one minute, and that both products need to spend one minute on the special machine. As finished products, each flywheel needs two square feet of storage while each crankshaft needs five square feet.
       The firm knows that when sold the flywheels will generate a unit profit of £20 while the crankshafts will generate a unit profit of £10.
       Kilminster's is hoping to use linear programming to help it calculate the outputs of flywheels and crankshafts needed to maximise its profits.

   (b) The information above includes a number of production constraints that are present during each shift. List these as a set of inequalities and then show this information on a graph.   (8)

   (c) One corner of the feasible region on the graph is the origin. Label the other three corners, in a clockwise direction from the origin, A, B and C.
       By analysing each of these points, state the outputs of flywheels and crankshafts Kilminster's should produce in order to maximise its profits.   (8)

   (d) Unfortunately these profit maximising outputs do not result in the firm minimising its costs as the special machine is idle for approximately sixty-six minutes per shift. Calculate whether the firm would be able to increase its daily profit if the daily production run was changed to four six-hour shifts, *and all other factors remained constant.*
       (8)

   (e) The profit maximisation problem above could be solved using a computer. Name a software package that could be used, and describe how you would use it.   (8)

   London Examinations

Tutorial note

The Examiner's Report noted that few candidates were able to identify the constraints, and could therefore not produce correct graphs.

Suggested answer

(a) An example of such a decision-making problem is where a firm wants to examine the effect of random behaviour. Simulation is the OR tool used here, for example in the form of a Monte Carlo simulation. This attempts to imitate the random behaviour of real life, so that alternative courses of action for the firm can be evaluated. The limitations of such a technique lie in the fact that it is just a simulation of the real thing: for example, it is difficult to establish the variables (e.g. arrival patterns of customers, number of customers, waiting time) and the interrelationships among these variables.

(b) The constraints are (x for flywheels, y for crankshafts):

❶ Acid bath: 4x + y is less than or equal to 400 (minutes: i.e. 8 hours less 80 minutes preparation). (Plotted on graph as 4x = 400/x = 100; y = 400)

❷ Special machine: x + y is less than or equal to 300 (minutes; i.e. 5 hours). (Plotted on graph as x = 300; y = 300)

❸ Storage: 2x + 5y is less than or equal to 1000 (square feet). (Plotted on graph as 2x = 1000/x = 500; 5y = 1000/y = 200)

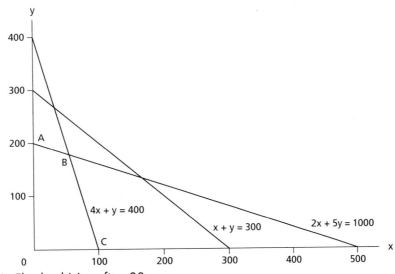

(c) Point A: Flywheel (x) profit = £0

Crankshaft (y) profit = 100 × £20 = £2,000. Total profit = £2,000

Point B: Flywheel (x) profit = (approx.) 60 x £20 = £1,200

Crankshaft (y) profit = (approx.) 180 x £10 = £1,800. Total profit = £3,000

Point C: Flywheel (x) profit = 100 x £20 = £2,000

Crankshaft (y) profit = £0. Total profit = £2,000

Point B maximises profit, at an output (read off the graph) of 60 flywheels and 180 crankshafts.

(d) New constraints are required for the acid bath and the special machine, as follows:

❶ Acid bath: 4x + y ≤ 280 (360 – 80)

❷ Special machine: x + y ≤ 180 (3 hours)

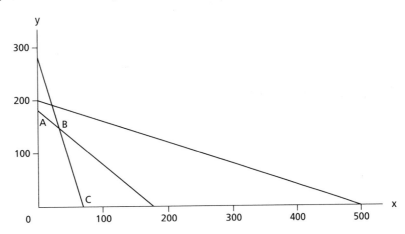

Point A: Crankshaft = 180 × £10 = £1,800 (total profit)

Point B: Flywheel = 40 × £20 = £800; Crankshaft = 140 × £10 = £1,400; total profit = £2,200

Point C: Flywheel = 70 × £20 = £1,400 (total profit).

Point B remains the most profitable: approximate output is 40 flywheels and 140 crankshafts.

(e) A commercial spreadsheet package such as Excel or Lotus 1–2–3 will enable linear programming data to be entered and calculated. Axes and cells need to be identified, and the formulæ entered at the appropriate points.

5 (a) Explain why some organisations find it difficult to implement change. (10)

(b) How may these difficulties be overcome? (10)

Tutorial note

Because this is a general question on the nature of change, you should try to limit your answer to three or four illustrations. This avoids getting bogged down in generalities and improves the structure of your answer.

Suggested answer

(a) Change is difficult to implement in organisations, because people resist it for many reasons. There may be personal reasons, such as prejudice against those introducing the change, a natural fear of the unknown, or just a low personal tolerance to change. Some people fear that the changes will cause their own economic circumstances to alter: for example, the introduction of new technology is often associated with an increased fear of unemployment. Employees may also lack the self-belief that they can cope with new equipment or new systems, or may simply dislike outside interference.

Management may fail in its duty to introduce change through negotiation and consultation. They may fail to provide adequate reasons for the changes being made, or may create mistrust in their motives. Their communication procedures may also be at fault, with staff misunderstanding the reasons given for the change. Managers sometimes use methods to bring about change which are disliked by staff who are content with their existing colleagues and work practices.

(b) Managers must seek to ensure that staff are consulted and that they (the managers) are also aware of the potential effects of introducing change into the organisation.

Before the change is implemented managers should give full information on why and how it is to be implemented, and should allow other employees the opportunity to feed ideas back. Proposed working parties, new groups and new processes should be discussed. During the process of change, the managers should liaise with staff to monitor progress and to counsel those staff with difficulties. A training programme for those staff affected by the changes provides important support. Finally, following the implementation of the change, all staff should continue to monitor its effects.

6 'Sensored' is having difficulty planning the time required for manufacturing their products. They have certain processes to complete. The foreman has estimated the number of hours each process is likely to take. They are as follows:

Process A – 6 hours, Process B – 4 hours, the other processes require the following number of hours work: C – 15, D – 10, E – 8, F – 6, G – 3, H – 9 and I – 4.

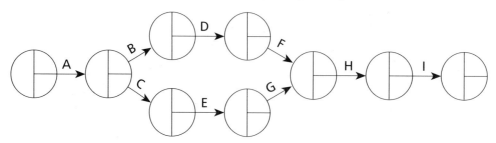

(a) Copy and complete the above network showing the earliest start time (EST) and the latest finish time (LFT) for **each** activity. (9)

(b) Discover the Critical Path. (3)

(c) Advise the 'Sensored' partners of the advantages this kind of analysis can have. (6)

WJEC

Tutorial note

Allow yourself plenty of space in your answer to construct the chart. If necessary, turn your page 90 degrees to construct the chart. As with NPV calculations, it is important to work logically through the information: listing the activities in order using a table is one way of achieving this.

Suggested answer

(a)

Activity	Duration	EST	LFT
A	6	0	6
B	4	6	10
C	15	6	16
D	10	10	26
E	8	21	29
F	6	20	32
G	3	29	32
H	9	32	41
I	4	41	45

(b) The critical path is where EST = LFT. It is therefore 1 – 2 – 4 – 6 – 7 – 8 – 9 (45 hours).

(c) The partners now know the 'critical time'; in other words, where there is no slack production time. Any time lost in any of these processes will affect the overall time spent in production. This allows the partners to prioritise and to ensure the processes run smoothly. Efficiency is therefore improved.

Practice questions

1 (a) Briefly explain the factors a business might consider when deciding to use
  (i) overdraft facilities;
  (ii) leasing arrangements.

(b) How might a change in interest rates affect the level of stock carried by a business? (10)

NEAB

Pitfalls

You need to distinguish between borrowing money and leasing. Your answer should acknowledge that there will be an overlap between the factors you identify.

Key points

(a) (i) Amount required; length required; cost.

(ii) Length of lease; ease of changing item leased (e.g. updating); cost.

(b) Stockholding ties up (working) capital and has costs associated with it. Increased interest rates raise the cost of capital/borrowing; reduced stock levels 'free up' cash, which can be made to work (or invested) by the firm.

2 A factory produces two types of chairs, 'straights' and 'rockers'. A 'straight' requires 6 hours of machine time, 6 hours of fabrication time and 12 hours in the assembly area. A 'rocker' requires 7 hours of machine time, 9 hours of fabrication time and 16 hours in the assembly area. The unit contributions to overheads and profits are £50 and £80 respectively. 420 hours are available in the machine shop, 450 hours in the fabrication area and 720 hours in the assembly area.

(a) Show the constraints and the objective function on a graph. (4)

(b) From the graph or otherwise, determine the optimal production plan and the associated contribution to overheads and profits. (1)

(c) If it transpires that in fact 960 hours (rather than 720 hours) are available in the assembly area, what would then be the optimal production plan and its associated contribution? (5)

NEAB

Pitfalls

The problems of LP in general are mentioned earlier (Tutorial note, question 4). There are three constraints here, but for this question you must also state the 'objective function' as an equation. Note that in this question hours are given, and can be used throughout (compare with the earlier question).

Key points

(a) Constraints ('s' straights; 'r' rockers):

① Machine shop: $6s + 7r \leq 420$

② Fabrication: $6s + 9r \leq 450$

③ Assembly: $12s + 16r \leq 720$

Objective function = maximum $50s + 80r$ (based on unit contributions).

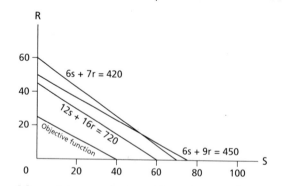

(b) Optimum line = $12s + 16r$, producing 45 rockers and £3,600 contribution (60 straights × £50 produces £3,000 contribution only; 42 straights plus 15 rockers generates £3,300).

(c) New constraint $12s + 16r = 960$. This moves the Assembly constraint line to axis points 80s and 60r.
Intersection now takes place on the graph at about s = 53 and r = 16.
This generates contribution as follows:
(where r = 0) s = 70 × £50 = £3,500;
(where s = 0) r = 50 × £80 = £4,000 (the maximum contribution); and
(at intersection) s = 53 × £50; r = 16 × £80; total £3,930.

TEST RUN

In this section:

Test your knowledge quiz

Test your knowledge quiz answers

Progress analysis

Mock exam

Mock exam suggested answers

- This section should be tackled towards the end of your revision programme, when you have covered all your syllabus topics, and attempted the practice questions at the end of the relevant chapters.

- The Test Your Knowledge Quiz contains short-answer questions on a wide range of syllabus topics. You should attempt it without reference to the text.

- Check your answers against the Test Your Knowledge Quiz Answers. If you are not sure why you got an answer wrong, go back to the relevant chapter in the text: you will find the reference next to our answer.

- Enter your marks in the Progress Analysis chart. The notes below will suggest a further revision strategy, based on your performance in the quiz. Only when you have done the extra work suggested should you go on to the final test.

- The Mock Exam is set out like a real exam paper. It contains a wide spread of question styles and topics, drawn from various examination boards. You should attempt this paper under examination conditions. Read the instructions on the front sheet carefully. Attempt the paper in the time allowed, and without reference to the text.

- Compare your answers to our Mock Exam Suggested Answers. We have provided tutorial notes to each, showing why we answered the question as we did and indicating where your answer may have differed from ours.

TEST YOUR KNOWLEDGE QUIZ

1 Explain the meaning of the term 'opportunity cost'.

2 State **two** functions of management.

3 Define 'limited liability'.

4 Identify **two** problems an Industrial Tribunal might handle.

5 Explain 'vertical integration' and give an example.

6 What is the difference between 'financial cost' and 'social cost'?

7 A firm reduces its product's price from £6.00 to £5.50. Following this, sales increase from 5,000 to 6,000 units a week. Calculate the product's price elasticity of demand.

8 Give **two** reasons why a potential investor in a public limited company should study the PLC's annual report and accounts.

9 Explain the difference between 'mark-up' and 'margin'.

10 Identify **two** increased costs that a firm might have to meet when improving the quality of its products.

11 What is the difference between 'field' and 'desk' research in marketing?

12 Outline briefly why a firm's short-term pricing policy might differ from its long-term one.

13 Identify **two** ways in which industry is affected by a high level of unemployment.

14 List the main objectives of a stock control system.

15 Name **two** groups with whom a firm must communicate effectively its financial information.

16 Explain 'just-in-time' manufacturing, giving **one** advantage and **one** disadvantage associated with it.

17 Name **two** methods of funding capital investment.

To answer questions 18, 19 and 20, first read the following information:

Superserve Ltd manufactures plastic cups used in vending machines. Last year's turnover was £4 million, and it had a 10 per cent net profit margin. The company now plans to change its distribution channel by eliminating wholesalers and selling direct to suppliers of vending machine drinks.

The managers estimate that sales will fall by 40 per cent and the new net profit will be £300,000. Fixed costs will increase from the existing £600,000 by 10 per cent, owing to increased storage and distribution costs.

18 Show how this policy change will affect the financial break-even point.

19 Calculate the sales Superserve needs to maintain the same profit as last year.

20 Advise the managers briefly on the proposed strategy.

TEST YOUR KNOWLEDGE QUIZ ANSWERS

The chapter and unit which explains the answer given is noted in brackets after the answer: e.g. (1.2) refers to Chapter 1, Unit 2.

1   The cost of something forgone: e.g. investment in project A means no finance for investment in project B. (1.1)

2   Control and co-ordination. (5.2)

3   No personal liability for business debts. (2.1)

4   Discrimination and unfair dismissal. (5.5)

5   Along the chain of production: e.g. an oil refiner acquiring a garage. (3.1)

6   Financial: incurred by a firm in meeting its obligations (e.g. payments to creditors). (6.1)
    Social: met by the community through a firm's operations, e.g. noise. (8.1)

7   20% demand and 8.3% price = 2.3 (price elastic). (1.3)

8   To assess the PLC's liquidity and profitability. (6.1, 6.2)

9   Mark-up: profit based as a percentage on cost.
    Margin: profit based as a percentage on selling price. (6.2)

10 Higher labour costs (e.g. better quality control) and higher material costs. (6.3, 8.2)

11 'Field' is original/primary: 'desk' is secondary. (7.2)

12 Short-term could be low (for market penetration): long-term will be higher (for profit, once sufficient market share has been obtained). (7.3)

13 Lower wage costs (unemployment levels used to control pay increases) and greater choice of new employees. (4.1, 5.3)

14 Security; cost control (e.g. to stop deterioration or obsolescence and to avoid too much money being tied up in stocks). (8.2)

15 Shareholders and employees. (6.2)

16 Manufacturing as and when required; better cashflow but greater reliance on suppliers being able to meet set deadlines. (8.1)

17 Share issue and debenture issue. (10.1)

18 Old break-even is £2.4m. sales: total costs are £3.6m. so variable cost is £3m.; 60 per cent sales required to cover the fixed costs (60 per cent of the £1m. difference between total sales and total variable costs). (8.2)

    New break-even is £1.65m. sales: total costs are now £2.1m.; profit £300,000 and fixed costs £660,000; break-even calculated by £2.4m. × (£660,000 as % of £960,000).

19 £2.65m.: variable cost is 60 per cent of sales so contribution 40 per cent; an extra £100,000 profit required; for every £1 profit, £2.50 sales are needed = extra £250,000 sales. (8.2)

20 A lower break-even point by £750,000; they need to consider output levels, the potential disadvantage of fewer outlets, whether extra warehousing and distribution is available and of the same quality, and the accuracy of their forecasts. (8.2)

PROGRESS ANALYSIS

Question	My answer ✓ or ✗ ?	Question	My answer ✓ or ✗ ?
1		11	
2		12	
3		13	
4		14	
5		15	
6		16	
7		17	
8		18	
9		19	
10		20	

My total mark is .... out of 20.

If you scored 0-5

You need to do some more work. The Mock Exam is intended as a test of exam technique: it will be wasted if your basic syllabus coverage is insufficient. Starting at Chapter 1, look at the list of Units at the beginning of each chapter, and if any of them look unfamiliar, make a note to go back over that chapter. You will then have a Further Revision Plan to work from. You will need to attempt the Test Your Knowledge Quiz one more time before you are ready to go on to the Mock Exam.

If you scored 6–10

You need to do a little more work. The Mock Exam is intended as a test of exam technique: it will not be really useful until you have filled in the current gaps in your syllabus coverage. If you have time, go through the list of Units at the beginning of each chapter, and plan to revise all those that look unfamiliar. If you don't think you'll have time to do this, look through the Practice Questions at the end of each chapter, and the notes on Points to include: this will be a 'whistle-stop' tour through key areas of the syllabus. You should then attempt the Test Your Knowledge Quiz again.

If you scored 11–15

You are just about ready to attempt the Mock Exam, but to get the best out of it, you might like to be a little more confident about your recall of some topics. If you have time, look through the Practice Questions at the end of each chapter, and the notes on Points to include: this will be a good guide to which syllabus areas are still unfamiliar. If you don't think you'll have time to do this, you should go back to the chapter whose reference is given in the Test Your Knowledge Quiz Answers for the ones you got wrong, and look over those chapters again. You should then be ready to go on to the Mock Exam.

If you scored 16–20

Congratulations. You have sufficient grasp of the syllabus topics to get real value out of attempting a Mock Exam in exam conditions. For your own satisfaction, though, you should go back to the specific Unit referred to in the Test Your Knowledge Quiz Answers for any questions you got wrong: reassure yourself that there is no real gap in your knowledge.

LETTS EXAMINATIONS BOARD
General Certificate of Education Examination

ADVANCED LEVEL
BUSINESS STUDIES

Paper 1
Time allowed: two and a half hours.

This paper contains three sections.

You are advised to allocate your time as follows:

Section A: 30 minutes
Section B: 1 hour
Section C: 1 hour

Mark allocations for each question are shown in brackets.

Paper 2
(Courtesy of London Examinations and NDTEF)
Time allowed: two and a half hours.

Attempt ALL questions.

The marks for each question are shown in brackets.

PAPER 1

Section A

Attempt ALL the questions in this Section. You are advised to allow no more than 30 minutes for this Section, which carries 25 marks out of 125 for the Paper. You are not required to write complete sentences as answers, e.g.

Question

Give **two** objectives of a stock control system.

Answer

(1) Minimise costs of stockholding.

(2) Ensure stocks available for production/customers.

A1 Identify **two** major differences between a public limited company and a public sector company. (2)

A2 Give **three** advantages that a person would gain from franchising rather than from setting up an independent business. (3)

A3 Suggest **two** reasons why a small business can still survive despite the growth of large-scale competitors. (2)

A4 Identify **three** problems which an organisation might face when locating its premises to another area. (3)

A5 Name **two** factors which will influence the method by which an entrepreneur raises finance. (2)

A6 List **three** methods used in investment appraisal. (3)

A7 Give **three** characteristics which are associated with the mass production method in manufacturing. (3)

A8 Suggest **two** ways in which a Marketing Department's decisions will influence the work of the same firm's Personnel Department. (2)

A9 Name **two** forms of non-price competition. (2)

A10 State **three** ways that 'high-street' banks might assist people to start up their own businesses. (3)

Section B

Attempt ALL the questions in this Section. You are advised to allow no more than 60 minutes for this Section, which carries 50 marks out of 125 for the Paper. You are expected to write complete sentences as answers to these questions.

B1 On an organisation chart, what is the difference between 'line' and 'staff' relationships? (4)

B2 Describe the main factors which influence a grocery outlet's decision to introduce 'own label' items. (4)

B3 Explain how job enrichment can improve the motivation of a firm's employees. (4)

B4 What major courses of action are available to a trade union if wage negotiations break down? (4)

B5 Why do many firms use direct marketing? (4)

B6 Suggest why an individual might decide to become an entrepreneur rather than continue as an employee. (4)

B7 Define the term 'depreciation'. In your answer, note the factors which affect an asset's life. (6)

B8 Outline the main problems that small firms face when attempting to recruit new employees. (6)

B9 Show, using a numerical illustration, how the FIFO system differs from the LIFO system of stock valuation. (6)

B10 A firm wishes to change its policy on disposing its own industrial waste: it currently uses the waste as 'land-fill' (filling old mining and quarrying sites), and now proposes to buy and use large machinery to crush and burn the waste. Identify the main costs associated with such a decision. (8)

Section C

Attempt **two** questions from this Section. You are advised to allow 1 hour for answering these questions, which carry 50 marks out of 125 for the Paper. You are reminded of the need for neat and orderly presentation of information in your answers.

C1 'More firms fail because of liquidity problems than through a lack of profitability.'
   (a) Explain why this is widely accepted as a true statement. (10)
   (b) Outline **three** ways that firms might try to avoid or overcome liquidity problems. (15)

C2 Critically examine the functions of trade unions in the 1990s. (25)

C3 (a) Evaluate the extent to which mass production techniques meet the needs of employees. Use an appropriate 'hierarchy of needs' model in your answer. (10)

   (b) How should managers set about creating a suitable environment and appropriate working practices to satisfy their staff? (15)

PAPER 2

You are advised to read the questions below prior to reading the extracts (taken from *Guardian* 14 October 1995). In answering the questions you should draw on appropriate knowledge of business studies that you have acquired through all of the modules you have studied.

1 (a) Identify FOUR business aims/objectives appropriate to a commercial bank. (4)

  (b) Analyse how take-overs such as those referred to in the extracts might help or hinder a commercial bank in achieving each of the aims/objectives which you identified. (12)

  (c) Discuss how such take-overs might affect the customer. (8)

2 The changes which are taking place in the banking industry have been partly brought about by developments in information technology.

  (a) Using examples referred to in the extracts and others with which you may be familiar, explain how firms in the financial sector can use information technology to improve their efficiency. (16)

  (b) State and explain FOUR ways in which customers in the financial sector may be affected by the use of information technology. (8)

3 The article states 'the number of staff employed in the banking sector has fallen by 110,000' (paragraph 5). This will have had a demotivating effect on many of those remaining at work in this industry.

  (a) Suggest FOUR reasons why these workers have become demotivated. (8)

  (b) Using your knowledge of motivational theories, evaluate FOUR possible ways in which managers might be able to improve the motivation of employees in the industry. (16)

4 (a) What does each letter of the term 'PEST' stand for? (4)

  The article suggests that 'there was very little sign of underlying growth in core lending' (paragraph 14).

  (b) Using PEST analysis, or any other appropriate technique, show how external factors may have contributed to this lack of growth in bank lending. (16)

  (c) Despite this lack of growth in bank lending, bank profits have continued to increase in recent years. Explain how such an increase in profits may have occurred. (4)

5 According to the article, Norwich Union is intending to change from a mutual business to a public limited company (paragraph 24).

  (a) Outline the procedure by which a business becomes a company. (8)

  (b) Explain who might benefit from Norwich Union becoming a public limited company. (4)

  (c) Suggest ways in which Norwich Union might manage the process of change successfully for:
  ● current customers
  ● future shareholders. (8)

  (d) What might be the effects on small insurance organisations of Norwich Union becoming a public limited company? (4)

London Examinations

Culling of the Clerks

1 They did not even say thank you. That is what really hurts 34-year-old Micky Thakur about the way she was sacked last week by NatWest. There was no pat on the back. No parting drink with a sympathetic manager. No recognition of the way she had grafted her way up the hierarchy after joining the bank straight after A Levels in 1979.

2 Just a terse letter she discovered on her doormat last week when she returned to her home in Bexley, Kent, after a two week holiday in Greece.

3 No wonder Ms Thakur, who earned £20,000 a year after winning a hugely sought after promotion to the bank's personal finance division, feels betrayed. Her ambition was to become one of the first female Asian bank managers and she had made it clear she was ready to be relocated if that helped keep her job. But all to no avail. And this led to last week's letter with the bald offer of an £18,000 pay-off. "There wasn't even a line to say 'thank you'. I thought it was really insulting," she says.

4 But this is clearly the way things are now done in the ruthless jobs shake-up sweeping the financial sector.

5 Ms Thakur has her own depressing story. But she is just one of 110,000 full-time bank employees to lose their jobs over the past four years. Official figures from the British Bankers Association show that only about 370,000 are currently employed in the industry – down from a peak of 445,000 in 1990. These were staff who, like Ms Thakur, joined the big banks for "a safe and secure career". Instead, their livelihoods have been thrown into jeopardy by an extraordinary revolution in the workplace which seems to spell the end of the road for the clerical classes and much middle management.

6 It was clear this week that the cull is far from over when Lloyds announced merger terms with the TSB with the likely loss of up to 10,000 jobs. This is likely to be followed by another mega-merger.

7 One of the biggest ironies of this week's Lloyds-TSB merger is that up to a dozen top directors have seen the paper value of their option packages soar because of the cost-saving benefits of getting rid of staff.

8 Decisions about any aspect of the bank's business can be made by one person and implemented at the touch of a button. Responsibility like that commands a £500,000 salary.

9 And for those that are left? Ironically, it would appear that the more technology develops, the faster what is left of the clerical sector becomes "deskilled". Instead of a career, the new-age bank clerk has a job. And because such a job demands relatively little training and little chance of career development in a world without middle management, it hardly offers a lifetime's employment.

10 Indeed, it seems inevitable that banks will increasingly favour younger and cheaper recruits. These are ideal breeding grounds for the kind of unspoken ageism which makes it so hard for the over-forties to find work. It has already started to happen. Barclays, for instance, has taken on 3,000 agency staff during the past year to replace more costly full-timers.

11 We are seeing here yet another stage of a structural change in the workplace which is every bit as radical as the industrial revolution's impact on 19th century Britain. It is a scenario vividly spelt out in Professor Charles Handy's work *The Empty Raincoat*, in which he distils the pressures on modern management into the formula: "Halve the number of managers in the core business in five years' time, pay them twice as much and produce three times as much productivity".

12 This formula, alas, is no longer academic. Such calculations have already reshaped the head offices of British industry, with dozens of the biggest FTSE names rationalising their headquarters and whittling away the decision-making cadre to a few dozen in a London office.

13 Other factors, too, are costing jobs in the financial services revolution. While information technology has rendered obsolescent large swathes of clerical staff, its computer terminals and optic fibre cables have short-circuited the traditional reporting hierarchy through middle management. More job losses.

14 Then there is competition. The high street is "over banked". And although last year the combined profits of the big four clearers bounced sharply up by £1.5 billion to £5 billion, this was due largely to a fall in bad debts. There was very little sign of any underlying growth in core lending. Like the manufacturing sector before it, the banking and finance industry is finding it cannot simply charge what it likes, often for a product no one wants.

15 So, slowly, with the introduction of such innovations as interest on current accounts and 24 hour a day telephone banking, the industry is having to haul itself closer to what consumers desire and are prepared to pay for.

16 Advances in technology have meant many of these improvements were introduced without increasing staff levels. Indeed, as profits are increasingly threatened by providing these "extras", banks have become even more determined to cut out any layer of "unnecessary" cost and, by and large, that has meant employees. Time was every bank had a manager and sub-manager. No longer. Throughout Britain, banks are "clustering" branches in chains of up to a dozen.

17 Out goes the traditional and expensive bank manager in every branch. Instead, traditional management functions are devolved by computer to a senior manager at a regional office.

18 As TSB chairman Sir Nicholas Goodison puts it: "The two main engines of change have been faster technological advances and the growing ascendancy of free-market thinking."

19 So where will it all stop? There is a bitter suspicion among unions and staff that this instinctively compliant workforce has been betrayed by its own management. Rory Murphy, general secretary of the 40,000 strong NatWest Staff Association, argues that the banks have taken advantage of a naturally docile workforce. He concedes that compulsory redundancies have not yet been the norm, but argues the banks have adopted a strategy of squeezing people out of work and forcing them to accept voluntary redundancy packages.

20 Many staff, he says, fear that if they do not accept they will receive a much smaller payout if they are subsequently compulsorily axed. The result has been the decimation of morale. No longer is a job in a bank a career for life, a world where employees pride themselves on their office amateur operatic association and branch darts league, a world where a bank worker would no more swap jobs than change allegiance to a local football team.

21 As Mr Murphy says: "The banks are not getting it right. Twenty years ago people were proud to work for a bank. Now it's not the sort of thing to admit in the pub. There are hundreds of staff who are demoralised and demotivated, who would like to leave."

22 Where the banks go, the rest of the financial services sector follows. There are many who now fear huge job losses have only just begun, particularly within the insurance sector, which employs 370,000 people.

23 Insurers have yet to grasp the nettle of advanced technology and a wave of cost-cutting takeovers is predicted, mirroring the shrinkage among the banks as they struggle to cut overheads.

24 Norwich Union, a large insurance company, intends to consider a £2 billion public quotation. This would change it from a mutual business to a public limited company.

**Adapted from *The Guardian*
14 October 1995**

Selected UK and Irish bank and building society purchases

Year	Buyer	£m	Bought
1995	Abbey National	1,351	National & Provincial
1994	Lloyds Bank	1,800	Cheltenham & Gloucester
1992	HSBC	3,828	Midland Bank
1991	Bank of Scotland	22	Bank of Wales
1991	Allied Irish Banks	111	TSB Northern Ireland
1990	National Australia Bank	877	Yorkshire Bank
1989	Alliance and Leicester	130	Girobank
1987	National Australia Bank	420	Clydesdale Bank, Northern Bank, Northern Bank (Ireland).

Source: *The Guardian*, 14 October 1995

MOCK EXAM SUGGESTED ANSWERS

PAPER 1

Tutorial note, Sections A and B

Both sections contain restricted-response and short-answer question forms. Those in Section A state the number of points required and your answers should be influenced by this.

Section B questions give no guidance on the number of points you need to make. There are typically more marks per question, especially for numbers 7–10, compared with Section A. Your answers are likely to be longer and more detailed, and should contain additional analysis. Question 9 asks for supporting numerical details: we advise you to use simple figures in such situations, so that you illustrate the principles involved rather than over-concentrate on the calculations.

Suggested answers

Section A

A1 Ownership: the PLC by shareholders, the public corporation by the state on behalf of the public.

Capital: the PLC from private individuals, the public corporation from public funds.

A2 Specialist support (eg in marketing); a nationally known trade name; a lower capital outlay required.

A3 A limited or local demand for goods/services; providing a personal service.

A4 Cost of land/premises; unsuitable local labour skills; refusal of existing staff to move with the organisation.

A5 Cost of the method; level of security expected by the lender.

A6 Discounted cash flow; payback; accounting rate of return.

A7 Large numbers of identical products; a flow-line operation; economies of scale.

A8 An advertising campaign leading to higher output and extra recruitment; a change of product requiring new labour skills leading to retraining of existing staff.

A9 Back-up service; product features.

A10 Loans; business advice; a business bank account.

Section B

B1 'Line' refers to functional responsibility, e.g. Marketing Manager in direct authority line; 'staff' refers to specialist (advisory) support, e.g. Personnel Officer.

B2 Gives control over the end quality; increases profits and total revenue; a suitable manufacturer is available.

B3 It reduces or prevents boredom; it increases personal challenge; it helps achieve self-esteem and self-fulfilment (Maslow).

B4 Go-slow; overtime ban; work-to-rule; strike action (following a ballot).

B5 It is a selective approach; it is cheaper than conventional advertising; the firm has greater control over its marketing.

B6   To gain satisfaction from working for himself/herself; for prestige/status; to achieve self-esteem/self-actualisation.

B7   The fall in value of a fixed asset over time. The factors affecting the asset vary according to the nature of the asset: e.g. depletion (mines and quarries), passage of time (leases and patents), obsolescence (machinery), and wear and tear (vehicles).

B8   A limited budget; they may be uncompetitive on pay; a probable lack of expertise on recruitment and selection procedures.

B9

Date	Receipts	Issues	Balance
1st			10 at £2.00
4th	10 at £2.50		
6th		15	

The FIFO method charges the 15 issued at £32.50, i.e.

(10 × £2.00) + (5 × £2.50), and closing stock is £12.50 (5 × £2.50).

The LIFO method charges the 15 issued at £35.00, i.e.

(10 × £2.50) + (5 × £2.00), and closing stock is £10.00 (5 × £2.00).

B10   Social costs (borne by the community through actions of the firm): increased pollution through burning.

      Financial costs: capital expenditure (purchase of machinery), revenue expenditure (depreciation of machinery, wages to operate it, maintenance, etc.).

      Opportunity cost: the cost of the alternatives required to land-fill, and the cost to the firm of buying the machinery (this capital expenditure is not available for alternative uses).

Tutorial note, Section C

Questions 1 and 3 have the same structure, and both are general in scope. The mark allocations suggest that part (a) should take you about twelve minutes, and part (b) about eighteen minutes, to answer. A good answer to question 1 part (a) should contain brief definitions of profitability and liquidity, and an explanation of how each affects the short-term survival chances of a typical firm. Part (b) concentrates exclusively on liquidity, and you can differentiate between factors such as better credit control which overcome problems, and other factors (e.g. ratio analysis) which help avoid the problem in the first place.

      Question 3 again expects a degree of evaluation to support the content points included. Maslow is an obvious illustration to use because the hierarchy lends itself to a discussion on motivation. Part(b) does not state the number of points you should make in the answer: a good answer is likely to include both specific illustrations and general statements relating to the importance of good communication and close negotiation.

      Question 2 is also general in scope, although your answer could include examples of unions. The question requires you to 'critically examine' the functions of unions: the answer should contain statements of content, together with some analysis and evaluation of this content.

Suggested answers

Question C1 (a)

The term 'liquidity' refers to the ability of a firm to meet its debts, and the term 'profitability' to the return it makes against some identified measure (normally capital employed, or net assets, as this is sometimes known).

      The statement in the question is widely regarded as true because the firm must be able to pay its way. Liquidity problems typically occur when there is a shortage of working capital: the excess of current assets over current liabilities. Current assets represent actual or 'near' cash, for example trade debts owed to the firm (debtors), and the finished goods, work in progress and raw material stocks it currently holds. Current liabilities represent its short-term debts, such as those owed to trade creditors (suppliers of raw materials on credit terms) and expense creditors (e.g. an unpaid electricity bill). If the firm's current liabilities equal or exceed its current assets, this means that the firm will shortly be asked to pay debts for which it does not have the money available. In such instances the creditors can press for payment, forcing the firm to borrow money which then creates an additional debt burden as well as leading to extra borrowing costs such as the interest charges on the amount borrowed. Creditors may also decide to withdraw their credit terms and make the firm pay cash, which increases the pressure on its liquid resources. Another example of the problems associated with low liquidity is the inability of the firm to take advantage of settlement discounts offered to it for prompt payment of its own bills.

The firm can survive, at least in the short term, without making reasonable profits. Annual profit levels can fluctuate widely anyway, and directors therefore often take a medium-term view of the trends in the amount of profits. Profitability remains important because it is the final measure of the worth of the investment, but the ability of the firm to pay what it owes – its liquidity – is far more important to its survival in the short term.

Question C1 (b)

Three ways available to a firm are:

(i) Close monitoring of the working capital situation. This is an avoidance strategy which relies largely on monitoring the key ratios:

- the current ratio of current assets to current liabilities, which has a 'textbook' 2:1 ratio;
- the 'acid test' of current assets minus stock to current liabilities, having a 'textbook' ratio of 1:1;
- the debtor and creditor turnover ratios, which compare these totals to sales and purchases (respectively) and measure the credit periods allowed and taken by the firm.

Regular monitoring will identify changes taking place and allow the managers to take appropriate corrective action.

(ii) Better credit control. This is a strategy which helps both to avoid and to overcome liquidity problems. The firm's credit controller will concentrate on the schedule of debtors (a list of debts outstanding, together with the age of the debts) to ensure regular and prompt payment. Extra action might be taken to chase doubtful debts, and credit terms allowed can be reviewed. Other control can be exercised on working capital, such as a review of the spending on stock and the associated costs of holding it.

(iii) Obtaining additional short-term finance. This is a strategy used to overcome liquidity problems. If the firm can obtain extra long-term capital (e.g. it can issue more shares if it is a company), some of the funds generated can be used to pay creditors or other short-term debts. The managers will be aware that any form of borrowing has an associated cost.

Question C2

The main functions of trade unions involve assisting individual and groups of workers in a variety of ways. Their functions include the improvement of the following.

❶ **Pay and minimum pay levels:** for example, there have been union-led campaigns to follow most of the rest of Western Europe in having a minimum statutory national wage, and to preserve Wages Councils which guaranteed minimum hourly wages in low-pay industries such as hairdressing (a minimum hourly wage of £2.88 in 1993, compared with the average national rate of £7.49), pubs and clubs (£3.01 in 1993), and clothing (£2.71 in 1993). In the 1980s and 1990s unions have had to acknowledge the effect of 'market conditions' on pay, as well as the fact that continuing high levels of unemployment have driven real pay down in some industries and areas of work.

② Employment conditions: such as hours of work, shiftwork and overtime, e.g. union campaigns in the early 1990s for a 48-hour maximum working week. Unions have benefited from closer links with the rest of the European Union, where the 'Social Chapter' and more favourable worker-oriented policies have been implemented. UK unions have used such policies to argue the case for improved conditions at home, though the Conservative government of the 1990s has been unwilling to support action for better pay and conditions, arguing the case for the control of wage levels and employment costs which otherwise would work through to increase firms' prices and reduce international competitiveness.

③ The work environment: there is union representation on the UK's Health and Safety Executive and on various EU health and safety committees. In reality, some forms of work are innately more dangerous than others, though – even with the contraction in the fishing and mining industries – unions continue to monitor all accident statistics.

Other specific union functions include protecting members from illegal or unfair working practices such as discrimination, representing members who have grievances concerning work (eg concerning unfair or constructive dismissal), representing members in consultations or disputes with employers, protecting members' job security, and using their collective power and economic strength to provide member services such as reduced insurance premiums, discount cards, etc. Unions have retained these functions, even though total membership has fallen (by some 4 million during the 1980s). The various legal restraints introduced in the 1980s to curb unions have reduced their power, and they play only a weak part in some industries (e.g. sections of the catering and tourism industries).

The quality of the functions and services offered by unions in the 1990s is sometimes criticised. For example, some unions have been criticised as not promoting opportunities for certain groups within their membership (e.g. women workers, and workers from minority groups). Another common criticism is that the officials are not always representative of the membership. The less than sympathetic stance of the Conservative government towards the unions throughout the 1980s and early 1990s has not always helped them to carry out effectively those functions they believe they should undertake: the range and effectiveness of these functions is influenced by external factors such as government policy and the relative increase in power and influence of the CBI and the Institute of Directors under the Thatcher and Major administrations.

The overall function of unions in the 1990s, however, remains that of retaining a good relationship with the various employers, because it is in the interests of both sides that business is successful. The harsh economic environment of the early 1990s has led to some modification of union activity, though they retain their key functions noted above.

Question C3 (a)

Mass production techniques are widely used in the manufacturing sector of the economy. The justification for their use is the reduction of unit costs through economies of scale. Mass production, with its low unit costs, has led to a range of goods being available in the economy at affordable prices: without mass production techniques, a much higher proportion of the population would be unable to afford the goods.

Mass production techniques normally include a flow-line production layout for the (identical) product which consists of specialised machinery and equipment, and employees who carry out tasks which are physically limited, repetitive and simple in nature. The end result is a speed of production and assembly which reduces unit costs, but which also is associated with employee boredom and dissatisfaction. Many workers suffer from low morale and poor job satisfaction when employed in a mass production environment.

Abraham Maslow identified a hierarchy of needs, which can be used to evaluate the nature of mass production work. The base of his hierarchical pyramid consists of physiological needs such as the need for air, water and food. These basic needs are followed (in order) by: security needs (the need for safety and order); social needs (the need to belong to a group); self-esteem needs (the need for self-respect and achievement); and, at the top of the hierarchy, self-actualisation needs (the need to be fulfilled and to realise one's potential). In many traditional mass-production oriented firms, employees have little opportunity at work to achieve the higher-order needs of self-esteem and self-actualisation, whereas the lower-order ones are often achieved easily. There tends to be little chance of achieving personal potential in a flow-line organisation, little sense of achievement, and a feeling of low self-esteem and worth.

Question C3 (b)

Management can attempt to create a suitable environment and appropriate working practices through the following strategies.

1 Ensure that there are adequate communication and negotiation networks to enable employees to contribute ideas and become involved in decision-making: this increases feelings of worth and self-esteem amongst the staff.

2 Introduce schemes such as job rotation and job enrichment, and improve training, to give employees the opportunity for greater self-fulfilment through greater job satisfaction.

3 Increase automation of the very basic tasks, giving the employees released from these tasks more demanding work: this improves self-esteem.

4 Encourage social activities (e.g. through improved sports and social facilities) and teamwork: this leads to an enhancement of social needs.

PAPER 2

Tutorial note

The theme of this paper is 'Change and Development in Business'. It seeks to integrate content from a number of modules/study areas. All questions are data response type, being linked to the *Guardian* article. You are also advised to draw on your general business studies knowledge. You therefore must **link general points made to the specific situations given** in the information component.

Question 1 requires you to identify aims for a particular type of business, then analyse this information in some depth. The actual choice of aims/objectives can determine how well you answer the main part of the question. Question 2 uses information technology to explore the theme of change: you are specifically asked to use 'examples referred to in the extract...'. Question 3 again requires you to apply general theoretical knowledge (of motivation) to a specific situation. You need to take care to evaluate how your suggestions in part (b) might affect banks. Question 4 sets the task of applying PEST analysis to the given case. Question 5 examines your understanding of business organisations, with quite a demanding last part.

Suggested answers

Question 1

(a) Four relevant business aims are survival, profitability (or profit maximisation), market share (or sales maximisation), and customer loyalty/satisfaction.

(b) Takeover would help achieve the survival objective in one sense (e.g. through economies of scale), although the individual bank does not survive as a separate entity. Sales and profit maximisation is more easily achieved due to greater market share and power. Customer loyalty and satisfaction might be the most difficult of the four to achieve on the basis that the bank's identity is lost or changed, and working practices altered, thereby affecting customers.

(c) Four effects on customers include: the possibility of fewer branches following rationalisation; less choice of financial institutions; a change in bank services/

charges following rationalisation; and the possibility that the customers will gain financially from the takeover (e.g. share offers).

Question 2

(a) Firms in the financial sector can use IT to improve efficiency in a number of ways. Firstly, a key development in the 1990s has been the introduction of 24-hour telephone banking (para. 15) which expands the firm's customer base and allows all-day operation. Secondly, the use of databases is referred to indirectly on a number of occasions in the text (e.g. paras. 15 and 16), enabling banks to store, retrieve and manipulate mass information quickly and efficiently. Thirdly, information technology allows customers greater access to bank services outside normal opening hours: in addition to telephone banking, there are the 'hole in the wall' machines which offer services such as cash withdrawal and confirmation of current account balances. Finally, the use of integrated specialist or 'open' software such as word processors and spreadsheets allows bank staff to generate relevant statistical information, transmit it, and communicate it efficiently to their customers.

(b) Customers receive a less personal service, often being 'dealt with' by computers rather than bank staff directly. They do, however, have greater access to these services (outside opening hours), for example from home. Thirdly, customers are offered a wider range of services, without having to make personal appointments. Finally, customers can obtain greater information about the financial sector in general (e.g. via the Internet).

Question 3

(a) One reason for worker demotivation is the fear of losing their jobs. This is mentioned several times in the article (e.g. para. 6). Secondly, the advent of deskilling (para. 9) can lead to reduced pay levels. Thirdly, there is the loss of the team ethos, due to higher labour turnover rates (para. 20). Finally, the introduction of new work practices and procedures (paras. 15 and 16) can affect motivation levels.

(b) Managers could offer improved working conditions (Herzberg hygiene factors) which would bring greater job satisfaction but at a cost to the banks (e.g. redesign of bank layout, refurbishing). Managers could change/improve promotion prospects (McGregor, 'Theory Y' seeking responsibility), establishing internal promotion as policy; this could have detrimental effects in the longer term, though. Managers could seek to ensure staff obtain greater job satisfaction through job rotation/enrichment (Maslow: social/esteem/self-actualisation), which would create little additional cost to the banks. Finally, managers might offer improved training (McGregor Theory Y, also Maslow's social needs) which, whilst increasing costs, would also lead to improved company efficiency.

Question 4

(a) Political, Economic, Social and Technological (alternatively expressed as Technical).

(b) External factors included in and implied by the article include the problems of negative equity, high rates of interest in the money markets, high unemployment levels, the greater availability of alternative forms of credit, poor levels of economic growth, deskilling of the clerical sector, and demographic change. Fundamentally, there is either (or both) an over-supply of finance with too little demand for it.

(c) Banks have managed to increase their profits through increasing revenue (e.g. increasing interest rates and bank charges), and by cutting costs such as through reducing staff levels.

Question 5

(a) The business will identify and appoint key officers such as directors and a company secretary; a Memorandum and Articles of Association will be drawn up; the officers will forward these and other relevant statements to the Registrar of Companies who will ensure they comply with the requirements of the Companies Acts; the company will be issued with its Certificates of Incorporation/Trading, and can sell shares to appropriate people.

(b) The present customers – who may indirectly hold shares through share accounts – will benefit (e.g. by share offers), and so will the directors (e.g. through future share and other options). Staff may also benefit, though this is less certain and may be more indirect (e.g. the creation of new posts and the opportunity of promotion in the new organisation).

(c) For its current customers, the Norwich Union should keep them informed of developments, together with reasons for these developments. It should also allow customers access (e.g. via dedicated telephone lines) to ask questions and gain additional information. For its future shareholders, the company should set up appropriate channels of communication, to enable these people to action their interest in the business.

(d) The small firm is likely to face increased competition in the market, and may well seek to merge with another institution in order to survive. Its profits are also likely to decline, and this could lead to a corresponding decline in confidence in the institution.

More invaluable exam question practice can be found in Letts *A Level Questions and Answers Business Studies*.

INDEX